REFERENCE BOOKS: HOW TO SELECT AND USE THEM

REFERENCE BOOKS: HOW TO SELECT AND USE THEM

SAUL GALIN and
PETER SPIELBERG

 Random House New York

Library of Congress Catalog Card Number: 69–16443
Manufactured in the United States of America
by H. Wolff Book Manufacturing Company
Designed by Andrew Roberts

CONTENTS

Part II
___

SPECIALIZED REFERENCE WORKS
for the HUMANITIES and SOCIAL SCIENCES

II. A. ANTHROPOLOGY

II. B. ART

II. E. HISTORY

BIBLIOGRAPHIES AND INDEXES

General

American

ENCYCLOPEDIAS, HANDBOOKS, HISTORIES, etc.

American

English

European

General and Others

II. F. LITERATURE

BIBLIOGRAPHIES AND INDEXES

HANDBOOKS, DICTIONARIES, HISTORIES, etc.

American

English

Part III

SPECIALIZED REFERENCE WORKS for the PHYSICAL SCIENCES

III. A. GENERAL REFERENCE WORKS

Part IV

AIDS FOR RESEARCH

INTRODUCTION

I: AIM AND SCOPE

This guide to reference works has been compiled for the bene-fit of the college student, as well as for others involved in research projects—high school students, graduate students, or laymen. The need for such a guide was brought to our atten-tion by the seemingly contradictory attitudes toward reference books we observed in our students. On the one hand, students, especially lowerclassmen, are confused, puzzled, and often even frightened when they are asked to work on a research project—a term paper or some other assignment involving the use of reference books. On the other hand, the reference sections in school libraries are mobbed by frantic students thumbing through the ever-increasing piles of encyclopedias, dictionaries, bibliographies, indexes, abstracts, etc. Observing this, we came to the conclusion that even though more and more students consult reference works, most are confused and pained because they don't know where to go or what to do.

The confusion is understandable. Wandering through the mass of reference works, the newcomer is overwhelmed and lost. The aim of this book is to guide him. We have provided the student or researcher with a descriptive list of essential reference books that gives a simple, clear, concise summary of the contents of each book, and thus enables the reader to find quickly the best-suited reference works for his particular research problem and to ignore what does not apply.

To make the process of selection as simple as possible, we have limited ourselves to about 200 basic reference books, which are, in our opinion, the most valuable and the most fre-quently used works. This guide emphasizes the humanities and social sciences (although some twenty-five basic works in the physical sciences are also listed). It should also be noted that the following areas are *not* included in our coverage: reference works in foreign languages, reference works that are more specialized and primarily of interest to graduate students, and works dealing with such highly specialized fields as medicine, law, architecture, engineering, television, etc.

II: DIRECTIONS

The main part of this guide, which lists and describes the basic reference books, is divided into three parts: I. *General Reference Works:* books of value to all fields of study listed by category. II. *Specialized Reference Works for the Humanities and Social Sciences:* listed according to special subjects, alphabetically from Anthropology to Sociology. III. *Specialized References Works for the Physical Sciences:* listed by subject.

We advise the researcher to first consult the section that deals with his special subject, in Part II or III. For example, a student doing research in philosophy should begin by consulting section II.H. However, it should be kept in mind that general reference works are described in Part I. Therefore, most researchers will consult the general as well as the special listings.

III: WARNING

Reference works have their limitations. They are not, and were never meant to be, a substitute for primary sources.

Such obvious storehouses of facts as bibliographies, indexes, almanacs, gazetteers, biographical dictionaries, wordbooks, and directories, pose no problems. They are tools that enable us to find facts or to locate essential pieces of information. But the same is not quite true of the reference works that condense, summarize, or describe—the encyclopedias, histories, handbooks, companions, and abstracts. These are often misused—read in place of the real thing (not to mention outline books, ponies, or trots, which are not included in this guide). Surely, we can all see that a plot summary of *Hamlet* is a sorry substitute for the play itself. Just so a chapter in an encyclopedia of mythology is a pale thing compared to Homer's *Odyssey* or to Ovid's *Metamorphoses;* similarly, an article in a companion to European history that summarizes the rise and fall of Napoleon cannot replace a more serious or complete treatise on the subject. This applies equally to an abstract of a critical article, which is meant to present only the barest outline.

Yet such outlines have their proper function; they may help us decide whether or not to read the full article, or the book-length treatise on Napoleon; they may also help weak memories by supplying us with the correct dates or the name of Hamlet's fickle schoolmates. In the hands of honest users, such reference works can be invaluable tools, not to avoid work, or to avoid confronting the real thing, but as a means of making our work easier, and as an aid to original thinking.

The compilers are grateful for the use they have been able to make of the resources of the Brooklyn College, Columbia University, and New York University libraries, and for the valuable and gracious aid offered them by the reference librarians at these institutions. We would also like to acknowledge our debt to the great standard work in the field, Constance M. Winchell's *A Guide to Reference Books* (Chicago: American Library Association, 8th ed., 1967), to which we refer those readers who wish to find a comprehensive list of the thousands of reference works presently in print.

S.G.
P.S.

Brooklyn College
City University of New York
1968

Part I

GENERAL REFERENCE WORKS

I. A.
ENCYCLOPEDIAS

DEFINITION: The general encyclopedia is a work (usually of many volumes) that contains a collection of articles giving essential general information about all the various branches of knowledge, arranged alphabetically by subjects and names for easy use.

The specialized encyclopedia is a collection of articles limited to a specific field of knowledge or area of interest.

WHEN TO USE AN ENCYCLOPEDIA: A student should begin here if he knows nothing or next to nothing about a subject, or if he wants to refresh his memory. Encyclopedias provide general, comprehensive summaries as well as specific and authoritative facts.

But it should be remembered that these works are meant to serve only as an introduction. Most students will want to delve deeper. The next logical step is to consult the books cited in the bibliographies that most of these works supply.

WHICH ENCYCLOPEDIA SUITS YOUR NEEDS? The works listed below are the most important and most widely used *general* encyclopedias.* To facilitate the reader's choice, we have arranged them in three groups: full and scholarly; shorter or simpler; and capsule size.

* *We have included one specialized work below,* The International Encyclopedia of the Social Sciences (*our no. 7*), *because it covers all the social sciences (anthropology, economics, law, penology, political science, and sociology) and could therefore not be assigned to one special field. For other specialized encyclopedias, see the sections of our book dealing with specific subjects; e.g., for an encyclopedia on banking and finance, see our section II. C. Economics & Business.*

3

» Full and scholarly
Encyclopedia Americana (our no. 1)   Strong on American topics.
Encyclopaedia Britannica (our no. 2)   Good coverage of both British and American subjects.

» Shorter or simpler
Chambers's Encyclopaedia (our no. 3)   Emphasis on British topics.
Collier's Encyclopedia (our no. 4)   Emphasis on simple explanations.

» Capsule size
Columbia Encyclopedia (our no. 5)   In one volume for quick reference.
New Century Cyclopedia of Names (our no. 6)   For quick identification of proper names.

ALSO NOTE: There is some overlapping among various kinds of reference works. Thus the reader will notice that encyclopedias give information that can also be found in dictionaries, yearbooks, atlases, or biographical dictionaries. The researcher should keep this in mind in case the encyclopedia consulted does not answer all questions. In such a case, the student might have to turn to another kind of reference work, one of the more specialized ones, to complete the research.

1] *Encyclopedia Americana*

New York: Americana Corp., 1927—.

CONTENTS: A compilation in 30 volumes of articles on important topics from all branches of knowledge. The individual articles vary in length from a 3-line explanation of "Atmolysis" to a 7-page article on "Pottery" to a 56-page chapter on "Africa" to a 170-page, book-length history of "World War II," plus numerous excellent illustrations (photographs, drawings, graphs, charts, maps). The stress is on "simple, clear writing." *

Most items are signed by the author, who also supplies the

* *Unless otherwise noted, all quotations of this sort are taken from the introduction or front matter of the work described.*

reader with a list of "books and other source materials for further research."

Frequent new editions are kept up to date by a "plan of continuous revision."

METHOD OF ORGANIZATION: Alphabetical. To fully understand the alphabetical system employed, see the "Guide to the Use of the Index" in the *Index Volume*, vol. 30 (e.g., "New York" comes before "Newark").

In any case, always consult the *Index Volume* first, since the main article on a subject does not necessarily contain all available information. Relevant material is often given in related articles that cannot be located without the index; e.g., if a reader were interested in cutworms, he would discover that the index lists not only the main article (8–345, i.e., vol. 8, page 345), but also related articles ("Moth 19–510; Army Worm 2–309; Wheat 28–694"). Furthermore, the index lists subjects about which there are no main articles, but which are covered elsewhere; e.g., although there is no article on Lake Alachua, Florida, information is given in an article on "Sink Holes 25–36" to which the index refers the reader.

Another useful portion of the *Index Volume* is a 30-page section entitled "Illustrated Chronology of World Events," which records the "important events of the past five years."

USEFULNESS: One of the best and most useful of general encyclopedias, this is noted for its full treatment of subjects in all branches of knowledge and its long essays (e.g., on the major countries of the world). It is especially strong on American topics.

EXAMPLES: The subjects treated by this work are wide and varied. As a brief illustration of its vast range, of its broad scope, consider the following sample list of topics, chosen at random:

Africa, Apache, Ballet, Bantu, Barrymore Family, Baths, Beethoven, Bible, California, Canonization, Cant, Cantata, The Canterbury Tales, Carnegie Institute of Technology, Croquet, Dementia Praecox, Ecumenical Movement, Egg, Ego, Elephantiasis, Engine, Leif Ericson, Fall Line, Fetish, Fur Trade, Galileo, Gall Bladder, Glaciers, Gonorrhea, Holbein, Hydrogen

Bomb, Inquisition, Iowa City, Jefferson Memorial, Kosygin, Lace, LSD, Mephistopheles, Migration of Animals, Mikado, Molecular Theory, Moscow, Nobel Prizes, Obiter Dictum, Quantum Theory, Poultry, Pound (Ezra), Pound (money), Radar, Steel, Succession Wars, Sulfonamides, Turtles, Usury, Vassar College, Windmill, World War I, Xanthippe, Zinc, Zoroastrianism.

ALSO NOTE: A supplement, *Americana Annual*, is issued yearly. These books review and interpret "outstanding political, economic, scientific, and cultural developments of the preceding year," from 1923 on.

As in the main volumes, articles are arranged alphabetically. The index at the back of the book should be consulted for rapid and full results. The book also contains two introductory sections: "Outstanding Dates of [the year]" and "Topical Survey of the Year," as well as a group of feature articles on topics of timely interest, and a "Necrology" of prominent persons who died during the preceding year.

RELATED REFERENCE WORKS: For British subjects, see *Chambers's Encyclopaedia* (our no. 3). Also see the specialized encyclopedias that treat subjects in specific fields.

2] *Encyclopaedia Britannica*

Chicago: Encyclopaedia Britannica, Inc., 1929—.

CONTENTS: A compilation in 24 volumes of articles on important topics from all branches of knowledge. The individual articles vary in length from a 4-line explanation of "Potato Races" to a half-page summary of the mechanics of "Proofreading" (including a chart of common proofreading symbols) to a 3-page article on "Salt" to a 50-page treatise on "Pottery and Porcelain" (plus 40-pages of illustrations) to an 80-page history of "World War II."

Most items are signed by the author, who also supplies the reader with a brief, selected bibliography at the end of the article.

Frequent new editions are kept up to date by a "plan of continuous revision."

METHOD OF ORGANIZATION: Alphabetical. To fully understand the method of organization, see the "Explanation of the Alphabetical System" at the front of vol. 1 (e.g., Van Gogh is alphabetized under "Gogh").

Most important of all: consult the *Index Volume* (vol. 24) first! This preliminary step is essential since the main article on a subject does not contain all available information. Much is given in related articles; e.g., if a student were interested in Wendell Willkie, he could find the main article on this figure by simply consulting the appropriate alphabetized volume (vol. 23), but he would not know that further information about Mr. Willkie is available in two other places. This information is supplied only in the *Index Volume*, which gives the volume and page number of the main article ("23–633") as well as the volume and page numbers of related articles ("national convention 16–137" and "U.S. history 22–809").

Moreover, some subjects are not treated in separate articles, yet information about these subjects is available under other headings; e.g., although there is no main article on the Metropolitan Museum of Art (a reader will look in vain in vol. 15, the *Index Volume* does have a listing for this museum and will send the reader to five related articles in which this subject is treated. The index also lists cross references; e.g., for Taiwan, see "Formosa."

The second half of the *Index Volume* contains a full-color *Atlas*, over one hundred pages long, with a pronouncing index (e.g., "Aachen—ä′kĕn") and a glossary of foreign geographical terms (e.g., "Praha = Prague").

USEFULNESS: The *Britannica*, probably the most famous reference work in the English language, is recognized as one of the best, and some say the best, of the general encyclopedias. It is noted for its full and scholarly treatment of subjects in all branches of knowledge.

Despite its title, it gives equally good coverage to British and American subjects. (The work has been published in the U.S. since 1910, but it still tends to use British spellings, e.g., "colour" instead of color.)

EXAMPLES: The subjects treated by this work are legion. As a brief illustration of its vast range, consider the following sample list of topics, chosen at random: Adobe, Adolescence, American College of Physicians, Bedbug, Birthmark, Cain, Calvinism, Cancer, Charles I, Cubism, Dialectic Materialism, Dwarfs, Existentialism, ex post facto law, Flatworm, Flax, Fugitive Slave Laws, Mt. Fujiyama, Girl Guides, Glasgow, Glass, Harmony, Harpoon, Harvard Univ., Hippocratic Oath, Hippopotamus, Hiroshima, Honey, Hymen, Hypnosis, Hundred Years War, Iowa, Jupiter, Kafka, Kaleidoscope, the Koran, Kurds, Labyrinth, Lace, Language, Latitude, Lead, Monarchy, Moneylending, Nutrition, Nymph, Osmosis, Pregnancy, Protozoa, Radiation, Raspberry, Rasputin, The Stamp Act, Totem, Utrillo, Vassar, Queen Victoria, Wagner, Welding, Whig Party, Woman's Suffrage, X-ray, Zoology.

ALSO NOTE: A supplement, *Britannica Book of the Year,* is issued annually. These books cover the "significant events of each succeeding year," from 1938 on. As in the main volumes, articles are arranged alphabetically by subjects. Consult the cumulative index (which indexes the current volume as well as those of the four preceding years) at the back of the book for rapid and full results.

A special feature of these volumes is a chronological listing of the major events of the past year, a day-by-day record of the march of events. Another section gives the obituaries of prominent individuals who died during the preceding year. Recent yearbooks include a special section for U.S. readers, "States Statistical Supplement."

RELATED REFERENCE WORKS: Most libraries stock early as well as the current editions of the *Britannica.* Some of these, particularly the 9th ed. (1875–89) and the 11th ed. (1910–11), are of interest since they contain fuller and more scholarly treatments of certain subjects.

Also see the various specialized encyclopedias that treat subjects in specific fields.

3] *Chambers's Encyclopaedia*

London: G. Newnes Ltd. New ed. (1950, 1959, 1967).

CONTENTS: A compilation in 15 volumes of articles on important topics from all branches of knowledge. Most of the items are short descriptive entries, although there are a substantial number of essay-length articles (e.g., five pages on tuberculosis) and a limited number of long main articles (e.g., fifty-four pages on World War II). Many illustrations, graphs, and tables are included.

Most articles are signed by the specialists who prepared them and are followed by brief bibliographies that list the "acknowledged standard works" on the subjects.

METHOD OF ORGANIZATION: Alphabetical.

Volume XV contains the *Index and Atlas.* Be sure to consult the "General Subject Index" first, since the main article on a subject does not necesarily contain all available information. Relevant material is often given in related articles that cannot be located without the index. Cross references are also given here.

A second index, "Classified List of Articles," lists the main articles included in the encyclopedia, classifying them under the appropriate subject headings, from "Agriculture" through "Zoology."

The 144-page full-color atlas included in vol. XV is indexed in an "Atlas Index," which also serves as a geographical dictionary.

USEFULNESS: One of the best known British encyclopedias, it is an excellent source for information on British topics. The emphasis of this work is on making general information available and understandable "to the educated layman" in relatively brief articles.

4] *Collier's Encyclopedia*

New York: Crowell-Collier, 1950—.

CONTENTS: A compilation in 24 volumes of articles on important topics from all branches of knowledge. The individual articles vary in length, from brief descriptive entries to chapter-length treatments (e.g., seventy-seven pages plus maps on "Africa," and twenty-six pages on "World War II"). The work uses large, readable type and stresses clear, simple, objective writing. Numerous illustrations and maps are included within the relevant articles.

Items are signed by the authors. Bibliographies are not appended to the articles, but are to be found in vol. 24 (a cumbersome system).

Frequent new editions are kept up to date by a "plan of continuous revision."

METHOD OF ORGANIZATION: Alphabetical.

Be sure to consult the index (vol. 24) first, since the main article on a subject does not necessarily contain all available information.

The "Bibliography" section of vol. 24 lists recommended books for further reading by subjects, under about 125 headings from Accounting to Zoology. This can be useful to the general reader or beginning student.

USEFULNESS: A general encyclopedia, which emphasizes clear, simple explanations. Not so full or scholarly as the *Britannica* or *Americana*.

ALSO NOTE: A supplement, *Collier's Year Book*, summarizing the important events and discoveries of the year, has been issued annually since 1939.

5] *Columbia Encyclopedia*

New York: Columbia University Press, 3rd ed., 1963.

CONTENTS: A one-volume encyclopedia. Brief entries give "simple and accurate information to the ordinary reader" on important topics—"places, persons, and subjects" from all branches of knowledge. Most items are of paragraph length, although some run to half a page, and a few to a whole page (e.g., "World War II"). A few black-and-white illustrations.

Brief bibliographies are given at the end of most items.

METHOD OF ORGANIZATION: Alphabetical. There are numerous cross references, but no index.

USEFULNESS: The best known and most widely used single-volume encyclopedia. Its capsule-size entries make it ideally suited for quick identifications and checks on facts. Obviously the work is limited by its size; for fuller treatments turn to the big encyclopedias.

Although the work is primarily intended for the American reader, it includes information of international interest as well. Pronunciations of foreign names are given.

EXAMPLES: The emphasis is on inclusiveness; the work has as many entries as the multi-volume sets. The following subjects are especially well covered: Latin America, the Bible (every proper name in the Authorized, King James Version), famous Americans, "all incorporated U.S. towns of 1,000 or more population."

RELATED REFERENCE WORKS: Among other abridged, one-volume encyclopedias, the following are widely used: *Columbia-Viking Desk Encyclopedia*, ed. by William Bridgwater, *et al.* (New York: Viking Press, 2nd ed., 1960); *Hutchinson's New Twentieth Century Encyclopedia*, ed. by E. M. Horsley (New York: Hawthorn Books, 1964); and *Lincoln Library of Essential Information* (Buffalo: Frontier Press, frequently revised and reissued).

6] *New Century Cyclopedia of Names*

New York: Appleton-Century-Crofts, 1954.
Ed. by C. L. Barnhart.

CONTENTS: Brief notes in 3 volumes identify and give the essential facts about proper names (more than 100,000 of them) "having importance in the English-speaking world."

The work covers "names of every description—persons [living and dead], places, historical events, plays and operas, works of fiction, literary characters, works of art, mythology and legendary persons and places, and any other class of proper names of interest or importance today."

METHOD OF ORGANIZATION: Alphabetical.

USEFULNESS: A good place to begin if a reader is looking for a quick identification of a name. Since the work lists all kinds of proper names (people, places, historical events, works, etc.), it is a good one-stop source for facts. It should be remembered, though, that the emphasis is on inclusiveness and briefness; thus the user should not expect to find more than succinct identifications. For more detailed treatments, turn to the big encyclopedias and biographical dictionaries.

EXAMPLES: Here is a typical short entry:

Borden, Lizzie Andrew. b. 1860; d. June 2, 1927. Daughter of a wealthy banker of Fall River, Mass., who was accused of murdering her father and stepmother. After the discovery (Aug. 4, 1892) of their bodies bludgeoned to death with an ax, she became the central figure in a celebrated trial, and was finally acquitted (June 20, 1893); the murder remains still unsolved. The fame of this case inspired the play *Nine Pine Street* (1933), the novel *A Study in Conjecture* (1939) by Mrs. Belloc Lowndes, and the ballet *Fall River Legend* (1948) by Agnes de Mille.

RELATED REFERENCE WORKS: For more detailed treatments of many of the names identified in this work, see the "big" encyclopedias and biographical dictionaries.

For a general one-volume encyclopedia that not only includes all sorts of proper names but also entries on curious words, phrases, and facts, see Ebenezer C. Brewer's *Dictionary of Phrase and Fable* (New York: Harper & Bros., 8th ed., 1963).

7] *International Encyclopedia of the Social Sciences*

New York: Macmillan & The Free Press, 1967.
Ed. by David L. Sills.

CONTENTS: A complication in 17 volumes of articles on important topics in the social sciences: anthropology, economics, geography, history, law, political science, psychiatry, psychology, sociology, and statistics. Most of the articles deal with "the concepts, theories, and methods" of these disciplines; in addition, the encyclopedia includes the biographies of some 600 persons who have contributed significantly to the social sciences.

Almost all articles are topical and of essay-length (e.g., "African Society," 30 pages; "Mass Society," 7 pages; "Migration," 13 pages; "Time: Psychological Aspects" and "Time: Social Aspects," 18 pages; "Utopianism," 8 pages; "Voting," 9 pages; "Welfare State," 10 pages).

The articles are signed. Selected bibliographies are appended. Terms and specific items can be readily located because of the numerous cross references both in the body of the encyclopedia and in its index.

Vol. 17, the *Index*, provides three kinds of indexes: the main alphabetical index, listing subjects, names, and article titles; an alphabetical list of all articles in the encyclopedia; and a classified list of articles, listing all essays in the work by 29 major fields, from "Anthropology" to "Statistics."

USEFULNESS: This is an up-to-date work, an entirely new encyclopedia, providing extensive coverage of all the disciplines of the social sciences. The articles reflect contemporary trends in the disciplines.

EXAMPLES: The subjects treated by this encyclopedia span the whole range of social sciences as well as the social aspects of other fields. As a brief illustration of its broad scope, here is a sample list of topics, chosen at random: Administrative Law; Adolescence; Adoption; Aging; Augustine; Blindness; Bureaucracy; J. Calvin; Capital Punishment; Cartels; Caste; Census; Morris R. Cohen; Conformity; Creativity; Cybernetics; Death; Duty; John Dewey; Havelock Ellis; Errors; Ethnology; Eugenics; Family; Famine; Feudalism; Game Theory; Groups; Hinduism; Honor; Ideology; Incest; Industrialization; Integration; W. James; Judicial Process; Laissez-faire; Leisure; J. Locke; Marriage; K. Marx; Minorities; Norms; Nuclear War; Obesity; Robert Owen; Pavlov; Police; Poverty; Property; Quantal Response; Race; Suicide; Syndicalism; Technology; Trade and Markets; Unemployment Insurance; Voting; Wages; G. Udny Yule; Zionism.

RELATED REFERENCE WORKS: The *Encyclopaedia of the Social Sciences*, ed. by Edwin R. A. Seligman (N.Y.: Macmillan, 1930–1935, 15 vols.), was until recently the standard work in the field. Although published more than thirty years ago and thus out of date in many respects, it is still a valuable reference tool, providing the reader with a historical document of its time. The new encyclopedia was "designed to complement, not to supplant, its predecessor." Note that the articles in the old work are generally briefer; thus, the work combines the characteristics of an encyclopedia and a dictionary or handbook. The older work also contains many more biographies (4,000).

I. B.
DICTIONARIES

DEFINITION: A reference book that lists the standard words of the English language alphabetically and gives their meanings, pronunciation, spelling, origin, idiomatic use, etc.

THE MAIN USES OF A DICTIONARY: A dictionary is used to:
» find the meaning (or the various meanings) of a word,
» check on the spelling of a word (or its syllabication and hyphenation),
» check on the pronunciation of a word,
» trace the history of a word, its origin, derivation, or etymology,
» determine the current acceptability of a word, its level of usage (e.g., archaic, rare, slang).

WHICH DICTIONARY IS THE ONE FOR YOU? For everyday needs, the standard desk dictionaries, or "collegiate" dictionaries, as they are often called, should be sufficient. But often the student will find that the information given in these standard or abridged dictionaries is insufficient or that the word he is interested in is not listed; then one will need an "unabridged" dictionary. We have described the three most widely used ones below:

Webster's Third International (our no. 8)
Funk and Wagnalls (our no. 9)
Random House Dictionary (our no. 10)

At other times the student might need to trace the history of a word: how and when and from where the word became part of the English language; what changes have taken place in its meaning and use over the years. To find this information, consult:

Oxford English Dictionary (our no. 11)
A Dictionary of American English (our no. 12)

OTHER WORDBOOKS

DEFINITION: Reference books that deal with a particular, specialized aspect of the English language.

WHICH SPECIALIZED DICTIONARY ANSWERS YOUR NEEDS?

» Slang
A Dictionary of Slang & Unconventional English
(our no. 13).
The American Thesaurus of Slang (our no. 14).
» Dialects
English Dialect Dictionary (our no. 15).
» Idioms
Handbook of American Idioms & Idiomatic Usage
(our no. 16).
» Clichés
A Dictionary of Clichés (our no. 17).
» Good usage
Dictionary of Modern English Usage (our no. 18).
Modern American Usage (our no. 19).
Dictionary of Contemporary American Usage (our no. 20).
» Synonyms
Roget's International Thesaurus (our no. 21).
Webster's Dictionary of Synonyms (our no. 22).
» Famous quotations
Familiar Quotations (our no. 23).
» Acronyms and abbreviations
Acronyms and Initialisms Dictionary (our no. 24).

ALSO NOTE: We have described only the most important and most widely used specialized wordbooks. There are many others, which fulfill even more specialized needs; for example, dictionaries of pronunciation, linguistics and etymology, rhymes, curious expressions, proverbs, famous last words, dates, battles, colors, plant names, crossword puzzles, literary terms, military terms, medical terms, as well as many handbook-type dictionaries for the various disciplines. Check the reference library for such ultraspecialized dictionaries. They can be extremely useful. (Note that we have listed some in our sections II and III, where we describe the most important reference books for each field of study; e.g., for a dictionary of literary terms, see our section II. F. Literature.)

GENERAL (UNABRIDGED)

8] *Webster's Third New International Dictionary of the English Language, Unabridged*

Springfield, Mass.: G. & C. Merriam & Co., 1961—
(1st ed., 1909—; 2nd ed., 1934—).

CONTENTS: A dictionary of standard English "as it is written and spoken today." More than 450,000 words are defined; their correct usage is demonstrated in illustrative quotations that help make the meanings clearly understandable.

METHOD OF ORGANIZATION: Alphabetical. Common foreign words and phrases, abbreviations, and symbols are included in the main vocabulary. (Note that the dictionary does *not* include proper nouns—there are no entries for Greece, Paris, Hercules, or Ivan the Terrible—but proper adjectives are included, as are common nouns formed from proper nouns.)

A key to pronunciation symbols and special symbols used in the dictionary is printed on the inside of the front and back cover.

Be sure to consult the "Explanatory Chart & Notes," pp. 15a–20a, where type faces, abbreviations, symbols, and order of items in each vocabulary entry are explained in detail.

Rules of hyphenation, compounds, spelling, plurals, capitalization, italicization, pronunciation, punctuation, and forms of address are given in the "Preface," where one will also find a full key to the abbreviations used in this dictionary and an addenda list.

USEFULNESS: Although the object of much controversy when it first appeared (some still prefer the second edition; most libraries stock both editions), the *Third International*, like its famous predecessors, is generally accepted as one of the best, if not *the* best, of the one-volume unabridged dictionaries.

The new edition is extremely valuable because it takes cognizance of the many changes that have taken place in the English language as it is used currently in this country. More than 100,-000 new words and definitions have been added. Its coverage of scientific and technical vocabulary, which has expanded at an unprecedented pace, is excellent.

EXAMPLES: Information given about each word includes the following (when applicable), in this order: spelling, syllabication and hyphenation; pronunciation; grammatical designation (part of speech); inflections (plural ending of noun, principal parts of verb when irregular); capitalization; etymology (derivation); status note (e.g., obsolete, slang, etc.); definitions (in historical sequence, oldest first); quotation to illustrate use of word; cross references; idioms formed with word; run-on entries (different forms of word, e.g., adjective formed from noun); synonyms.

RELATED REFERENCE WORKS: *Webster's New International Dictionary of the English Language, Second Edition*, 1934—, although replaced by the new third edition, is still a valuable reference tool, containing some 600,000 entries compared to 450,000 in the new work. It includes many obsolete words dropped from the new work. It also includes proper nouns in its main vocabulary, antonyms as well as synonyms, and two valuable appendixes: "A Pronouncing Gazetteer" and "A Pronouncing Biographical Dictionary"—all dropped from the third. Furthermore, the second edition was stricter in its acceptance of words and usage as standard English; much that the third edition accepts as standard was labeled as "colloquial" by the older dictionary. (The status label "colloquial" is no longer used in the new edition.)

The "New Words" section in the front pages of the second edition is often useful.

For other one-volume unabridged dictionaries see our nos. 9 and 10.

9] *Funk and Wagnalls New Standard Dictionary of the English Language*

New York: Funk & Wagnalls, 1913—.

CONTENTS: A dictionary in which "all live words of the English language as used in standard speech and literature of the day" are defined. More than 450,000 words are included.

METHOD OF ORGANIZATION: Alphabetical. Proper nouns and abbreviations are included in the main alphabet.

A key to pronunciation is given in the introductory pages. Consult the "Introductory" section, which summarizes the purpose and method of the dictionary, as well as explaining in detail the type faces, abbreviations, symbols, and order of items in each vocabulary entry. The introductory section also gives basic rules of spelling, pronunciation, hyphenation, and compounding. A list of commonly used foreign words and phrases is found in the appendix.

USEFULNESS: The emphasis is on present-day usage (thus, the most common and current meaning of a word is given first). Although no complete revision of the dictionary has taken place since 1913, the work is kept up to date by incorporating changes and additions in the new printings.

EXAMPLES: Information given about each word includes the following (when applicable), in this order: spelling, capitalization, syllabication, and hyphenation; pronunciation; grammatical designation (part of speech); inflections (when irregular); usage labels (colloquial, rare, etc.); definitions (most common and current meaning first); quotations to illustrate use of word; etymology (derivation); synonyms (in many cases); antonyms (in some cases); cross references; run-on entries (different forms of word, e.g., adjective, adverb); idioms formed with word.

RELATED REFERENCE WORKS: For other one-volume unabridged dictionaries, see our nos. 8 and 10.

10] *Random House Dictionary of the English Language, The Unabridged Edition*

New York: Random House, 1966.

CONTENTS: A dictionary of the English language in which more than 260,000 words are defined. In addition to the main vocabulary, the dictionary contains two major supplementary sections: a complete atlas of the world, and four concise bilingual foreign language dictionaries—French, Spanish, Italian, German.

METHOD OF ORGANIZATION: Alphabetical. Common foreign words and phrases, abbreviations, symbols, and proper nouns are included in the main vocabulary.

Keys to pronunciation and etymological abbreviations used in the dictionary are printed on the front flyleaf. Be sure to consult "A Guide to the Dictionary," pp. xxv–xxxi, where the type faces, abbreviations, symbols, and order of items in each vocabulary entry are explained in detail.

In addition to the two main supplementary sections (the atlas and concise foreign language dictionaries), there are a number of other useful supplementary sections (a list of "Signs and Symbols," "A Directory of Colleges and Universities," "A Basic Manual of Style," a list of "Major Dates in World History," and a key to foreign alphabets).

USEFULNESS: Although the newest of the one-volume, unabridged dictionaries, the *Random House Dictionary* is already established as one of the most popular reference works. Because of its recent publication date, it is most up-to-date, citing such recently coined words as "psychedelic" and "Franglais." However, the total number of words is only about half of that in *Webster's Third* or *Funk & Wagnalls*.

EXAMPLES: Information given about each word includes the following (when applicable), in this order: spelling, syllabication, hyphenation, and capitalization; pronunciation; grammatical designation (part of speech); inflections (when irregular); restrictive labels (such as U.S., Physics, Archaic); definitions (most frequently encountered definition first); idioms formed with word; sample phrases or sentences to illustrate usage; cross references; abbreviation; etymology (derivation); run-on entries (different forms of word, e.g., adjective formed from noun); synonyms (in many cases); antonyms (in some cases).

RELATED REFERENCE WORKS: For other one-volume unabridged dictionaries see our nos. 8 and 9.

11] *Oxford English Dictionary (OED)* *(New English Dictionary)*

Oxford: Clarendon Press, 1888–1933. A reissue of the *New English Dictionary on Historical Principles (NED)*, 10 vols. + supplement, 1884–1933. Also known as *Murray's Dictionary*, after its editor, Sir James A. H. Murray. A new supplement is scheduled for publication in about 1975.

CONTENTS: A listing in 12 volumes plus supplement of most standard words in the English language known to have been in use between 1150 and 1933. The origin, history, and meaning of each word (414,825 words) are given in detail, illustrated by quotations from English authors (nearly 2 million quotations).

The emphasis of this giant dictionary is on the *historical development* of English words. It shows "when, how, in what shape, and with what signification [meaning]" each word came into the written language; "what development of form and meaning it has since received; which of its uses have, in the course of time, become obsolete, and which still survive; what new uses have since arisen, by what process, and when." These facts are illustrated "by a series of quotations ranging from the first known occurrence of the word to the latest."

METHOD OF ORGANIZATION: Words are listed alphabetically by modern or most usual British spelling. The supplement contains a second alphabetical listing of those words that were not included in the main volumes, mostly new words, and additions or corrections of listings in the main alphabet.

For a detailed guide to the use of this work see the "General Explanations" at the beginning of vol. 1, pp. xvii–xxiv. Keys to pronunciation and abbreviations appear at the front of each volume.

EXAMPLES: Information given about each main word includes:

» "The Identification": usual modern spelling (British),
  pronunciation, grammatical designation (part of speech),
  specification (if used in specific field, e.g., music),
  status, if peculiar (e.g., obsolete, archaic, colloquial),
  earlier forms of spelling, inflections (plurals and
  principal parts of verbs when other than ordinary);
» "The Morphology or Form History": derivation
  (origin of word), subsequent form history
  (phonetic changes, corruptions, obsolescence, revival, etc.);
» "The Signification" (i.e., meaning): arranged historically
  from early to present, with marking of obsolete senses,
  erroneous uses, etc.;
» "The Illustrative Quotations": arranged chronologically
  to illustrate each sense of a word, about one quotation
  for each century (original spelling is retained in quote;
  all quotes are identified and full bibliographical data
  is available in the bibliography of last volume).

USEFULNESS: This is the most authoritative, scholarly, and complete English dictionary. However, it is not the most convenient dictionary for everyday use; for other than historical or etymological purposes, the student will find the ordinary one-volume unabridged dictionaries (our nos. 8, 9, 10) more convenient.

Indispensable for learning the derivation of a word (the etymology) and the changes in the meaning of a word; e.g., if a student needs to know the meaning of a word in Chaucer's time or in Shakespeare's time, this is the dictionary to consult.

RELATED REFERENCE WORKS: The *Shorter Oxford English Dictionary on Historical Principles.* (1st ed. 1933, 3rd ed. 1955) is an authorized abridgment of the *OED*.

A Dictionary of American English on Historical Principles (our no. 12).

12] A *Dictionary of American English on Historical Principles*

Chicago: Univ. of Chicago Press, 1936–1944.
Compiled by William Craigie and James R. Hulbert.

CONTENTS: A 4-volume dictionary that aims to list all words originating in America, as well as English words having acquired special American senses or having an American record of interest.

The dictionary, whose primary interest is the "historical aspect" of American English, defines each word listed and illustrates its history with quotations from its earliest recorded use in America to its latest (i.e., from the colonial days to the end of the nineteenth century, the cut-off date of the work).

METHOD OF ORGANIZATION: Alphabetical. Note that words of American origin are indicated by a plus sign (+); words originating in England are indicated by an asterisk (*). See the prefatory pages entitled "Explanation of Special Lettering and Symbols."

EXAMPLES: The principal information given for each word consists of its definition(s) and its American history; dated quotations, which show how the word was used, are arranged chronologically from its earliest recorded appearance to the end of the nineteenth or beginning of the twentieth century. Other information given includes variant spellings and the etymology in some cases (e.g., if the word is of American Indian origin).

USEFULNESS: The *DAE* is the best-known and most important dictionary dealing with American English on historical principles. It should be used in conjunction with the *OED* (our no. 11) for those American words originating in England if the complete history is wanted. It is also an extremely valuable and fascinating source book for information on American customs and folklore.

RELATED REFERENCE WORKS: Another important reference tool for those interested in American English is *A Dictionary of Americanisms on Historical Principles*, ed. by Mitford M.

Mathews, (Chicago: Univ. of Chicago Press, 1951, 2 vols.). This works lists fewer words than the *DAE*, but includes material from the twentieth century and is in many ways stricter and more accurate in its attempts to distinguish words originating in America.

OTHER DICTIONARIES and WORDBOOKS

13] A *Dictionary of Slang and Unconventional English*

New York: Macmillan, 6th ed., 1967.
Compiled by Eric Partridge.

CONTENTS: A dictionary of unconventional speech—mostly British, with such Americanisms as have come into British usage.

METHOD OF ORGANIZATION: The ;lang words and phrases are listed alphabetically. Note that there are two alphabetical listings: the main dictionary, and a supplement that includes slang of more recent vintage.

USEFULNESS: The best dictionary to consult if a reader wants to know the meaning or history of a slang expression. Most of the words listed are not included in the standard dictionaries. So-called "vulgarisms," for example, are well represented.

Note that this dictionary works *from* slang *to* conventional English—it does not translate conventional English into slang, nor is there an index. Therefore, it is of principal use to those who have run across a slang term in their reading or conversation and wish to check its meaning.

The emphasis is on British usage, although American slang that has crossed the Atlantic (and slang is one of our chief exports) is included.

EXAMPLES: Here is the entry for "peach"—the noun (entries for other parts of speech follow in standard order: verb "to peach," participle "peaching," etc.). [Our explanations are added in brackets.]

peach. A detective; esp. one employed by omnibus, and formerly by stage-coach, proprietors to check receipts: from ca. 1835; ob. [obsolescent] F. & H. [according to Farmer and Henley's *Slang and its Analogues*, 1890–1904—see front of book for explanations of abbreviations] 2. [second meaning] An attractive girl or (gen. young) woman: orig. (1870's), U.S.; anglicised before 1889. Barrère & Leland [source of information *A Dictionary of Slang, Jargon, and Cant*, 1889–90]. Gen. *a regular peach* or *a peach of a girl*. Occ. (mostly U.S.) *a peach from Peachville:* C. 20 [20th Century] Cf. [compare with] *daisy*, q.v. ["which see"—look up "daisy"].

RELATED REFERENCE WORKS: John S. Farmer & W. E. Henley, *Slang and its Analogues* (London: Routledge, 1890–1904, 7 vols.); Eric Partridge, *Dictionary of the Underworld, British & American* (New York: Macmillan, 1949); *The American Thesaurus of Slang* (our no. 14).

14] *The American Thesaurus of Slang*

New York: Crowell, 2nd ed., 1953.
Compiled by Lester Berrey and Melvin Van Den Bark.

CONTENTS: A dictionary of unconventional speech—mostly American.

METHOD OF ORGANIZATION: Terms are grouped *by subjects*. The quickest and easiest way to use this work is to consult the Index, which lists, under one alphabet, both slang terms and standard English subjects, and sends the reader to the appropriate place in the dictionary. (Note that one is given the group number here, not the page number.)

A forty-eight-page appendix, "Slang Origins," gives the history and dates for a good number of slang expressions.

USEFULNESS: The best of the thesaurus type of slang dictionaries. Its index makes it possible to find both slang synonyms for standard English words and definitions of slang expressions one has come across.

The emphasis is on American slang. The coverage given to the slang of particular groups (e.g., dope addicts or members of the U.S. Navy) is particularly good.

EXAMPLES: The following is a typical entry [our explanations are added in brackets]:

353.2 **Infatuation.** Affectionate jag, beguin, case, case of spoons, crush (on), crusheroo, heavy crush,—case & c. [i.e., heavy case, etc.], mad pash, mash (on), pash (on), rave, sweet mash, sweet on, yen (on). *Spec.* [specific—terms following have a specific or restricted meaning and are defined in the italicized passages] calf love, pooch pash, puppy love, ooly-drooly, *transitory infatuation of a boy or girl.*

RELATED REFERENCE WORKS: Harold Wentworth and Stuart B. Flexner, *Dictionary of American Slang* (New York: Crowell 1960); Hyman E. Goldin, *et al., Dictionary of American Underworld Lingo* (New York: Twayne, 1950); *A Dictionary of Slang and Unconventional English* (our no. 13).

15] *English Dialect Dictionary*

London: Frowde, for the English Dialect Society,
1898–1905. 6 vols. Ed. by Joseph Wright.

CONTENTS: "Being the complete vocabulary of all dialect words still in use, or known to have been in use during the last two hundred years [1700–1900] in England, Ireland, Scotland, and Wales."

The 6-volume dictionary lists and defines English dialect words, giving the exact pronunciation in each case, the exact geographical area, the etymology, and quotations (with dates and bibliographical identifications) to illustrate the use of each word.

METHOD OF ORGANIZATION: Alphabetical. Keys to pronunciations and abbreviations used in this dictionary are given at the beginning of vol. I.

Note that the second half of vol. VI contains a "Supplement," an alphabetical listing of dialect words that were not included in the main vocabulary. Vol. VI also contains a "Bibliography" and an "English Dialect Grammar."

USEFULNESS: The largest and most comprehensive English dialect dictionary. Excellent for those who have come across a dialect word in their reading and wish to check its meaning or its origin or its local habitation. In addition, the 6 volumes are a storehouse of information on English superstitions, popular games, and customs.

EXAMPLES: Here is a brief sampling of entries, chosen at random: abide (to endure, tolerate); Adam's wine (water); betwattled (confused); blind-bucky-davy (game of blindman's bluff); clarty (dirty, sticky); grob (to search, grope, probe); lamploo (boy's game); looker (an eye); ormy-gormy (a simpleton); shortsome (amusing, merry); zounds (an oath, i.e., "God's wounds").

RELATED REFERENCE WORKS: Those interested in American dialect words should consult Harold Wentworth's *American Dialect Dictionary* (New York: Crowell, 1944), which lists more than 15,000 dialect terms, United States "localisms, regionalisms, and provincialisms; folk speech, urban as well as rustic; New England and Southern U.S. dialects viewed in their deviations from General Northern, or Western."

16] *Handbook of American Idioms and Idiomatic Usage*

New York: Regents Publ. Co., 1953.
Ed. by Harold C. Whitford and Robert J. Dixson.

CONTENTS: A listing of more than 4,500 American idioms. "Each idiom is defined, and its use is illustrated in a sentence."

METHOD OF ORGANIZATION: Idioms are listed alphabetically, from "about face" to "young ones."

USEFULNESS: A good place for writers to check their use of idioms. A handy place for readers to find the definitions of idioms they have encountered in their reading. An excellent book for anyone who wishes to perfect his command of idiomatic American-English.

EXAMPLES: Here is a typical entry:

hold the bag   be victimized, made liable for: —We all agreed
to share in the rent of the cottage, but when it came time to
pay, the others left me holding the bag.

RELATED REFERENCE WORKS: William Freeman, *A Concise
Dictionary of English Idioms* (New York: Crowell, 1951) lists
common British and American idioms.

Also see *Standard Handbook of Prepositions, Conjunctions,
Relative Pronouns, and Adverbs* (New York: Funk & Wagnalls,
1953).

17] *A Dictionary of Clichés*

New York: Macmillan, 4th ed., 1950.
Compiled by Eric Partridge.

CONTENTS: Lists, defines, and dates over 2,000 clichés—that
is, trite, stereotyped expressions that by their repeated use have
become offensive to the ear or have lost their meaning or point.

"A cliché is an outworn commonplace; a phrase, or short sentence, that has become so hackneyed that careful speakers and
scrupulous writers shrink from it because they feel that its use
is an insult to the intelligence of their audience or public," says
Mr. Partridge in the preface, and then goes on to classify
clichés into four groups:
» Idioms that have become clichés," e.g., "far and wide,"
  "safe and sound," "for love or money,"
» "Other hackneyed phrases," e.g., "add insult to injury,"
  "sick at heart," "generous to a fault,"
» "Stock phrases and familiar quotations from foreign
  languages," e.g., *"cherchez la femme,"* "sic transit
  gloria mundi,"
» "Quotations from English literature (usually misquoted),"
  e.g., "their name is Legion," "alas, poor Yorick!"
  "water, water, everywhere, and not a drop to drink."

METHOD OF ORGANIZATION: The clichés are listed alphabetically. There is, unfortunately, no index and too few cross references; thus clichés are hard to locate unless one knows them
word by word.

USEFULNESS: *First and foremost,* to help writers recognize clichés and henceforth *avoid* them *like the plague. Last but not least,* to help readers understand clichés that have because of their repeated use and misuse lost all *rhyme or reason.* It's also fun to read.

EXAMPLES: The following information is given for most items: definition and/or explanation of cliché, origin, date when it came into prominence, example in use or quote in some cases. The most "objectionable" clichés are starred (*).

Here is a typical entry:

go in at one ear and out of the other, to. (Of a warning, a discourse) to make no impression: C. 18–20. 'The professor's lecture went in at . . .'

18] *Dictionary of Modern English Usage*

Oxford: Clarendon Press, 2nd ed., 1965.
By Henry W. Fowler, rev. by Ernest Gowers.

CONTENTS: A guide to usage (grammar, syntax, style, idioms, and choice of words), spelling and inflections (formation of plurals, etc.), pronunciation, and punctuation.

METHOD OF ORGANIZATION: Entries are arranged alphabetically, from an article on the correct use of the indefinite articles "a" and "an" to an article on the use of "zz" instead of "z" at the end of such words as buzz, fizz, and jazz. There is no index. There are some cross references, but it is occasionally difficult to find the information wanted.

EXAMPLES: Here is a brief sampling of entries, chosen at random from the first few pages, to show the range of the book: abdomen (on pronunciation); —able, —ible (on the difference between the two suffixes); aborigines (on the non-use of the singular of this word); abridg(e)ment (on spelling); absolute construction (an article on this grammatical and syntactical question); act, action (on the distinction between meanings); addle, addled (on inflectional changes); adjective noun (definition and discussion); adverse (on the correct idiom: "adverse to," never "adverse from"); affect, effect (on the difference in meaning); aged (on the number of syllables in word, "aged 21" and "an aged man"); Americanisms (on the difference between English and American English, followed by a comparative list of words, e.g., boot—shoe, dust-bin—garbage can, goods train —freight train, lorry—truck, nappy—diaper, perambulator— baby carriage).

USEFULNESS: A famous work by an eccentric scholar; "*Modern English Usage* is personal: it is Fowler." Although somewhat out of fashion, since Fowler is a prescriptive grammarian, the work refuses to die, probably because of its lively style and the author's sense of humor.

Note that the point of view is British (especially on pronunciation, spelling, and punctuation).

RELATED REFERENCE WORKS: An adaptation of Fowler's work for Americans is available: Margaret Nicholson, *A Dictionary of American-English Usage* (New York: Oxford Univ. Press, 1957).

19] *Modern American Usage: A Guide*

New York: Hill & Wang, 1966.
By Wilson Follett and Jacques Barzun, *et al.*

CONTENTS: A guide to American usage: grammar, syntax, style, idioms, choice of words, spelling and inflections (formation of words), pronunciation, and punctuation.

METHOD OF ORGANIZATION: Entries are arranged alphabetically, from an article on the correct use of "a," "an," and "the" to an article on the correct pronunciation of "x" in "exult" (as in "egs") and in "luxurious" (as in "luks").

For matters of style, first consult the "Inventory of Main Entries" on pp. viii–x, and find the title of the fitting article (e.g., "and/or"; "in terms of"; "jargon"; "popularized technicalities"; "we, editorial"), then look in the main part of the lexicon for the article in its alphabetical place.

Two appendixes follow the alphabetical listings: on the

usage of "shall (should), will (would)"; and on the conventions of punctuation.

EXAMPLES: Here is a brief sampling of entries, chosen at random: awed, awesome (on the difference between the two words); and (on the legitimacy of beginning a sentence with "and"); ax to grind (definition of the idiom); compatible (on its overuse and misuse); imply, infer (on the difference between the words); Latin and Greek plurals (e.g., criterion—criteria); on, upon, up on (on the bookishness of "upon" in place of "on"); subjunctive (on the subjunctive mood); that, which (on when to use "which," when "that").

USEFULNESS: A handbook for educated usage and good taste in writing American English. A good place to check the usage or grammatical correctness of a word or phrase.

RELATED REFERENCE WORKS: *Dictionary of Contemporary American Usage* (our no. 20); H. L. Mencken, *The American Language: An Inquiry into the Development of English in the United States,* abridged edition edited by Raven I. McDavid, Jr. (New York: Knopf, 1963).

20] *Dictionary of Contemporary American Usage*

New York: Random House, 1957.
By Bergen and Cornelia Evans.

CONTENTS: A guide to American usage: grammar, syntax, style, idioms, choice of words, spelling and inflections (formation of words), and punctuation.

METHOD OF ORGANIZATION: Entries are arranged alphabetically, from an article on the use of the indefinite articles "a" and "an" to an article that clarifies the meaning and usage of the verb "zoom."

EXAMPLES: Here is a brief sampling of entries, chosen at random from the first few pages: abandoned, depraved, vicious (on the difference in meaning); abbreviations; abide (on its past tense); abject apology (a cliché); accept, except (on the confusion of these words); adjective (on grammar); adumbrate (on its level of diction); advertising (on its effect on our language); aerie (on spelling); agent (difference between English and American usage); agnostic, atheist, heathen, infidel, pagan (on the difference in meaning); alliteration (defined and discussed); America (on its common use as the equivalent for the U.S.A.); apropos (on correct idiom, "apropos to" or "apropos of").

USEFULNESS: A useful and often amusing handbook on current American usage. "It attempts to list the questions that most people ask, or should ask, about what is now good practice and to give the best answers available." The authors are more permissive than Fowler (our no. 18).

RELATED REFERENCE WORKS: *Modern American Usage: A Guide* (our no. 19).

21] *Roget's International Thesaurus*

New York: Crowell, 3rd ed., 1962.
Originally compiled by Peter M. Roget.

CONTENTS: A listing of synonymous words. A word finder, that groups related words together, making it possible for the user to locate the exact word he needs to express his idea.

METHOD OF ORGANIZATION: The synonyms are grouped according to ideas, or subject categories (not in alphabetical order), in the main portion of the book. Therefore consult the alphabetically arranged Index Guide (in the second half of the book) first.

For quick, sure results, this method of procedure is recommended:

» Look up the word or idea for which you want a list of synonyms in the Index Guide.
» Turn to the numbered section in the main portion of the book to which you have been referred by the index. (Remember that the numbers refer to subject category numbers, not page numbers.) Antonyms can be located

by looking at the nearby categories—"love" (# 929)
follows "hate" (# 928).

A handy illustration of how to use the thesaurus is printed on
the inside covers; the introductory section has more detailed
instructions.

EXAMPLES: For a synonym for the adjective "stupid," look in
the alphabetical Index Guide. Under "stupid," you will find
several possible references. Choose the one that is closest to
your meaning, e.g., "foolish" rather than "unintelligent." The
reference number given for "foolish" is "469.8." Then turn to
category 469, paragraph 8. Now you have a list of synonymous
adjectives from which to choose: "foolish . . . stupid, dumb
(slang), asinine, silly, dizzy (coll.) . . . inane, senseless, wit-
less, thoughtless," etc.

USEFULNESS: The best-known of the dictionaries of synonyms,
comprehensive, and easy to use. The latest edition is up to
date, giving good coverage of American slang and colloquial-
isms (so labeled); many obsolete words have been dropped.

Warning: this thesaurus does not define or distinguish between synonyms; thus, unless the student knows the denotation
and connotation of the words selected, he may misuse (mis-
employ, misapply, misappropriate, misdirect, pervert, abuse,
prostitute, profane, desecrate, or maltreat) them.

22] *Webster's Dictionary of Synonyms*

Springfield, Mass.: G. & C. Merriam & Co., 1942.

CONTENTS: "A dictionary of discriminated synonyms, with antonyms and analogous words [near synonyms] and contrasted
words [near antonyms]." A word finder that groups synonyms
and analogous words together, defining each and carefully distinguishing the differences in implication, connotation, and application by illustrative quotations from noted authors.

METHOD OF ORGANIZATION: Alphabetical. Cross references to
entries in which related words (analogous words or antonyms)
are discussed are indicated by an asterisk (*) prefixed to the
words. Thus the main entry for "stupid" shows in detail the

exact meaning and use of "stupid" and its closest synonyms, "dull, dense, crass, dumb," and then gives a list of analogous words, "foolish, silly, *simple, fatuous, asinine: sluggish . . . *lethargic: inert . . . *inactive: phlegmatic, stolid, *impassive"—thus sending the reader to four different main entries (marked by *) in which analogous words are treated.

For more detailed instructions, see the introductory section.

USEFULNESS: One of the most useful dictionaries of synonyms because it carefully discriminates among synonyms. It provides users "with the means of making clear comparisons between words of common denotation," clearly distinguishing "the differences in implications, connotations, and applications."

EXAMPLES: To show the distinction between two synonyms, "childlike and childish," for example, the dictionary first provides definitions, and then gives a series of quotations to illustrate the difference in usage.

RELATED REFERENCE WORKS: The following are the best-known of the many dictionaries of synonyms: *Roget's International Thesaurus* (our no. 21); *Crabb's English Synonyms*, ed. by George Crabb (New York: Grosset & Dunlap, 1945); *Funk & Wagnalls Standard Handbook of Synonyms, Antonyms, and Prepositions*, ed. by James C. Fernald, *et al.* (New York: Funk & Wagnalls, 1947); *March's Thesaurus–Dictionary*, new edition ed. by Norman Cousins, *et al.* (Garden City: Hanover House, 1958); *A Dictionary of English Synonyms*, by Richard Soule, revised by Alfred D. Sheffield (Boston: Little, Brown & Co., 1938).

23] *Familiar Quotations*

Boston: Little Brown & Co., 13th ed., 1955 (1st ed., 1855). Compiled by John Bartlett.

CONTENTS: An anthology of more than 110,000 familiar quotations, principally from the world's great literature, spanning the ages from ancient Egypt (*ca.* 2,675 B.C.) to the mid-twentieth century.

METHOD OF ORGANIZATION: Quotations are arranged chronologically by author in the main section of the book. A shorter section follows containing anonymous quotations, and passages from the Bible, the Book of Common Prayer, and the Koran.

An alphabetical index of authors at the front of the book makes it possible to find quotations by a particular author quickly. But to find the full text, author, source, and date of a familiar quotation, or to find famous quotations on a specific subject, the reader should use the main "index" at the back of the book. This over-500-page index is so complete, listing each quotation under a number of key words, that a seeker can locate a quote with only a vague recollection of the original. (Note that page references also indicate whether the quote is printed in the left column (*a*) or right column (*b*).)

EXAMPLES: The following example should show the ease with which a quotation can be found:

Dante's famous line "Leave all hope, ye that enter" can be found by looking in the "Index of Authors" under "Dante"; or by looking under "Leave" in the main index; or by looking under "Hope" in the main index.

USEFULNESS: Bartlett's *Familiar Quotations* is the best-known of the dictionaries of quotations. It is accurate, comprehensive, and easy to use.

RELATED REFERENCE WORKS: Since every new edition of Bartlett's adds new quotations but drops some of the old ones, readers might in some cases find it profitable to consult the older editions of the work.

Among other well-known dictionaries of quotations are the *Oxford Dictionary of Quotations* (London: Oxford Univ. Press, 2nd ed., 1953); *Home Book of Quotations* by Burton E. Stevenson (New York: Dodd, 9th ed., 1958); *Hoyt's New Cyclopedia of Practical Quotations* by Jehiel K. Hoyt (New York: Funk & Wagnalls, 1922); *New Dictionary of Quotations* by H. L. Mencken (New York: Knopf, 1942). Also see the *Oxford Dictionary of English Proverbs,* ed. by William G. Smith (Oxford: Clarendon Press, 2nd ed., 1948).

24] *Acronyms and Initialisms Dictionary*

Detroit, Mich.: Gale Research Co., 2nd ed., 1965.
Ed. by Robert C. Thomas, *et al.*

CONTENTS: A key to over 45,000 acronyms (or initialisms or abecedisms), contractions, and similar condensed appellations. The emphasis is on American terms, although foreign acronyms that Americans are likely to encounter are included. (Standard "outright abbreviations," e.g. "lb." for pound, "Mr." for mister, or "Mme." for madame, are not included; neither are acronyms for colleges and universities.)

METHOD OF ORGANIZATION: In alphabetical order, according to the acronym.

EXAMPLES: The dictionary lists acronyms from all fields and areas, physical sciences, social sciences, humanities, business, sports, transportation, military, government, etc. Here is a handful, taken at random from the many thousand entries: AT&T = American Telephone & Telegraph Co.; CID = Criminal Investigation Division; CORE = Congress of Racial Equality; D&D = Drunk & Disorderly; DI = Drill Instructor (Marine Corps); DOA = Dead On Arrival; DVOT = Dog Vomit On Toast (creamed tuna on toast; military slang) INRI = Iesus Naxerenus Rex Iudaeorum (Jesus of Nazareth, King of the Jews); JFK = John Fitzgerald Kennedy; LSD 25 = Lysergic Acid Diethylamine Tartrate; LSD = Doctor of Library Science; OED = Oxford English Dictionary; PC = Peace Corps; SANE = National Committee for a Sane Nuclear Policy; SPQR = Senatus Populusque Romanus (The Senate and People of Rome); SRO = Standing Room Only (Theater); ZIP = Zone Improvement Plan (Post Office code).

USEFULNESS: Good for quick identification and comprehension of acronyms (many of which are not listed in standard dictionaries).

RELATED REFERENCE WORKS: There are many other dictionaries of abbreviations and acronyms. Ralph De Sola's *Abbreviations Dictionary* (New York: Duell, Sloan & Pearce, 1964) lists abbreviations, acronyms, contractions, signs, and symbols, including standard abbreviations and acronyms of colleges and universities. Be sure to consult a recently published work, because acronyms multiply as fast as fruit flies.

I. C.
BIOGRAPHICAL DICTIONARIES

DEFINITION: A book that lists and identifies notable persons. Usually arranged alphabetically. Length and coverage vary, from skeletal listings of essential facts to long interpretive essays.

WHICH BIOGRAPHICAL DICTIONARY IS THE ONE FOR YOU?

The works listed below are the most important and most widely used ones. Note that we have divided them into three groups: American, British, and international.

To find the dictionary that best suits one's reference needs, the researcher should consider the following questions:

1. Into which national group does the man about whom information is desired fit?

2. Is he living or dead?

3. How much information is wanted—the bare facts of his life and accomplishments, or a succinct but broader summary and evaluation?

Next, consult the following oversimplified table, which notes the special value of each biographical dictionary:

» American
Who's Who in America (our no. 25)   Facts about living Americans.

Who Was Who in America (our no. 26)   Facts about dead Americans.

Dictionary of American Biography (our no. 27)
Facts about and evaluations of dead Americans.

National Cyclopaedia of American Biography (our no. 28)
Facts about and evaluations of dead and living Americans.

» British
Who's Who (our no. 29)   Facts about living
British notables.

Who Was Who (our no. 30)   Facts about dead
British notables, 1897—.

Dictionary of National Biography (our no. 31)
Facts about and evaluations of dead British notables.

⁕ International
International Who's Who (our no. 32)   Facts about
living notables of all nations (revised annually).

Chambers' Biographical Dictionary (our no. 33)
Detailed facts about dead and living notables of all nations
(*ca.* 15,000 entries).

Webster's Biographical Dictionary (our no. 34)
Facts about and evaluations of living notables of all nations.
(*ca.* 40,000 entries).

Current Biography (our no. 35)
Facts about and evaluations of living notables of all nations.

Biography Index (our no. 36)   Index to biographical
materials in current books and periodicals.

Now, the researcher should look at our description of the
one or two works that seem to fit his needs.

ALSO NOTE

There is some overlapping among various kinds of reference
works. Biographical information can also be obtained in encyclopedias (especially about major figures) and in some yearbooks, as well as in certain directories and in the obituary columns of newspapers.

But the first step should always be to consult the most likely
source of information: in seeking brief and general information
about the life and fame of a notable, one reaches for a biographical dictionary.

25] *Who's Who in America*

A Biographical Dictionary of Notable Living Men & Women.
Chicago: Marquis, 1899—. Revised and reissued every
two years.

CONTENTS: Brief biographical sketches of prominent living
Americans, notable either for their accomplishments or their
official positions. There are approximately 66,000 names listed
in the latest volume. Some prominent persons from other countries are included.

METHOD OF ORGANIZATION: Alphabetical. Also check the section "Latest Listings & Sketch Additions," following the end of
the main alphabetical listings, for names not found in the main
section and for occasional additional information about those
who are in the main section. Be sure to consult the current
volume for the latest information.

USEFULNESS: The emphasis is on brief descriptions and the inclusion of many names. Do not expect to find more than short
summaries of the lives—the bare, minimal facts. Note that the
facts are supplied by the subjects of the biographies; hence the
subject himself is responsible for the completeness and accuracy of his sketch.

EXAMPLES: The following information is given for each person listed: occupation, place and date of birth, names of parents, education and degrees received, marital status, names of
children, honors received (fellowships, prizes), major positions
held, present position and business address, works published,
religion (in some cases), place of domicile, mailing address.
    An asterisk (*) following a sketch signifies that the informa-
tion has not been verified by the biographee and may be out of
date.

RELATED REFERENCE WORKS: "Current Series" of the *National
Cyclopaedia of American Biography* (our no. 28).
    For sketches of deceased Americans once included in *Who's
Who in America,* see *Who Was Who in America* (our no. 26).

See also the various *specialized* biographical dictionaries. These works are both more *inclusive*, since they list many who are not in the general volume, and more *exclusive* or specialized, since the individual works are limited according to regional, professional, or other categories. The *Biography Index* (our no. 36) can direct you to the appropriate publications.

26] *Who Was Who in America*

Chicago: Marquis, 1897—.

CONTENTS: Brief biographical sketches in 3 volumes of prominent deceased Americans, notable either for their accomplishments or their official positions, whose biographies have been dropped from *Who's Who in America* (our no. 25) because of death. Nearly 50,000 men and women who have died since 1897 are included.

METHOD OF ORGANIZATION: Names are listed alphabetically in each volume.

Vol. I contains biographies of notables who died between 1897 and 1942; vol. II covers through 1950, and vol. III through 1960.

Vol. IV, covering 1961–1970, is scheduled to appear in 1970. But note that vols. II and III also contain some biographies omitted from earlier volumes. Therefore, a reader should check all three volumes in case he can't find the name he is looking for in the first volume.

USEFULNESS: The emphasis is on brief descriptions and the inclusion of many names. Do not expect to find more than short summaries of the lives—the bare, minimal facts. *Who Was Who* is valuable, however, for its information about minor notables not available elsewhere.

The information given here is the same as was given in the latest sketch printed in *Who's Who in America*, supplied by the biographee himself, plus the date of death, and the interment location if available.

EXAMPLES: For a summary of the information supplied in each biographical sketch, see our no. 25.

RELATED REFERENCE WORKS: A related volume, published in the same place, is the *Historical Volume: 1607–1896.* It contains 13,300 sketches of notables "both of the United States of America and of other countries, who have made contributions to, or whose activity was in some manner related to the history of the United States, from the founding of Jamestown Colony" to 1896. The format is the same as that followed in the other volumes; however the information was not supplied by the biographees themselves, but rather researched and compiled by the editors. The *Historical Volume* plus the three volumes of *Who Was Who in America* plus the latest volume of *Who's Who in America* are sometimes referred to by the collective title of *Who's Who in American History;* information on 120,-000 notables of interest to students of America are gathered in five related volumes.

27] *Dictionary of American Biography* (*DAB*)

New York: Scribner's. 20 vols. and *Index*, 1928–1937;
Supplement One, 1944; *Supplement Two*, 1958.
Ed. by Allen Johnson, *et al.*

CONTENTS: Twenty-two volumes of articles on the lives and accomplishments of prominent deceased Americans. Each article is signed, and is followed by a bibliography. The work contains 14,870 biographies of Americans from the colonial days to 1940.

METHOD OF ORGANIZATION: Alphabetical. The 20 main volumes include biographies of people who died before 1927; the supplements bring the coverage up through 1940, and also include some biographies omitted from the earlier volumes.

The *Index Volume* (for vols. 1–20) is divided into six lists: (1) biographees, alphabetically; (2) the authors of the biographies, alphabetically; (3) biographees, according to birthplace; (4) biographees, according to schools attended; (5) biographees, according to occupation; (6) a subject index. The uses to which these indexes can be put are obvious: e.g., to find prominent Americans of Chinese origin, or from Nebraska, consult index no. 3.

USEFULNESS: The *DAB*, prepared "under the auspices of the American Council of Learned Societies," is the most famous and most reliable of all American biographical dictionaries. It is *the* work to consult for information on the life and accomplishments of a deceased American. The bibliographies found at the end of all articles add further to its value.

EXAMPLES: Each biography gives dates of birth and death; occupation; place of birth; names of parents, spouse, children; education; accomplishments or publications; history of career; analysis of character; analysis of influence; a bibliography of works about the subject of the biography. They vary in length from half-page sketches to chapter-length essays.

RELATED REFERENCE WORKS: *Concise Dictionary of American Biography* (New York: Scribner's, 1964), an abridgment of the *DAB* and its supplements. *National Cyclopaedia of American Biography* (our no. 28). *Who Was Who in America* (our no. 26).

28] *National Cyclopaedia of American Biography*

New York: J. T. White & Co., 1892—. 49 vols. (volumes are identified by numbers); plus 10 vols. in the "Current Series," plus *Index*. (Volumes are identified by letters).

CONTENTS: Detailed accounts of the lives and accomplishments of prominent Americans, deceased (in the "Permanent Series") and living (in the "Current Series"). The work contains more than 52,000 biographies of Americans from the colonial days to the present who have made significant national contributions.

METHOD OF ORGANIZATION: Because the biographies are *not* arranged alphabetically (but grouped more or less chronologically), readers must use the *Index Volume,* which indexes both the "Permanent" and "Current" series. This alphabetical index not only lists the names of the men and women whose lives are included, but also indexes subjects (e.g., petroleum, trade unions, abolitionists, N.A.A.C.P., First National Bank, "My Country 'tis of Thee," World War I, strikes, etc.).

USEFULNESS: Since this work is much more inclusive than the *DAB* (our no. 27), listing many lesser-known as well as major figures, it should be consulted if a researcher cannot find the deceased American he was looking for in the *DAB.* In general, the articles in the *DAB* are longer, and provide more information and evaluative commentary; therefore, look there first.

The volumes in the "Current Series" are an excellent source for information on living Americans, and give much fuller information than the who's-who sort of biographical dictionaries (e.g., *Who's Who in America,* our no. 25).

EXAMPLES: The information given for each person listed is fuller than, but similar to, the sort in *Who's Who in America* (our no. 25); see "Examples" there. The biographies vary in length from paragraph-length sketches to longish essays.

RELATED REFERENCE WORKS: *White's Conspectus of American Biography* (New York: J.T. White & Co., 1937) provides another index to the volumes in the "Permanent Series." In it the past leaders of American life are listed, not alphabetically, but by their reason for fame. Here one can find answers to such questions as: Who was the American ambassador to Russia in 1809? Who is known as the Father of the American Auto Industry? (The answer is not Henry Ford.) Who was the president of the American Gynecological Society in 1899?

Dictionary of American Biography (our no. 27), *Who's Who in America* (our no. 25), *Who Was Who in America* (our no. 26).

British

29] *Who's Who*

London: A. & C. Black, Ltd., 1849—.
Revised and reissued annually.

CONTENTS: Brief biographical sketches of prominent living persons, principally British. A few distinguished persons of other countries are also included. The more than 20,000 included are notable either for their accomplishments or their official positions.

METHOD OF ORGANIZATION: Alphabetical.

USEFULNESS: In this, the grandpapa of all who's whos, as in all other biographical dictionaries of the who's-who ilk, the emphasis is on briefness. Do not expect to find more than short summaries of the lives—the bare, minimal facts. Note that the facts are supplied by the subjects of the biographies; hence the subject himself is responsible for the completeness and accuracy of his sketch.

EXAMPLES: The following information is given for each person listed: titles, honors, degrees, current profession, date of birth (place of birth is not given, except for foreigners), names of parents, name of spouse, name of spouse's father, date of marriage, number and sex of living children, education, important professional positions held, publications (with dates), "recreations," address, and a list of clubs.

As one can see, here is the skeleton only. For the meat, the reader must look elsewhere—to biographies, magazine and newspaper articles, and to the works of the man in question.

The section, of close to 30 pages, entitled "Abbreviations Used in this Book," which precedes the alphabetical listings, can be extremely useful, especially to the work's American users who may not be familiar with British initials and abbreviations (e.g., M.B.E. = Member of the Order of the British Empire, C.B.S.A. = Clay Bird Shooting Association).

RELATED REFERENCE WORKS: *Chambers's Biographical Dictionary* (our no. 33), *Current Biography* (our no. 35).

For sketches of deceased Englishmen once included in *Who's Who*, see *Who Was Who* (our no. 30).

30] *Who Was Who*

London: A & C. Black, Ltd., 1897—. 5 vols. The 6th vol. is scheduled to appear in 1970.

CONTENTS: Brief biographical sketches of prominent deceased persons, principally British. These volumes contain "the biographees removed from *Who's Who* each year on account of death, with final details and date of death added."

METHOD OF ORGANIZATION: Names are listed alphabetically in each volume. Vol. I contains biographies of those who died between 1897 and 1915. Vol. II covers 1916–1928; Vol. III, 1929–1940; Vol. IV, 1941–1950; Vol. V, 1951–1960. Each volume contains between 8,000 and 12,000 biographies.

For an explanation of the numerous abbreviations, see the key supplied at the beginning of each volume.

USEFULNESS: The emphasis is on briefness and inclusiveness. Do not expect to find more than succinct summaries of the lives —the bare, minimal facts. *Who Was Who* is valuable, however, for its information about minor notables not available elsewhere.

EXAMPLES: The following information is given for each person listed: titles, honors, degrees, current profession, date of birth (place of birth is not given, except for foreigners), names of parents, name of spouse, name of spouse's father, date of marriage, number and sex of living children, education, important professional positions held, publications (with dates), "recreations," address, and a list of clubs.

As one can see, here is the skeleton only. For the meat, the reader must look elsewhere—to biographies, magazine and newspaper articles, and to the works of the man in question.

RELATED REFERENCE WORKS: *Dictionary of National Biography* (our no. 31).

31] *Dictionary of National Biography* (*DNB*)

London: Oxford University Press, 1921—. 21 vols. plus
supplements. A reissue of the original (1885—) 66-vol. ed.
Further decennial vols. to follow. Ed. by Leslie Stephens
and Sidney Lee.

CONTENTS: Authoritative, well-written articles on the lives
and accomplishments of approximately 17,500 deceased "noteworthy inhabitants of the British Isles and the colonies, from
the earliest historical period to the present time." Each article is
signed, and is followed by a bibliography.

METHOD OF ORGANIZATION: Alphabetical. Vols. I–XXI contain
biographies of those who died before January 22, 1901 (the
date of Queen Victoria's death). There is an index at the end of
each volume.

Vol. XXII, also known as the *1st Supplement*, lists persons
who were "accidentally omitted from the main volumes." The
2nd Supplement, 1901–1911, covers January 22, 1901–December 31, 1911. The *3rd Supplement* covers 1912–1921; *4th Supplement, 1922–1930*; *5th Supplement, 1931–1940*; *6th Supplement, 1941–1950*. The index at the end of the most recent
supplement is cumulative; it gives volume and page references
for all the twentieth century volumes.

USEFULNESS: The *DNB* is the most famous and most reliable
of all British biographical dictionaries. It is *the* work to consult
for accurate and concise (yet full) information on the life and
accomplishments of a deceased British notable. Its value is further enhanced by the bibliographies found at the end of all articles; consult the books listed there for fuller information.

EXAMPLES: The following information is given for each person listed: dates of birth and death, profession or other classification, family background, education, synopsis of life, analysis
of career, reputation, works, facts on marriage and children,
place of burial, epitaph, plus a bibliography of works about the
subject of the biography.

The biographies vary in length, from half-page sketches
(e.g., on William Burke, senior partner of the nineteenth-
century mass-murder team of Burke and Hare) to chapter

length (e.g., 15 pages on Hogarth, 35 on Wellington, 50 on Shakespeare, and 112 on Queen Victoria).

RELATED REFERENCE WORKS: The 2-vol. *Concise Dictionary of National Biography* (London: Oxford University Press, 1952, 1961) is a summary of the *DNB*.

Who Was Who (our no. 30); *Modern English Biography* (limited to nineteenth century Englishmen), ed. by Frederick Boase (Truro: Netherton, 1892–1921); *Who's Who in History* (limited to the British Isles), ed. by C. R. N. Routh (Oxford: Blackwell, 1960—).

International

32] *International Who's Who*

London: Europa Publications, 1935—.
Revised and reissued annually.

CONTENTS: Brief biographical sketches of eminent living personalities of all nations. "The compilers have attempted to include everyone whose name is known outside his country." The current volume lists about 14,000 persons of international repute.

METHOD OF ORGANIZATION: Alphabetical. A list of the "Reigning Royal Families" precedes the alphabetical listing.

USEFULNESS: A valuable source for biographical information about current international figures, gathered in one listing, and written in English. The book is especially useful if the person one needs data on is from one of the smaller countries that are not covered by a national who's who.

The emphasis in this work is on brief descriptions and the inclusion of many names. Do not expect to find more than short summaries of the lives—the bare, minimal facts.

The facts for the biographies are supplied either by the subject of the sketch or by various agencies such as embassies, chambers of commerce, or other associations.

EXAMPLES: The following information is given for each person listed: titles, honors, degrees, nationality, profession, date of birth, education, a summary of his career and accomplishments (publications, exhibitions, prizes), address.

RELATED REFERENCE WORKS: *Dictionary of International Biography*, compiled by Geoffrey Handley-Taylor (London: Dict. of Int. Biog. Co., 1963); *World Biography*, 5th edit. (Bethpage, N.Y.: Institute for Research in Biography, 1954).

If the researcher knows the nationality of the man he wants to find listed, he could look in the appropriate regional or national biographical dictionary, e.g., *Who's Who in France, Who's Who in Communist China.*

33] *Chambers's Biographical Dictionary*

New York: St. Martin's; London: W. & R. Chambers, Ltd., 1897—. Periodically rev. and brought up to date (new ed., 1962). Ed. by J. O. Thorne, *et al.*

CONTENTS: Brief biographical sketches of prominent individuals, both living and dead, of all nations. The latest edition lists over 15,000 major and minor figures. The infamous as well as the famous appear. Major Biblical figures are also listed. A short bibliography is given in many cases.

METHOD OF ORGANIZATION: Alphabetical. An especially useful subject index follows, unusual in this sort of biographical dictionary with its brief entries. The researcher can use this index to locate men by the subject or work or event associated with them. For example, if a reader were looking for a biographical sketch of the author of *Dr. Fu Manchu* but did not know the name of the author, he could simply look up the title of the book in the subject index—under the category Literature & Drama—and be referred to Rohmer, the author.

The subject index is divided into the following categories: Art & Architecture, Cinema, Exploration & Geography, History, Literature & Drama, Music, Nicknames & Personalities, Philosophy & Theology, and Science & Industry.

USEFULNESS: A valuable one-volume source for biographical information about past and present world figures. Although the work emphasizes brief descriptions and the inclusion of many names, and consequently presents only short summaries of the lives, it attempts to be more than just a catalogue of facts. It tells the life stories in complete sentences and adds "human interest and critical observations" to the facts.

This work tends to give more detailed information than its closest relative, *Webster's Biographical Dictionary* (our no. 34), but lists fewer names.

EXAMPLES: The following information is given for each person listed: pronunciation of name (when necessary), titles, dates, designation (profession or field of renown), birthplace, reason for fame (with list of works where applicable), reputation, bibliographical references (in many cases).

Entries vary in length, from a few lines to a full page.

RELATED REFERENCE WORKS: *Webster's Biographical Dictionary* (our no. 34); *New Century Cyclopedia of Names* (our no. 6); *Universal Pronouncing Dictionary of Biography & Mythology* (also known as *Lippincott's Pronouncing Biographical Dictionary*), ed. by Joseph Thomas (Phila.: Lippincott, 5th ed. 1930).

34] *Webster's Biographical Dictionary*

Springfield, Mass.: G. & C. Merriam Co., 1943—.
Revised every few years.

CONTENTS: Brief biographical listings of prominent individuals, both living and dead, of all nations.

This work attempts to be all inclusive. More than 40,000 major and minor figures are sketched in the latest edition; both the famous and the infamous. Figures in the Bible are also listed.

METHOD OF ORGANIZATION: Alphabetical. A most useful appendix, "Pronouncing List of Prenames," lists the correct pronunciation of given names in all languages. Other appendixes give lists of U. S. presidents, Popes, heads of foreign states, and other information.

USEFULNESS: A valuable source of biographical facts about past and present notables. The emphasis in this work is on inclusiveness; thus it is a good one-stop, catch-all source. However, the listings are limited to the bare, minimal facts.

Although this work gives less detailed information than its closest relative, *Chambers's Biographical Dictionary* (our no. 33), it lists many more names.

EXAMPLES: The following information is given for each person listed: pronunciation and syllabification of name (e.g., Flau'bert [flō bâr], Mao Tse-tung [mä' ō dzu' doong']), dates, nationality, city of residence, designation (profession or field of renown), city of birth, family relationships, education, details of career, other significant activities (discoveries, inventions, publications).

Entries are very brief (the average item takes less than 10 lines), and are given in outline form as in most other who's-who type of dictionaries.

RELATED REFERENCE WORKS: *Chambers's Biographical Dictionary* (our no. 33), *New Century Cyclopedia of Names* (our no. 6).

35] *Current Biography*

Who's News and Why. New York: H. W. Wilson Co., 1940—.
Published monthly (except August) and then gathered into annual and finally decennial volumes.

CONTENTS: Brief articles about living persons in all nations who have come to the general public's attention because of their newsworthiness. Limited to about 350 biographies a year. Monthly, with annual and decennial accumulations.

METHOD OF ORGANIZATION: Alphabetical. The index of the latest monthly issue lists the names of the figures included in all of the year's monthly issues. The cumulated index in the latest annual volume also lists the names of those included in the previous annual volumes, back to the last decennial volume. To locate an article a user should start with the index to the latest monthly issue and then work backwards till his man is found —to the index of the latest annual volume, then the 1951–1960 index, and finally the 1940–1950 index.

USEFULNESS: Article-length portraits summarize the lives and accomplishments of currently newsworthy persons; well-written, lively, and informative. Citizens of all countries are included, but Americans are particularly well represented.

Following each article is a list of the sources upon which the sketch has been based. These short and selective bibliographies point the way to a next possible step in research.

At the end of the annual volumes, the names of the biographees are also listed according to their professions, under such classifications as Advertising, Agriculture, Architecture, Art, etc.

EXAMPLES: The following coverage is given to each person included: pronunciation of name, date of birth, occupation and reason for newsworthiness, address, followed by a biographical sketch (average length: 2 pages), a photograph (in almost all cases), and a list of the sources used.

RELATED REFERENCE WORKS: For vital statistics about living persons, see the various national, regional or professional who's whos. For sources giving fuller information, check the listings in the *Biography Index* (our no. 36).

36] *Biography Index*

New York: H. W. Wilson Co., 1946—. Published quarterly, then gathered into annual and finally triennial volumes.

CONTENTS: This quarterly is an *index* (it does not itself contain any biographical material), a listing of current biographical books and articles published in English, on the world's notable living and dead.

"All types of biographical material are covered: pure biography, critical material of biographical significance, autobiography, letters, diaries . . . genealogies, fiction, drama, poetry, bibliographies, obituaries, pictorial works, and juvenile literature" as well as "incidental biographical material such as prefaces and chapters in otherwise non-biographical books." There are annual and triennial cumulations.

METHOD OF ORGANIZATION: Alphabetical. To obtain a list of all the biographical work done on someone since January, 1946, one consults each of the triennial volumes, plus the current annual volume(s), plus the current quarterly issues not as yet bound into annual volumes.

USEFULNESS: The best available tool for locating biographical material published in English since 1946. Its scope is universal, "ranging from bootblacks to presidents, assassins to saints, children to centenarians."

Also note that each volume contains an "Index to Professions and Occupations," in which all the figures included in the main alphabetical section are listed under some 1,000 appropriate categories, from "Abbots" to "Zoologists." This can be useful for researchers who are interested in a field but are unfamiliar with the names of individuals (e.g., the names of Hungarian poets, or pirates, or child prodigy musicians).

EXAMPLES:

Eichmann, Adolf, 1906–1962. German Nazi leader
Arendt, Hannah. Eichmann in Jerusalem; a report on the banality of evil.   rev and enl ed Viking '61 313 p bibliog
Papadatos, Pierre Achille. Eichmann trial. Praeger '64 129 p. bibliog

A key to periodical abbreviations used is found at the front of each issue and volume.

RELATED REFERENCE WORKS: See our section I.D., which describes indexes to periodicals and newspapers, and our section I.E., which lists bibliographies.

I. D.

INDEXES TO PERIODICALS
AND NEWSPAPERS

DEFINITION: To put it as simply as possible, an index is a guide that tells one where and how to find publications on a particular subject. Indexes are arranged either by subject or by author or both. The indexes in this section tell where and how to find what has been published in magazines and newspapers.

WHICH INDEX SUITS YOUR NEEDS?: The following indexes show which periodicals have articles on the subject or by the author a researcher is looking for:

» *Readers' Guide to Periodical Literature* (our no. 37)
  Indexes about 135 of the most popular as well as a few
  scholarly and scientific American magazines from 1900
  to the present.
» *International Index*, vols. 1–18, and *Social Sciences and
  Humanities Index*, vol. 19 (our no. 38)   Indexes about
  172 scholarly periodicals, almost exclusively American,
  British, and Canadian, in the humanities and social sciences.
» *Poole's Index to Periodical Literature* (our no. 39)
  Indexes 470 nineteenth-century American and British
  periodicals of a general nature.
» *Nineteenth Century Readers' Guide to Periodical Literature*
  (our no. 40)   Indexes 51 American and English periodicals,
  most of them general and literary, mainly from 1890–1899.

To find which library has the issues of the periodical needed, the researcher consults:

» *Union List of Serials in Libraries of the United States and
  Canada* (our no. 41)   Lists and often describes over 150,000
  periodicals in 891 American and 65 Canadian libraries.

To find articles, reviews, feature stories, news and editorial matter—with the exception of advertising—in newspapers, a researcher would turn first to the following:

» *New York Times Index* (our no. 42)   *Gives a* condensed, classified history of the world as it is printed every day in the *New York Times.*

» *Times* [*London*]: *Official Index* (our no. 43)   The English counterpart of the *New York Times,* specializing in British and European news.

Finally, to find reviews of books, one consults the following:

» *Book Review Digest* (our no. 44)   Contains short quotations from selected reviews of books for the general reader from about 75 popular American and English periodicals.

» *An Index to Book Reviews in the Humanities* (our no. 45) Indexes reviews of books in over 650 magazines, general as well as scholarly.

» *Book Review Index* (our no. 46)   Lists almost every review in over 220 magazines, general as well as scholarly. No quotations.

37] *Readers' Guide to Periodical Literature*

New York: H. W. Wilson Co., 1900—.
Biweekly with cumulations every two years.

CONTENTS: Published two times a month (once a month in July and August), the *Readers' Guide* indexes the contents of about 135 of the most popular as well as a few scholarly and scientific American magazines published from 1900 to the present. This means that the *Readers' Guide* gives, among other things, a detailed alphabetical key to magazine articles, their authors, where and when the articles were published, and the exact pages where they can be found.

METHOD OF ORGANIZATION: Each magazine article is listed alphabetically under the author, the subject, and often under the title (titles given only for works of fiction; titles of poems and movies are listed alphabetically under "Poems" and "Moving Picture Plays"). This organization resembles the organization of the card catalog in the library.

USEFULNESS: The *Readers' Guide* is one of the most important reference works in the library, for it shows the history of our time as recorded in the most widely read general magazines published in the United States. *Time, Life, Sports Illustrated, Reader's Digest, The Atlantic, Harper's Magazine, The New Yorker,* and *Science* are just a few of the magazines covered by the *Readers' Guide.*

EXAMPLES: Here are two sample entries from the 1963–1964 volume:

Play Guide to play and playthings. R. M. Goldenson. il Parents
Mag 39: 62–3 O '64
Playfair, Giles Word of Christine. New Repub 149:11–13 D 21
'63

In the first entry, the subject is play; R. M. Goldenson's article, "Guide to Play and Playthings," is illustrated, and is in *Parents Magazine,* vol. 39, pages 62 and 63 and other pages, in the October 1964 issue. In the second sample, "Playfair, Giles" is the author of the article "Word of Christine," which appeared in *New Republic* magazine, vol. 149, pages 11–13, in the December 21, 1963, issue.

The first few pages of each volume explain the abbreviations of periodical names used.

38] *International Index Vols. 1–18, Social Sciences and Humanities Index Vol. 19—*

New York: H. W. Wilson Co., 1907—. Annual supplements available to permanent 3-year volumes. Supplements also available every 3 months.

From 1909–1919 this index was called *Readers' Guide to Periodical Literature Supplement,* and from 1920 to 1964 the *International Index.* In 1965 its name was changed to *Social Sciences and Humanities Index.*

CONTENTS: This important work indexes about 172 scholarly periodicals, almost exclusively American, British, Canadian, with the majority being American, in the humanities and the social sciences. Up to 1916 no foreign language periodicals were included; from 1916 to 1940 French, German, Swiss, Swedish, Japanese, Dutch, and Italian periodicals were listed. From about 1941 on foreign magazines were dropped. Up to 1955 it also listed articles on the physical sciences, but from 1955 on those periodicals were dropped.

METHOD OF ORGANIZATION: Alphabetically arranged by author and subject. For example: "Preface to *Les Misérables*" by R. T. House may be found under R. T. House and under Victor Hugo.

USEFULNESS: This index is one of the most valuable reference works covering scholarly articles mainly in the humanities and the social sciences. It provides a record of the published history of scholarship in these disciplines for the past sixty years. (*American Journal of Philology, American Journal of International Law, Philosophical Review,* and publications of the Modern Language Association of America, are just a few of the magazines listed in the *International Index.*)

EXAMPLES: See "Examples" under *Readers' Guide to Periodical Literature* (our no. 37). Explanations there apply to *International Index.*

RELATED REFERENCE WORKS: *British Humanities Index* (London: Library Association, 1962—). This quarterly, with annual cumulations, indexes about 270 British periodicals concerned with the arts and politics.

39] *Poole's Index to Periodical Literature*

Boston: Houghton, 1802–1881, 2 vols. Thereafter in 5 supplements: 1882–1886, 1887–1891, 1892–1896, 1897–1901, 1902–1906.

CONTENTS: This is the most important magazine index for the nineteenth century. It lists about 600,000 articles, mostly of a general nature (medical, legal, botanical, and the purely professional and scientific periodicals have been excluded), in 470 American and British periodicals.

METHOD OF ORGANIZATION: Alphabetically arranged by subject, *never* by author. Authors are included only when they are treated as subjects. For example, Lord Macaulay's articles are not under his name but under the appropriate subject—Bacon, Church and State, Machiavelli, etc. When his name does appear, it is in a list of articles *about* him.

USEFULNESS: This is the reference work to use for locating nineteenth century magazine articles on social, political, economic, scientific, and literary topics, mostly of a general nature.

The drawbacks to this index are: there are no listings under the author's name; brief articles and notes are omitted; minor book reviews are omitted; the index is not always complete; and the day, month and year of an article are not given.

EXAMPLES: The following information is given for each article listed: title of article; name of author, in parentheses, whenever author's name is given or can be identified; name of periodical; volume and page number. Only the page number of the beginning of article is given, and so one can't tell how long an article is. No dates.

Check the introductory pages of vol. 1 for abbreviations, full titles, place of publication, dates and number of volumes of each periodical.

40] *Nineteenth Century Readers'* *Guide to Periodical Literature*

New York: H. W. Wilson Co., 1944.

CONTENTS: This work indexes 51 American and British periodicals, most of them general and literary, mainly from between 1890 and 1899. Fourteen of the 51 are indexed beyond 1899; the *National Geographic* up to 1909, and *PMLA* to 1919.

METHOD OF ORGANIZATION: This guide is arranged alphabetically, by author, subject, and title.

USEFULNESS: More thorough, accurate, and comprehensive than *Poole's Index to Periodical Literature* for the nine years that it covers, *Nineteenth Century Readers' Guide* gives date of publication (day, month, and year) and includes seven important magazines not included in Poole's:

American Historical Review, Cornhill Magazine, Critic, Edinburgh Review, Harper's Weekly, Nation, Quarterly Review, and *The Yellow Book.*

It also enables readers to find an entry under the author's name.

One very useful feature is that it often identifies anonymous articles, sometimes written by famous men of letters. Sir Arthur Conan Doyle did not sign his name to an article entitled *Duello in France.* Under the title the reader is referred to "A. C. Doyle," and under "Arthur Conan Doyle" is given the information about the article, including the fact that it was published anonymously.

EXAMPLES: See "Examples" under *Readers' Guide to Periodical Literature* (our no. 37). Explanations there apply to this work, with one exception: in this guide, the name of the author comes first followed by the name of the article; in the *Readers' Guide,* it is the name of the article that comes first, followed by the author.

41] *Union List of Serials in Libraries of the United States and Canada*

New York: H. W. Wilson Co., 3rd ed., 1965. 5 vols.

CONTENTS: This comprehensive reference work lists over 150,-000 periodicals in 891 American and 65 Canadian libraries. It lists which libraries a periodical can be found in, and tells how complete each library's holdings are. Often it gives a brief description of a periodical, and then goes on to tell when the periodical began publication, when it ceased publication, and with what volume.

Periodicals listed are in all languages and go back as far as the eighteenth century. The closing date for the third edition is 1949.

The *Union List* excludes the following categories:
» Government publications (except periodicals and monographic series issued by governments).
» Administrative reports of societies, universities, corporations, etc.
» Almanacs.
» American newspapers.
» English and other foreign newspapers published after 1820.
» Law reports and digests.
» Publications of agricultural and other experimental stations.
» Publications of local, religious, labor and fraternal organizations, boards of trade, chambers of commerce.
» Publications of national and international conferences, congresses, etc.
» United Nations publications.
» Alumni, undergraduate, and inter-collegiate fraternity publications.

METHOD OF ORGANIZATION: Arranged alphabetically. Readers should read introductory pages on the special characteristics of the third edition and the list of abbreviations of all libraries.

USEFULNESS: An indispensable reference source for those working with periodicals. If the periodical needed is not available at the local college or public library, the *Union List* will give the name and the location of the library that does have it.

An inter-library loan or a photo reproduction of the pages needed can then be arranged.

EXAMPLES:

Photography: a monthly supplement to "World Press News." London. 1, Ag 1932+

CL (1)	NN 1+
IU (4–6)	NRE 1+
MH 1+	OT 4– (7)
MdBE 4+	PP (1–4)+

"1, Ag 1932 +" shows that this series began in August, 1932, and is still being published.

The initials—CL, IU, etc.—indicate libraries; the code is given in several pages at the beginning of the volume. MH, NN, and NRE have complete files from Vol. 1 on, and subscribe currently (remember that "currently" means as of 1949). MdBE has a complete set beginning with Volume 4 and subscribes currently.

CL has an incomplete set of volume 1; IU has only volumes 4–6, all incomplete. OT has volumes 4–7, volume 7 being incomplete. The absence of a plus sign means that the library does not subscribe to the publication currently.

PP has volumes 1–4, all incomplete, and a current subscription beginning with volume 5.

RELATED REFERENCE WORKS: For the periodicals from 1950–1964, see *New Serials Titles* 1950–1960, 2 vols., and *New Serials Titles* 1961–1964, 2 vols. Both are published by the Library of Congress and give the same information as the *Union List.*

British Union-Catalogue of Periodicals, ed. by James D. Stewart (London: Butterworths Scientific Publishers, 1955–1958), gives the most comprehensive record of the periodicals of the world, from the seventeenth century to the present, in British libraries. About 142,000 periodicals in 438 libraries are listed.

42] *New York Times Index*

New York: *New York Times,* 1913—.
Semimonthly, with annual cumulation.

CONTENTS: This index of the final Late City Edition gives a
condensed, classified history of the world as it is printed every
day in the *New York Times.*

Indexes from the *Times's* first issue—September 18, 1851—to
1913 are all on microfilm, and some of those are in print. Indexes from 1913 on are in print, but frequency of printing has
varied over the years.

METHOD OF ORGANIZATION: This index is made up of summaries of news and editorial matter, under headings that are arranged alphabetically. Entries under each heading are arranged chronologically. Whenever possible, entries are made
under subject, and cross references are frequent.

USEFULNESS: The extensive coverage of national and international news by the *New York Times* makes this an extremely
valuable index. It is especially valuable for its accurate and extensive coverage of obituaries; for its publication of the complete texts of important documents and speeches; for its reviews of books, movies, plays, art shows, and fashion shows; for
its thorough and precise business reports, and for its coverage
of sports throughout the world.

This is probably the best single newspaper reference work
available.

EXAMPLES: Here is a sample entry:

General Mills Inc. See Educ-US-Gen Je 7. Flour F23, Mr 23, Je
4, Je 6

J. F. McFarland named exec vp, Ja 3, III, 7:3; L. H. Crites
elected dir, My 25, 65:2

"Educ-US-Gen" is the heading; look it up alphabetically. The
next step is to check the entries under this heading, which are
listed chronologically. Under "Je [June] 7" will be "Gen. Mills
Co. offers educ. premiums on cereal boxes, Je 7, 60:3"—a very
brief synopsis of the article, the month and date of publication,
the page number (60), and the column (3).

The next heading to look up—alphabetically—is "Flour."

Under "Flour" the entries wanted—February 23, March 23, June 4, and June 6—will also supply the page and column.

For the article on McFarland see the *Times* of January 3, section 3, page 7, column 3.

For L. H. Crites, see the May 25 *Times*, page 65, column 2.

43] *Times* [*London*]: *Official Index*

> London: *The Times*, 1906—. Published every month from 1906–June 1914, every three months from July 1914–1956, and every two months from 1957. No cumulations.
>
> From 1906–1913 it was known as *The Annual Index;* from 1914–1957 it was known as *The Official Index*.

CONTENTS: This is the English counterpart of the *New York Times Index* but it is not so detailed or so comprehensive. It has excellent coverage of British and European news.

METHOD OF ORGANIZATION: This work is arranged alphabetically by subject and name, followed by date, page, and column. No cross references except with plays and books reviewed.

For example, under "Rusk, Mr. D. (U.S.A.)—in Australia" one finds the date, page, and column of the article. But there is nothing about the article under either U.S.A. or Australia. However, *The Last Battle* by Cornelius Ryan is listed under Ryan and under Books.

USEFULNESS: Extremely valuable because of its accurate and extensive coverage of British and continental European news and events as they appear every day in the *Times*. Should be used with the *New York Times Index* for complete newspaper coverage of the world in English.

EXAMPLE: Here is a sample entry from the July-August 1966 *Index:*

Bread—article, Aug. 27, 11a;—
    Consumers' Assn. survey, Aug. 8, 11d;—
    Labour: productivity agreement frozen,
    Aug. 2, 9c; meeting sought with Minister,
    15, 1g;—Wheat content: article, July 25, 8a

"Bread" is the subject. An article on bread appears in the August 27 edition, page 11, column 1 (letters of the alphabet stand for column numbers). "Consumers' Assn. survey" is a synopsis of an article on August 8, page 11, column 4. There are two articles on the subject of bread under the subtopic "Labour," and one under the subtopic "Wheat content."

44] *Book Review Digest*

New York: H. W. Wilson Co., 1905—.
Monthly, with semiannual and annual cumulations.

CONTENTS: This digest gives short quotations from selected reviews of books for the general reader, from about 75 popular American and English periodicals.

The book reviewed must be hardbound and published in the United States. And to be included in this digest, a non-fiction work must have had two or more reviews and a work of fiction four or more reviews in the periodicals listed.

METHOD OF ORGANIZATION: Arranged alphabetically by authors of the books reviewed, with a subject and title index at the back. A cumulative index is printed every four years.

USEFULNESS: A good source for finding reviews, either favorable or unfavorable, of a work of fiction or non-fiction by the magazines listed in the *Book Review Digest*.

The great limitation here is that the books selected are always for the general reader and that the reviews selected are not from special or scholarly journals. Also the quotation used may be out of context and therefore destroy the intention of the reviewer.

EXAMPLES: The following information is given for each book listed: name of author and book, number of pages, illustrations, publisher, price, and brief description. Following this information come excerpts from the selected reviews (each about 110 words long) with the name of the author of each review, and the periodical, along with the day, month, year, page, and column, in which the review was published. The key to abbreviations of periodicals is given at the beginning of each volume.

45] *An Index to Book Reviews in the Humanities*

Detroit: Philip Thomson, 1960—.
Published every three months, with annual cumulations.

CONTENTS: This quarterly indexes reviews of books (fiction and paperbacks are included) in over 650 magazines and newspapers, general as well as scholarly. Almost all of the magazines whose book reviews are listed are devoted to the humanities and the social sciences. The magazines listed, which are published in the United States and abroad, are all in English, but the books reviewed may be in any language.

METHOD OF ORGANIZATION: This index is alphabetically arranged by the author of the book being reviewed.

USEFULNESS: Excellent source for finding recent reviews if the reader knows the name of an author. Both scholarly and popular magazines are included. A good companion to the *Book Review Digest* (our no. 44).

EXAMPLES:

> Beach, Sylvia. *Shakespeare and Company*
> Carl L. Anderson, 83: Spring–176
> Kay Deck, 512:7/13–69
> Patricia Hutchins, 362:7/14–66
> 617:6/24–393

Beach, Sylvia, is the name of the author, and *Shakespeare and Company* is the name of the book. Carl L. Anderson is the name of the reviewer, 83 is the number of the magazine, Spring is the date of publication, and 176 is the page. The periodicals in which the reviews appear are identified in this index by a number—the key is given at the beginning of each issue.

Kay Deck is the name of the reviewer, 512 is the number of the magazine, 7/13 is the date of publication, and 69 is the number of the page.

The last entry indicates that the review is unsigned.

46] *Book Review Index*

Detroit: Gale Research Company, 1965—.
Monthly, with quarterly cumulations.

CONTENTS: This is a "current guide to current reviews of current books" in the humanities, social sciences, fiction, poetry, and general non-fiction in about 220 periodicals, general and scholarly (e.g., *Life* is indexed as well as *Journal of Philosophy* and *Modern Philology*). Every review in every periodical listed is included in this index, which is published monthly, with annual accumulations.

METHOD OF ORGANIZATION: Arranged alphabetically by author, with alphabetical listing of magazines in which review appears beneath the author.

USEFULNESS: An excellent source for evaluation of a book by scholars and popular writers. One great advantage of this index is that all reviews are listed about six weeks after they are published.

EXAMPLES: Here is a sample entry from the index:

Saroyan, William—One day in the Afternoon of the World.
Books and Bookmen—A. Horner—v.11 Dec 65—p 42

The name of the author of the book being reviewed is William Saroyan and the title of the book is *One Day in the Afternoon of the World*. The review appeared in the magazine *Books and Bookmen;* the name of the reviewer is A. Horner. It appears in volume eleven in the December 1965 issue on page 42.

BIBLIOGRAPHIES

DEFINITION: Bibliographies are lists of sources of information on a given subject or author. Such lists cover books, pamphlets, periodicals, bulletins, etc. They are sometimes complete, sometimes selective, often authoritative.

Some bibliographies give the title of the book, the name of the author, the date of publication, the name of the publisher, and the number of pages and nothing more; others give this information as well as a brief description of the work and where it can be found.

WHICH BIBLIOGRAPHY SUITS YOUR NEEDS? The bibliographies in this section contain the following information:

» *The Bibliographic Index* (our no. 47) This work lists bibliographies, mostly in English, published in about 1,500 general and scholarly books, pamphlets, periodicals, and bulletins.

» *The United States Catalog* and *The Cumulative Book Index* (our no. 48) Together both works list almost every book printed, from 1899 to the present, in the United States.

» *Publisher's Trade List Annual* and *Books in Print* (our no. 49) Compiled from a collection of yearly catalogs, these works list books in print in the United States.

» *Essay and General Literature Index* (our no. 50) This work lists about 200,000 essays, articles, and symposiums in books, published since 1900.

47] *Bibliographic Index*

New York: H. W. Wilson Co., 1937—.

CONTENTS: This reference work gives a list of bibliographies, mostly in English, published in about 1,500 general and scholarly books, pamphlets, periodicals, and bulletins.

The *Index* is published every 4 years in a cumulative volume; every year as a supplement to the 4-year volume, and again every 3 months (every 6 months from 1965).

METHOD OF ORGANIZATION: This index is arranged alphabetically by subject only. Under each subject, books and pamphlets are listed by their author; periodicals and bulletins are listed by their title.

USEFULNESS: Good for all subjects, but especially for those that are limited and minor and are not often covered in the large subject indexes. The periodicals listed range from such well-known popular magazines as *House and Garden* to such obscure ones as the *Edison Electric Institute Bulletin*.

EXAMPLES:

Ability

Testing Greene, Edward Barrows. Measurements of human behavior. N.Y. Odyssey ('41) P 734–62

The subject is Ability. The bibliography is on Ability Testing and will be found in Edward Barrows Greene's *Measurements of Human Behavior,* published by the Odyssey Press, Inc., in 1941, on pages 734–62.

Abrasives Bibliography on blast cleaning with metallic abrasives. R. Hopp. Heat treat & Forg 27: 280, 289–90, 328–32 Je-Jl '41 annot

The subject is Abrasives. The bibliography is entitled *Bibliography on Blast Cleaning with Metallic Abrasives* by R. Hopp. It can be found in the periodical *Heat Treating and Forging,* volume 27, pages 280, 289–290, 328–332, which appeared in June and July, 1941. Items listed are annotated.

RELATED REFERENCE WORKS: *A World Bibliography of Bibliographies,* by Theodore Besterman (Geneva: Societas Bibliographica, 1955–1956, 4 vols.). This vast reference tool, international in scope, is a bibliography of about 84,000 separate bibliographies of books and manuscripts.

48] *United States Catalog* and *Cumulative Book Index*

Minneapolis: H. W. Wilson Co., 1899–1928;
New York, H. W. Wilson Co., 1928—. 4th ed.

CONTENTS: These two indispensable works together list almost every book printed, from 1899 to the present, in the United States. They also list many books in English published abroad.

But these reference works are much more than a mere listing of books in print. The *United States Catalog* gives the edition, the price, the name of the publisher and his address, the number of pages, and the name of the translator and editor should there be one. The *Cumulative Book Index*, the logical continuation of the *U.S.C.* and really a series of supplements to it, gives all that the *U.S.C.* gives, but in addition includes such important items as works published by university presses, societies, institutions (e.g., Smithsonian National Museum), and selected works of the national and state governments. It also tells if a book has a foreword, the name of the author of the foreword, if a book has been revised, and whether new material has been added.

Published in cumulative volumes every 4 years, every 2 years, yearly, and quarterly.

METHOD OF ORGANIZATION: Arranged alphabetically by author's real name or pseudonym, by title, and by subject. The entry under the author is fuller than that under title (under title one is not given year of publication, paging, and the Library of Congress card number).

USEFULNESS: Both reference works together make up the most comprehensive record of books printed in the United States from 1898 to the present.

RELATED REFERENCE WORKS: *English Catalogue of Books* (London: S. Low & Publishers' Circular, 1906—). This is the British counterpart of the *United States Catalog* and the *Cumulative Book Index.*

49] *Publishers' Trade List Annual (PTLA)* and *Books in Print*

New York: R. R. Bowker, 1873—; 1948—.
Both are annuals.

CONTENTS: These two annual companion sets, compiled from a collection of yearly catalogues from almost all of the important publishing houses, are the best source for books in print in the United States. The *PTLA* has much more detailed information than *Books in Print;* but in both the amount of information given depends, of course, on how much a publisher chooses to put into his catalogue.

METHOD OF ORGANIZATION: The *PTLA* is arranged alphabetically by the publisher's name. *Books in Print* is made up of three indexes in three separate volumes, one listed by authors, one by titles, and one by subject; all are arranged alphabetically. E.g., Kenneth Burke's *Philosophy of Literary Form* appears under his name, under the name of the book, and under the subject.

USEFULNESS: Both are invaluable for checking whether a book is or is not in print. For more detailed information than found in *Books in Print,* the reader should look up the same book in *PTLA* under the name of the publisher.

EXAMPLES: A sample entry from *Books in Print* is:

Scheff, Thomas J. Being Mentally Ill. 1966. 5.75. Aldine

The same book appears in the 1966 volume of *PTLA* under "Aldine" (the publisher):

Being Mentally Ill: A Sociological Theory by Thomas J. Scheff, Associate Professor of Sociology, University of California, Berkeley. A highly original and controversial appraisal of the kinds of deviant behavior that society defines as "mental illness." Observations. 1966. L.C. 66–15207 [Library of Congress number]. 192 pp. Fwd., acks., notes, app., index. $5.75

The information given in *Books in Print* will always be just about as shown here; the information given in *PTLA* will depend on the amount of information in the publisher's catalogue.

RELATED REFERENCE WORKS: *Paperbound Books in Print* (New York: Bowker, 1955—). This monthly, with cumulative issues three times a year, lists available paperbacks under (1) subject, (2) author, and (3) title, all in one volume.

Publishers' Weekly (New York: Bowker, 1872—). "The standard American book-trade journal, containing lists of new publications, lists of books announced for publication, news notes, editorials and articles, advertisements of books wanted, etc."

50] *Essay and General Literature Index*

New York: H. W. Wilson Co., 1900—. Annual.

CONTENTS: This annual is a detailed index to about 200,000 essays, articles, and symposiums, in books published since 1900. The works selected are from all fields—mathematics, medicine, law, literature, economics, music, philosophy—and they must be in English.

The selection of the books indexed is based on a list voted on by about 50 libraries of various sizes throughout the United States.

METHOD OF ORGANIZATION: Arranged alphabetically by author, subject, and occasionally by title. Excellent cross references. A list of the books indexed is appended at the back.

USEFULNESS: This is a valuable work in that it (1) lists essays by an author as well as essays about an author, his individual works, and the characters in these works, (2) refers to material on a given subject on which there may be no whole books, (3) identifies the source of the essay, (4) gives the variant titles of the same essay if variant titles exist.

EXAMPLE: Here is a sample entry from the 1965 volume; our explanations are in brackets:

Hardy, Thomas

About Gross, H.S. Modern poetry in the metrical tradition [title of essay by Gross]
In Gross, H.S. Sound and form in modern poetry [title of book in which essay is printed] p 42–78

Karl, F. R. Thomas Hardy's "Mayor" and the changing novel
In Karl, F.R. An age of fiction p 295–322

About individual works Jude the obscure [title of Hardy novel]
Horne, L. B. Fawley's quests: a reading of Jude the obscure
In Tennessee studies in literature [name of magazine in which above article appears] V 9 p 117–27

Characters—Henchard Karl, F.R. Thomas Hardy's "Mayor" and the changing novel [title of chapter in book below]
In Karl, F. R. An age of fiction p 295–322

RELATED REFERENCE WORKS: *Biography Index* (our no. 36).

I. F.

YEARBOOKS, ALMANACS,
AND OTHER BOOKS OF FACTS

DEFINITION: Yearbooks, almanacs, and other fact books, although less authoritative and often less objective than encyclopedias, should be used in conjunction with them because of the range of facts, the detail, and the concrete data they cover.

The items of information found in yearbooks, almanacs, and other books of facts are:

» Summaries of up-to-date political events. Many yearbooks publish important treaties and agreements concluded and signed during the year.
» Major developments in science and technology.
» Statistical information about most fields, especially in economics.
» Chronological listing of the important events of the year.
» Brief biographies of important living persons as well as obituaries of leading figures in all fields.
» Detailed statistical breakdown of all important sports events (i.e. pitching records, touchdowns, etc.).
» News items unlikely to be published in large reference works.

51] *Europa Year Book*

London: Europa, 1959——. 2 vols. Annual.

CONTENTS: This work is made up of two annual volumes. Vol. I covers the organization, function, and history of important international organizations and the countries of Europe, including Turkey and the Vatican. Vol. II covers the countries of Africa, the Middle East, North and South America, and Asia.

73

Both volumes have accurate and up-to-date information on trade and industry, the press, transportation, the constitution, religion, insurance, learned societies, museums, and scientific and cultural organizations.

METHOD OF ORGANIZATION: Part I of vol. I describes international organizations, in alphabetical order; part II of vol. I describes the European countries—in alphabetical order.

Vol. II describes all the other countries—in alphabetical order.

The index for vol. I lists the international organizations; the index for vol. II lists alphabetically the countries of the world.

USEFULNESS: This is a good source for brief descriptions and statistical data on the countries of the world and fairly extensive coverage of international organizations. It is strong on names and addresses of important organizations. There are no bibliographies.

EXAMPLES: Vol. I gives detailed information about the U.N. and other large international organizations, as well as the function, membership, address and the date of foundation of hundreds of lesser known organizations.

Part II of vol. I and vol. II offer the following data: statistical information on populations, births, deaths, marriages, divorces, and the whole economy of a country; names of government officials; description of judicial systems and names of important jurists; names and addresses of religious organizations, newspapers, publishers, important banks (and important information pertaining to them), trade organizations; and lists of universities with their addresses and numbers of teachers and students.

RELATED REFERENCE WORKS: *International Yearbook and Statesmen's Who's Who* (London: Burke's Peerage, 1953—). This annual covers international organizations and biographies of important people in government, church, commerce, industry, and education.

52] *Statesman's Year-Book*

New York: St. Martin's Press, 1864—. Annual.

CONTENTS: Over 1,600 pages long and revised each year, this comprehensive yearbook gives in short, well-written paragraphs and in statistical charts precise and accurate information on the political, economic, social, historical, educational, religious, and military aspects of every country in the world. There is a selected bibliography for each country and international organization.

METHOD OF ORGANIZATION: In four parts. Part one is devoted to international organizations, including the United Nations; part two is devoted to Great Britain and the Commonwealth; part three covers the United States, and part four the rest of the world.

The detailed, 100-page index is arranged alphabetically by place, name, and subject. Names of people are not included.

USEFULNESS: This is one of the best and most comprehensive of the international yearbooks. The information on the countries of the world is often much more extensive than in the *Europa Year Book.*

Another important feature is the selected bibliography, both in the original language and in English, which is a good general introduction to the make-up of any country in the world.

EXAMPLES: The following information is given about the United States, but the same basic data is supplied about any other country in the world: Detailed information on the constitution, the presidency, the congress, the states and local governments, area and population, vital statistics (live births, deaths, marriages, divorces), immigration, religion, education, finance, army, navy, air force, agriculture, forests, currency, the national anthem, the flag, etc. A breakdown of each state into its government, area and population, religion, education, welfare, finance, production, and communication is also given.

RELATED REFERENCE WORKS: *Worldmark Encyclopedia of the Nations,* in 5 vols., ed. by Benjamin A. Cohen (New York: Worldmark Press, 1960), contains condensed factual information about the geographical, historical, political, social, and economic status of Africa, North and South America, Asia and Australia, and Europe. Good section on the United Nations.

53] *Information Please Almanac*

New York: Simon and Schuster, 1947—. Annual.

CONTENTS: The basic information here is made up of facts and statistical data on the social, geographical, historical, political, economic, religious, and educational aspects of the United States. There is, however, a section on the history of each country in the world and another section devoted to reviews of the important political and economic events of the preceding year. Authors of these reviews are often identified. There are also signed articles and special features published only in that year.

METHOD OF ORGANIZATION: Fully indexed at the end, alphabetically and almost exclusively by subject.

USEFULNESS: This is an excellent companion to the *World Almanac* (our no. 54). The information is more readable, but not so comprehensive as in the *World Almanac*.

EXAMPLES: Here is the kind of information one can expect to find in this almanac: important data on states, cities, and territories of the United States and the rest of the world; statistical breakdown on how consumers spend their dollars, on employment and unemployment, on United States exports and general imports; a biographical section, a sort of who's who of famous living men and women throughout the world, and a list of celebrated persons of the past, from Aeschylus to Douglas MacArthur (places and dates of birth given for the living, place, date of birth, and occupation given for the dead); extensive miscellaneous material on things like income tax information, postal regulations, aviation, and the flag. There is also a good section called "Review of the Year," which includes books, movies, performing arts, and music.

The signed articles in the 1967 edition are on Vietnam, U.S. elections, new stories of 1966, the world today, the space race, and parliamentary procedure.

The special feature is the crossword puzzle guide. The 1955 edition lists recipes from the most famous restaurants in the world.

54] *World Almanac*

New York: Newspaper Enterprise Association, Inc. 1868—. Annual.

CONTENTS: This is an important book of facts and statistical data. It is also the most detailed and most comprehensive almanac published in the United States. It has up-to-date and reliable information on social, industrial, political, financial, religious, educational, and many, many other subjects. The section on sports is excellent. Most of the information is about the United States, but there are good small sections on the history and present conditions of every country in the world.

METHOD OF ORGANIZATION: The book is fully indexed, alphabetically by subject, occupation, and profession; the index begins the book. If the reader wanted to look up Cardinal Spellman, the Archbishop of the Archdiocese of New York, he would not find him under his name, but under Roman Catholic, Churches, and Religion. However, some famous men, both American and foreign, living and dead, are indexed under their name.

USEFULNESS: A good book for brief, factual information and fairly extensive statistical data, often accompanied by sources. For best results it should be used in conjunction with *Information Please Almanac*.

EXAMPLES: This book has information and statistics on all 50 states, including population by state and county and population of chief cities of foreign countries. There are short biographies of U.S. Presidents and their wives.

It has information and statistics on astronomical and meteorological events, art galleries, museums, historic sites, farm prices and wages, political assassinations, major and minor disasters and earthquakes, and sports events. Brief descriptions are included of the resources, history, government, and religion of foreign countries; the names of all cabinet officers of the U.S. Government from 1789 to date, U.S. Government officials, and the signers of the Declaration of Independence are listed.

It also includes the names of famous actors, actresses, musicians, and singers, with their place of birth and date of birth.

55] *Whitaker, Joseph. An Almanack*

London: Whitaker, 1869—. Annual.

CONTENTS: Known as "Whitaker's Almanack," this 1,200-page annual British counterpart of our *World Almanac* has thorough, accurate, and up-to-date facts about almost every aspect of British life. There is a small section on the United States and the other countries of the world.

METHOD OF ORGANIZATION: A comprehensive, alphabetical index of about 90 pages lists well over 19,000 items. Arrangement is by subject, name, or profession. Almost all names of people are excluded.

USEFULNESS: Excellent source for brief, factual information, very often in the form of statistical data, about the United Kingdom. Particularly useful for the vast variety of miscellaneous facts covered in the index. The *World Almanac* (our no. 54), the *Information Please Almanac* (our no. 53), and this work, used together, offer the most complete coverage of almanac information.

EXAMPLES: The 1966 issue has details of the General Election held at the end of March, foreign exchange rates, a long and fascinating section on calendars, astronomy, population, weather, a complete list of all peers, baronets, knights, M.P.s, ministers, senior civil servants with their salaries, information on churches, schools, cities, towns, insurance companies and their rates, and postal regulations, to name just a few.

There is also a good section on reviews of the year in science, literature, drama, movies, and sports.

56] *Facts on File*

New York: Facts on File, Inc., October, 1940—. Weekly.

CONTENTS: This four- to eight-page weekly offers a precise factual summary—but not the sources—of the important facts in most news events, as gathered from metropolitan newspapers in the United States and abroad.

METHOD OF ORGANIZATION: *Facts on File* is fully indexed every two weeks, and the index is made cumulative every month, every three months, and every year. The indexes are carefully and precisely arranged, so that Martin Luther King, for example, could be found under either Negroes, national affairs, civil rights, religion, or any other appropriate heading.

News items are usually arranged under such subjects as World Affairs, National Affairs, Foreign Affairs, Latin America, Finance and Economics, Arts and Science, Education and Religion, Sports, Obituaries, Miscellany.

USEFULNESS: This is a good survey of standard news items—also a good reference source, a sort of encyclopedia of current events. This is the place to look for a quick summary of the most important events of the week.

EXAMPLES: Aside from synopses of such standard items as World Affairs (Vietnam War, China, etc.), there are numerous other facts summarized, such as: critics' reactions to plays and movies, changes in the leadership of leading companies and universities, announcements of births, marriages, divorces, and deaths, and the dates of publication of important books.

RELATED REFERENCE WORKS: *Keesing's Contemporary Archives* (London: Keesing's, 1931—). A close equivalent of our *Facts on File*, this important British weekly gives you the events in all countries, "including texts of speeches and documents, obituaries, statistics, etc."

57] *U.S. Bureau of the Census: Statistical Abstract of the United States*

Washington: Government Printing Office, 1879—. Annual.

CONTENTS: Each volume gives the most important statistics on the political, social, economic, and industrial, educational, judicial, geographical, and scientific aspects of the United States. Data for statistics are supplied by the statistical agencies of the United States government and by private agencies. The emphasis here is on national data. Statistics cover a period of 15–20 years before publication date.

METHOD OF ORGANIZATION: Each volume has a detailed and precise index arranged by subject, name, and profession, which is often well over 40 pages long. No names of people are included in the index.

USEFULNESS: Probably the best source of statistics about all aspects of the United States, this work is also extremely important because sources for most of the statistics are given.

EXAMPLES: A full statistical profile of America, each volume gives statistical tables on population (sex, age, race, marital status, etc.), vital statistics (health and nutrition, births, deaths, life expectancy, marriage, divorce, mental institutions, national health expenditures), immigration and naturalization (immigration quotas, passports issued, naturalization), and then goes on to give detailed breakdowns on education, law enforcement, federal courts, prisons, social insurance and welfare service, prices, elections, banking, insurance, transportation, and fisheries, to name just a few.

This is a fascinating and invaluable reference work.

RELATED REFERENCE WORKS: *Vital Statistics of the United States* (Washington: United States Government Printing, 1939—). This annual gives you basic information on birth, marriage, divorce, and death, in the United States and its possessions.

58] *Statistical Yearbook / Annuaire Statistique*

New York: United Nations, 1948—. Annual.

CONTENTS: Prepared by the statistical office of the United Nations, with the text on each page printed in English and in French, this yearbook provides statistical tables about every country in the world. The tables cover such subjects as Population, Agriculture, Mining, Manufacturing, Finance, Trade, Education, Culture, Housing, and Social Statistics. The book gives source of information and has notes, whenever necessary, explaining the statistical tables.

METHOD OF ORGANIZATION: By subject and by countries, alphabetically arranged, under the subject. Indexed by countries at the end of each volume.

USEFULNESS: Good source for statistics about the world and about 150 countries and territories. References for sources are important because they tell where to go for information in depth. Notes about statistics are important because they suggest the correct use of the information they explain. This yearbook also gives an excellent economic profile of the world and the countries and territories in it.

EXAMPLES: Here is a breakdown for almost every subject needed for a statistical analysis of every country in the world.

For Population, there are statistical tables on sex, rate of population increase, area and density of each country, birth and death rates, and infant mortality rates. For Finance, there are exchange rates, money supply, international liquidity, rates of discount of central banks, money market rates, government bonds yields, market price of industrial shares.

A similarly detailed breakdown for the other 22 subjects is given.

ATLASES AND GAZETTEERS

DEFINITION: Both atlases and gazetteers are essentially sources of geographical information.

The gazetteers are geographical dictionaries, listing places and giving statistics about them. The information may range from brief notes to long essays.

Atlases are collections of maps, showing at a glance the kind of world the atlas wants to show (i.e., political, social, economic, historical, biblical, commercial, etc.).

Both can become dated quickly, especially atlases published since World War II. Information should always be checked against up-to-date sources, such as almanacs or yearbooks.

59] *Encyclopaedia Britannica: World Atlas*

Chicago: Encyclopaedia Britannica, Inc., 1949—.
Revised in 1957, 1961, and 1964.

CONTENTS: In color maps and in charts, this atlas gives information about world population distribution, physical characteristics of countries, location of places, important human patterns, the uses to which man has put his environment, and the world political geography, in a single volume.

METHOD OF ORGANIZATION: The atlas is divided into five sections: The Political-Physical Maps, The World Scene, Geographical Summaries, Geographical Comparisons, and Glossary and Index. Each section develops carefully the countries of the world from its own point of view.

USEFULNESS: The reader can locate, identify, and compare countries, continents, oceans, seas, rivers, and any other place or body of water in the atlas, quickly and visually. The scope is wide, and the maps are generally up to date and well indexed.

EXAMPLES: The atlas gives the precise location of countries and their political subdivisions, towns, villages, land and water features, as well as statistics on population distribution, languages spoken, world climates, state of soils and vegetation, mining, transportation and trade, mountain heights, river lengths, dam heights, and bridge spans, to name just a few.

60] *Rand McNally Commercial Atlas and Marketing Guide*

New York: Rand McNally & Co., 1869—. Annual.

CONTENTS: Revised carefully every year, this one-volume atlas, mostly about the United States and designed chiefly for businessmen, is the best and most comprehensive of its kind. The maps are large, detailed, in color, and designed to illustrate some aspect of our economy. The statistics cover almost every part of life likely to interest the business community, e.g., Agriculture, Communications, Manufacturing, Retail Trade, Population, Transportation, etc.

About one-fifth of the pages are devoted to Canada and the rest of the world.

METHOD OF ORGANIZATION: It is arranged in three parts: the first part is devoted to the United States and is the largest, taking up about 500 out of the 550 pages; part II is devoted to every other country in the world with the exception of Canada; part III is devoted to Canada.

USEFULNESS: The best atlas and one of the best reference books about the way businessmen look at the United States. Extremely useful because it is always up to date and gives statistics, both in map form and in charts, about our economy.

EXAMPLES: This work offers detailed, precise, and accurate information about scheduled airlines, trunk airline routes, population distribution in cities, towns, and villages, retail sales, growth of counties, principal business centers, and other cities of 20,000 or more, and an index of towns, cities, and counties, transportation lines, banks, and post offices in every state.

61] *Times Atlas of the World*

London: The *Times*, 1955–1959. 5 vols.

CONTENTS: In this large world atlas, vol. I includes the world, Australia, and east Asia; vol. II, southwest Asia and Russia; vol. III, northern Europe; vol. IV, southern Europe and Africa; vol. V, the Americas.

These five volumes have 120 double-page maps, and each map measures about 19½ by 12½ inches. This size page (it is very large even for an atlas) allows for extensive coverage, with great detail. Most of the cities and towns in a given area as well as highways, railways, canals, airports, county, state, and national boundaries and all important physical contours, are included in all volumes.

There is also a detailed index of place names at the end of each volume.

METHOD OF ORGANIZATION: The parts of the world treated in each volume are divided into logical sections. For example, vol. V, *The Americas*, is broken down into the various parts of Canada, the United States, Mexico and Central America, South America, and the Pacific Ocean.

USEFULNESS: Detailed and accurate maps of the world, with the location, latitude, longitude, and map reference to about 200,000 place names. Also provides coverage of islands and gives inset maps to cities.

EXAMPLES: The coverage of cities is vast and in depth, and includes such small and out of the way places as West Alexandria, Ohio; Vanderhoof, British Columbia; Crane Valley, Saskatchewan; Dolphin Head Mountain, Jamaica; Joe's Hell, Christmas Island, Pacific Ocean; Simong, India; Shegarkhang Lung, Tibet.

Also given are statistics in table form, as well as many-colored maps concerning the location of volcanoes, world climates and vegetation, world air routes, distribution and density of population, languages, races, and religions.

62] *Historical Atlas*

New York: Barnes and Noble, 1964. 9th ed.
Ed. by William R. Shepherd.

CONTENTS: Accurate and concise, this important general atlas of the world covers a time span from about 2500 B.C. to 1964.

No text, no charts, and no graphs. The 226 pages are devoted exclusively to color maps.

METHOD OF ORGANIZATION: Arranged historically, beginning with a Reference Map of Ancient Egypt and ending with Europe in 1964. There is an index at the back.

USEFULNESS: Excellent for a quick, visual presentation of much of the history of the world on maps. The reader is given the precise location or distribution in space of kingdoms, empires, major war campaigns, medieval commercial and ecclesiastical domains, treaties, and other major historical events.

This work should be used in conjunction with Rand McNally's *Atlas of World History,* in which pages of explanatory text accompany the maps and elucidate them.

EXAMPLES: The maps here cover such subjects as: The Ancient Near East, 1375 B.C.; The Orient, 600–500 B.C.; Plan of Athens; Territorial Expansion of Rome; Development of Christianity to 1300; Central Europe about 1477; The Conquest of Mexico, 1519–1521; The Growth of Russia in Europe, 1300–1796; The Waterloo Campaign; The Western Front, 1914–1918; Campaigns of the American Revolution, 1775–1781; Slavery and Emancipation in the United States, 1777–1865; and The World at War, 1939–1945—to name just a few.

63] *Atlas of World History*

New York: Rand McNally, 1957. Ed. by R. R. Palmer.

CONTENTS: This is a good, short, illustrated history of all parts of the world since ancient times.

There are 125 maps, 75 in color and 50 in black and white. Asia, Latin America, and Africa are represented, but the treatment of the United States, Canada, and Europe is more detailed, especially for the nineteenth and twentieth centuries. Pages of explanatory text often accompany the maps.

METHOD OF ORGANIZATION: The book is arranged in five sections: Ancient Times; Medieval Europe; Modern Europe; Asia, Africa, and America; The Twentieth Century. A detailed place name index is found at the back.

USEFULNESS: At a glance, these maps illustrate world history from ancient times to the present. For example, the civilization maps show, for various periods, the concentration of civilization in certain places, or its distribution, or "the movement of its center of gravity from time to time."

EXAMPLES: The maps and commentary here cover such subjects as: Ancient Mesopotamia; The Near East and Greece about 1400 B.C.; The Journeys of Paul; Europe in 1360; European Civilization during the Renaissance; The Ottoman Empire; The English Revolution; Languages of Europe in the Nineteenth Century; China under the Han Dynasty, 100 B.C.; Partition of Africa; Campaigns of the Civil War; and Defeat of Germany and Japan, 1943–1945, to name just a few.

64] *Columbia Lippincott Gazetteer of the World*

New York: Columbia University Press, 1962.
Ed. by Leon E. Seltzer.

CONTENTS: This comprehensive, geographical dictionary of the world, lists about 130,000 places and gives pertinent statistics about them. The contents range from brief notes about villages to long essays about rivers. The emphasis is on the modern world, but the ancient world has not been neglected. It also gives pronunciations and variant spellings. Neither maps, charts, nor graphs are included.

METHOD OF ORGANIZATION: Alphabetically arranged in dictionary form.

USEFULNESS: This is a good source for accurate information about and descriptions of most of the important places of the world.

Caution: Readers should not use this work as a substitute for an encyclopedia. The articles in the *Gazetteer* have more geographical detail and are more informative on certain places, but in all other respects are not so well developed and not so many-faceted and comprehensive as those in a good encyclopedia. Also, this work should not be used in place of an atlas.

EXAMPLES: Here is a typical entry from the *Gazetteer:*

Montmartre (mōmärt′rú), a N district of Paris, France, occupying an eminence (*Butte de Montmartre*) which rises 330 ft. (highest point of Paris) above right bank of the Seine. It is topped by 19th cent. basilica of Sacré-Coeur surmounted by a large dome of Byzantine style. Parts of old quarter on its slopes were long a favorite residence of artists. Montmartre is also noted for its night clubs, of which the Moulin Rouge is best known. The cemetery of Montmartre contains the tombs of Stendhal, Berlioz, Renan, Heine, and Alfred de Vigny. From earliest times the summit was a place of worship first of the Druids, and later of the Romans who built temples to Mercury and to Mars. A Benedictine Abbey and the Church of St. Pierre de Montmartre were founded here in the 12th century.

RELATED REFERENCE WORKS: *Chambers' World Gazetteer,* ed. by T. C. Collocott and J. O. Thorne (London: Chambers, 1954), is a small, useful, handy gazetteer with emphasis on Great Britain.

UNITED STATES GOVERNMENT PUBLICATIONS

65] *U.S. Superintendent of Documents: Monthly Catalog of United States Government Publications*

Washington, D.C.: Government Printing Office, 1895—.
Monthly, with annual cumulations.

CONTENTS: This is the *only* index that gives a bibliography of publications issued by every department and bureau of the federal government from 1895 to the present.

Each monthly issue has instructions for ordering a publication as well as the identity of the author, the title and a brief description of the publication, the price, the date, the number of pages, and often the Library of Congress catalog number. There are annual cumulations.

METHOD OF ORGANIZATION: Arranged alphabetically by department, bureau, and then title of publication. Each annual volume has an index. Also available: *Decennial Cumulation Index 1941–1950*.

USEFULNESS: Absolutely indispensable for a bibliography of government publications since 1940—no other publication gives this information.

EXAMPLES:

INTERIOR DEPARTMENT *Washington, D.C., 20240*
Annual report, 1964, Governor of Guam to Secretary of Interior, fiscal year. 1965. iii + 172 p. il. * Paper, 50c. L.C. card 53–29762.

Interior Department is the author, and *Annual Report* is the title. This is the report of the Governor of Guam to the Secretary of the Interior about the fiscal year 1964. Published in 1965. Three introductory pages and 172 pages of text, illustrated. For sale (by the Superintendent of Documents) in paperback for $.50. The Library of Congress catalog number is 53-29762.

66] *A Descriptive Catalogue of the Government Publications of the United States, September 5, 1774–March 4, 1881*

Washington, D.C.: Government Printing Office, 1885.

CONTENTS: This work lists and briefly describes most of the publications of the legislative, executive, and judicial departments of the federal government from 1774–1881.

METHOD OF ORGANIZATION: Arranged chronologically by date of publication. There is a subject–author index at the end of the volume.

USEFULNESS: This is a valuable work because it gives all the necessary information with which to track down the U.S. Government publications that it lists, and because it gives a brief synopsis of these publications.

It is not complete, however, for it omits about 10,000 publications. The index is also incomplete.

EXAMPLES: For each work listed the following information is given: the title of the book, pamphlet, or document; the name of its author; the date of its publication; where it is to be found, and a brief abstract of its contents.

67] *Comprehensive Index to the Publications of the United States Government, 1881–1893*

Washington, D.C.: Government Printing Office, 1905. 2 vols.

CONTENTS: This work indexes all publications of the Government from 1881, the date at which *A Descriptive Catalogue of the Government Publications of the United States* (our no. 66) terminates, to 1893, the date of publication of the first volume of *Catalog of the Public Documents* (our no. 68).

METHOD OF ORGANIZATION: The index is arranged in three columns. The left-hand column gives the author of the publication or the department that issued it. The middle and most important column lists the publications, in alphabetical order, and gives a concise description of the subjects treated. The right-hand column tells where to locate the publication.

There is a good author index at the back of vol. 2.

USEFULNESS: This comprehensive, complete, and highly detailed reference work fills the 13-year gap (1881–1893) between the *Descripitive Catalogue* and the *Catalog of the Public Documents*.

EXAMPLES: Here is a sample entry:

| Reagan, J.H. Commerce . . . | **Adulterate Foods and Drinks,** Importation of, Prohibition of, Recommended. Apr. 1, 84 H.B. 6405 | H.R. 48–1, V. 4 No. 1036, 2 P. |

Reagan, J.H. is the author; Commerce represents the name of the committee from which the document comes. *Adulterate Foods and Drinks* is the title of the document and "importation of, etc." is a brief description of the subject. April 1, 1884, is the date of publication; H.B. tells us that the bill came from the House and that its number is 6405.

H.R. tells us that the above information was made public in a House Report of the first session of the 48th Congress, and that the document can be found in vol. 4 of the *House Series*. The serial number of the document is 1036 and it takes up 2 pages.

68] *U.S. Superintendent of Documents: Catalog of the Public Documents of Congress . . . March 4, 1893– December 31, 1940*

Washington, D.C.: Government Printing Office, 1896–1945. 25 vols.

CONTENTS: This index continues the work of the *Comprehensive Index* (our no. 67) up to 1941. It is the most complete catalogue of all government publications, congressional as well as departmental, for the period from 1893–1940.

METHOD OF ORGANIZATION: Arranged alphabetically under author, subject, or title when necessary. Each volume covers two years, or one session of congress.

USEFULNESS: Besides giving all the necessary information about all government publications from 1893–1940, the *Catalog* often includes descriptions of each work. It also refers the reader to all editions in which the document has appeared.

EXAMPLES:

Abbot, Charles Greeley. Radiation of the sun. (In Smithsonian Institution. Report, 1912–1913. p. 153–165, il. 4 p of pl.) (Reprinted with revision and addition, from Science conspectus, Boston, V.2, no. 5, Apr. 1912.)

Charles Greeley Abbot is the author and "Radiation of the Sun" is the name of the article. It can be found in the 1912–1913 reports of the Smithsonian Institution, on pages 153 to 165. The article is illustrated and has 4 pages of plates. It is a reprint with revisions and additions from the magazine *Science Conspectus*, published in Boston, vol. 2, no. 5, April 1912.

SPECIALIZED
REFERENCE
WORKS

A NOTE OF INSTRUCTION

The reference works described in our sections II and III, below, are arranged by subjects from anthropology to sociology, and from biology to physics. The reader is advised to consult our descriptions of the works listed under the category of his particular interest.

If the reference works listed there do not answer his needs, he should first check the works described in our section I, which lists general reference works useful to all researchers no matter what their fields of interest. If he is still not satisfied, he should then consult one of the bibliographies in his field in our sections II and III—that is, one of the books that list (and in some cases describe) the major reference works of interest in his field; for example, students of history will find the *Guide to Historical Literature* (our no. 101) a valuable summary of the books available in their field. Note that we have listed bibliographies at the beginning of most subject areas.

For those who want to pursue their research further, we recommend Constance M. Winchell's *A Guide to Reference Books* (Chicago: American Library Association, 8th ed., 1967), which provides a comprehensive, annotated list of reference works available on all subjects.

Part II

SPECIALIZED REFERENCE WORKS for the HUMANITIES and SOCIAL SCIENCES

ANTHROPOLOGY

69] *International Bibliography of Social*
and Cultural Anthropology

Paris: UNESCO, 1955–1959. Annual.
Chicago: Aldine, 1960—. Annual.

CONTENTS: This annual bibliography, printed in English and
French on the same page, lists the titles of between 3,500 and
5,000 books and articles, published throughout the world and
in any languages, that the editors think represent "a definite
contribution to the science of anthropology."
The information on books often include a one- or two-line
description of the book. A one-line description accompanies
most entries for articles. Over 275 periodicals, most of them
scholarly and in every language in the world, are listed.

METHOD OF ORGANIZATION: The entries are arranged under
nine headings: Anthropology; General Studies; Material and
Methods of Anthropology; Morphological Foundations; General Ethnographic Studies of Peoples and Communities; Social
Organizations and Relationships; Religion, Magic and Witchcraft; Problems of Knowledge, Arts and Science, Folk Tradi-
tions; Studies of Culture and Personality, "National Character";
Problems of Acculturation and Social Change; Contact Situ-
ations; Applied Anthropology.
There is an author and subject index in the back of each
annual.

USEFULNESS: An excellent source for locating scholarly books
and critical articles on anthropology published throughout the
world.

EXAMPLES:

HENTZE, C. *TOD AUFERSTEHUNG, WELTORDNUNG. DAS MYTHISCHE BILD IM ÄLTESTEN CHINA* (Death resurrection, world order. The mythical picture in the oldest China). Zürich, Origo Verlag, 55, 192 P.

The book is published in Zürich by Origo Verlag; "55" indicates the year of publication.

Siroto, L. "A mask style from the French Congo," *Man* 54, Oct. 54: 149–150.

Siroto, L., is the name of the author, and "A mask style from the French Congo" the name of the article. It appeared in vol. 54 of *Man*, in the October 1954 issue, pages 149–150.

RELATED REFERENCE WORKS: *Biennial Review of Anthropology*, ed. by Bernard J. Siegel (Stanford: Stanford University Press, 1959—). International in coverage, this valuable review "describes and evaluates" important papers and monographs in anthropology. Subject index and bibliography.

70] *U.S. Bureau of American Ethnology: General Index*

Washington, D.C.: Government Printing Office, 1876–1931. vols. 1–48. Annual reports.

CONTENTS: An important reference work for those studying the cultural anthropology of the United States. It has attempted to preserve in its annual reports information on languages and customs of North American Indian tribes, many of whom have disappeared or are fast disappearing. No other series of books has such detailed somatological, psychological, linguistic, sociological, religious, and aesthetic information.

METHOD OF ORGANIZATION: Divided into two parts: part one is a detailed subject index of 1148 pages; part two gives in 35 pages a list of annual reports of the Bureau of American Ethnology with an index to authors and titles.

USEFULNESS: This is probably the best source available if one wants to know, among the countless things which make up a people, the way the Indian tribes of North America worshipped their gods, wrote their language, fought their wars, made their tools, cultivated their land, and raised their children.

EXAMPLES: The articles in these reports deal with every aspect of life among the North American Indians, with the following tribes included:

Zuñi, Iroquois, Navaho, Omaha, Cherokee, Seminole, Maya, Osage, Central Eskimo, Ojibwa, Point Barrow Eskimo, Siouan, Menomini, Seri, Hopi, Pawnee, Pima, Tewa, Seneca, Antillean, Winnebago, Fox, Creek Indian, and Chichasawa.

71] *Anthropology Today: An Encyclopedic Inventory*

Chicago: University of Chicago Press, 1953.
Ed. by A. L. Kroeber.

CONTENTS: This is a broad survey of modern anthropological knowledge as presented in 50 papers by 50 of the best scholars in the field, American and foreign.

Each paper concentrates on a particular area of anthropology, has a good, detailed bibliography appended to it, and deals with methods and results of research in such areas as social structure, folklore, cultural history, biological basis of human behavior, historical linguistics, human ecology, applied anthropology, and field work, to name just a few.

METHOD OF ORGANIZATION: Divided into three parts:

Part I, Problems of the Historical Approach, has 21 essays, 3 concerned with method, 13 with results, and 5 with theory;

Part II, Problems of Process, has 19 essays, 5 concerned with method, 11 with results, and 3 with theory;

Part III, Problems of Application, has 10 essays, all concerned with results.

An index and short biographies of contributors appear at the end.

USEFULNESS: *Anthropology Today* is a good survey of modern anthropology. It is especially useful because of the selected bibliographies at the end of each paper.

This work should be used in conjunction with *Yearbook of Anthropology* (our no. 74).

EXAMPLES: Paleopathology; New World History: South America; Historical Approach in Anthropology; Social Structure; Advances in Folklore Studies; National Character; and Cultural Values, are the titles of some of the papers you will find here.

72] *Funk and Wagnalls Standard Dictionary of Folklore, Mythology, and Legend*

New York: Funk & Wagnalls Co., 1950. 2 vols. Ed. by Maria Leach.

CONTENTS: Leading scholars in anthropology, folklore, and primitive and folk music are the contributors to this reference work. They have gathered together in these two volumes, without attempting to be complete, "a representative sampling of the gods of the world, the folk heroes, culture heroes . . . the folklore of animals, birds, plants, insects, stones, gems, minerals, stars . . . dances, ballads, folk songs, festivals and rituals . . . and the supernatural beings of folk belief and story, such as demons, ogres, fairies . . . werewolves, vampires, zombies."

The well over 7,000 entries range from a one-line definition of Aarvak ("In Norse mythology, one of the sun gods; the dawn") to a 12-page, double-column, highly detailed article on Spanish folklore.

The longer articles are signed, and have bibliographies appended to them.

METHOD OF ORGANIZATION: Alphabetical.

USEFULNESS: This work is extremely useful because here are brought together thousands of terms in mythology, folklore, and legend scattered in books, both in and out of print, memoires, diaries, manuscripts, ancient records, letters, journals, and the oral tradition of a people. Definitions are well written and easy to locate.

EXAMPLES: Atlantis, Cats, Door Signs, Flea, Friday, Gremlin, Hex, May Day, Moon, Oedipus, Paul Bunyan, Semitic Mythology, Shoes, and Twins are some of the entries.

RELATED REFERENCE WORKS: *Larousse Encyclopedia of Mythology*, ed. by Felix Guirand with an introduction by Robert Graves (New York: Prometheus, 1959), contains sophisticated essays on the folklore, legend, and religious customs of various countries from ancient times to the present.

Mythology of All Races, ed. by Louis Herbert Gray (Boston: Marshall Jones Co., 1916–32). This is the most comprehensive and probably the most valuable reference work in mythology. Covers all periods in depth. In 13 volumes, with the last volume the general index.

73] *The Golden Bough*

London: Macmillan, 1890; 2nd ed., 1900; 3rd ed.,
rev. and enl., 1911–1915. 12 vols. By Sir J. G. Frazer.

CONTENTS: Probably no other work in anthropology has contributed more to our understanding of ancient societies by seeking, as Frazer said himself, "to trace the growth of human thought and institutions in those dark ages which lie beyond the range of history." *The Golden Bough* is now a classic; though much of it has been superseded, it is considered by many to be the great work in our time on primitive beliefs and customs and their place in the comparative history of magic and religion.

METHOD OF ORGANIZATION: In 12 volumes. Vols. 1–2, *The Magic Art and the Evolution of Kings;* vol. 3, *Taboo and the Perils of the Soul;* vol. 4, *The Dying God;* vols. 5–6, *Adonis, Attis, Osiris; studies in the history of oriental religion;* vols. 7–8, *Spirits of the Corn and the Wild;* vol. 9, *The Scapegoat;* vol.

10–11, *Balder the Beautiful; the fire festival of Europe and the doctrine of the external soul;* vol. 12, *Bibliography and General Index.*

A word about vol. 12: the bibliography, 141 pages long, includes works in English, French, Latin, German, Dutch, Italian, and just about all the works on anthropology and fields related to it that were known when this monumental work was published. The index is 389 pages long.

Aftermath, often called vol. 13, is a supplement, with fresh information on subjects in *The Golden Bough.*

USEFULNESS: A great storehouse of information about the beliefs and institutions of mankind, especially as they pertain to magic and religion.

EXAMPLES: These chapter headings should illustrate the scope and depth of this work: Magic and Religion; Magicians as Kings; Incarnate Human Gods; The Omnipresence of Demons; Public Scapegoats; Human Scapegoats in Classical Antiquity; The Crucifixion of Christ; The Worship of Trees; Tabooed Acts; Tabooed Persons; Tabooed Things; Tabooed Words; The Myth of Adonis; and The Reincarnation of the Dead. These are just a few of the subjects Frazer treats in this classic reference work.

RELATED REFERENCE WORKS: *The New Golden Bough,* ed. by Theodor H. Gaster (New York: Criterion, 1959). This is a one-volume abridgment of Frazer's great work.

74] *Yearbook of Anthropology*

New York: Wenner-Gren Foundation for Anthropological Research, 1955. Ed. by William L. Thomas, Jr.

CONTENTS: This volume is a record of the accomplishments in anthropology through scholarly and popular articles of wide scope during the years 1952–1954.

There are 35 essays here, with extensive selected bibliographies for each, on such topics as cultural development and history, "Fossil Man and Human Evolution," complex civilizations, "Comparisons in Cultural Anthropology," and anthropology in government, education, business, and industry.

METHOD OF ORGANIZATION: Divided into six parts:

Part I introduces the volume with an essay on cultural and biological evolution by Julian H. Huxley;

Part II has 9 essays on "Man's Past: Environments, Relics, and Ancestors";

Part III has 8 essays on current theories in anthropology;

Part IV has 6 essays about new developments in applied and practical anthropology;

Part V has 13 essays examining critically work in Europe and southwest Asia;

Part VI deals with miscellaneous reference data (dissertations, awards, memorial lectures, etc.).

A subject and author index is included.

USEFULNESS: A good guide to recent trends of thought in anthropology. The appended, carefully selected bibliographies are extremely important should one want to do any additional reading.

75] *Art Index*

New York: H. W. Wilson Co., 1929—. Quarterly, with an
annual cumulation in September and a permanent
cumulation every 3 years.

CONTENTS: This quarterly bibliography indexes about 120 of
the leading American, English, French, German, Italian, and
Spanish periodicals, museum bulletins, and annuals in the fields
of art, archeology, architecture, ceramics, decoration and orna-
ment, graphic arts, landscape architecture, painting, and sculpture.

METHOD OF ORGANIZATION: Articles are arranged under subjects and authors in one alphabetical file; book reviews are indexed under the author reviewed; exhibitions generally appear
under the name of the artist exhibiting.

USEFULNESS: This is the reference work to use if one wants to
locate articles and reviews about artists, their work, and their
exhibitions. It is basic and invaluable in the field.

EXAMPLES: A sample entry is:

Classicism Some antique motifs in trecento art. A.M. Telpaz.
bibliog f il Art Bul 46: 372–6 S 64

An illustrated article with bibliographical footnotes on the subject, "classicism," entitled "Some Antique Motifs in Trecento
Art" by A. M. Telpaz will be found in volume 46 of *Art Bulletin,* pages 372–376 in the September 1964 number.

RELATED REFERENCE WORKS: *Index to Art Periodicals* (Boston:
G. K. Hall, 1962). A valuable reference work because it indexes

literature not found in *Art Index.* Arranged by subject. Within each subject, periodicals are arranged alphabetically.

76] *Index to Reproductions of American Paintings*

New York: H. W. Wilson Co., 1948. First Supplement, 1964.
By Isabel and Kate Monro.

CONTENTS: This is mainly an index to reproductions of paintings; it lists the work of artists of the United States occurring in 520 books and in more than 300 catalogues of annual exhibitions held by art museums. Often locations of originals have also been included.

METHOD OF ORGANIZATION: Alphabetical. There are three ways to find the listing of a picture here. The first way and the best is to look under the name of the artist. The user will be given the title of the picture and the name of the book in which it is reproduced.

The second way is to look under the title or titles of the picture. Here one will be given the artist and nothing more.

The third way is to look under the subject. Here one will find the name of the artist and the picture.

USEFULNESS: A quick, easy way to find the name of the artist and his date of birth and death, the title of the picture, the name of the book in which it appears and the museum in which it hangs.

EXAMPLES: See "Examples" under *Index to Reproductions of European Paintings* (our no. 77).

RELATED REFERENCE WORKS: *Index to Portraits Contained in Printed Books and Periodicals,* ed. by W. C. Lane and N. E. Browne (Washington: Library of Congress, 1906). "An index to portraits contained in 1181 sets (6,216 volumes), including both books and periodicals through the year 1904. Indexes some 120,000 portraits of about 40,000 persons."

77] *Index to Reproductions of European Paintings*

New York: H. W. Wilson Co., 1956. By Isabel and Kate Monro.

CONTENTS: This index is a guide to paintings by European artists that are reproduced in about 328 books, all of them in English and all of them general enough to be included in the average college library. Often locations of originals have also been included.

METHOD OF ORGANIZATION: See "Method of Organization" under *Index to Reproductions of American Paintings* (our no. 76).

USEFULNESS: A time-saving work, enabling the student in a few moments to find the name of the artist and his date of birth and death, the title of the picture, the name of the book in which it appears, and the museum in which it hangs.

EXAMPLES:

[1] **Chardin, Jean Baptiste Simeon,** 1699–1779
[2] The benediction. See The blessing
[3] The blessing (The benediction; Grace before meat; Saying grace) FPL
[4] Bryant. French pictures
[5] Gardner. 1926, 1936, 1948 eds.
[6] Kent. (col)
[7] Masters in art V6 pt 65
[8] Grace before meat. See The blessing
[9] Saying grace. See The blessing

Line [1] shows the name of painter, with date of birth and death. Lines [2], [8], and [9] are references to alternative titles and title used. Line [3] is the title used, followed by alternative titles. Lines [4], [5], [6], and [7] are brief forms used for books indexed where reproductions can be found—full entries are given in the List of Books in the front of the volume.

There are entries under titles, too, in alphabetical order, which give only the name of the painter.

RELATED REFERENCE WORKS: *Index to Portraits Contained in Printed Books and Periodicals* (see under our no. 76).

78] *Encyclopedia of Painting*

New York: Crown Publishers, Inc., 1955.
Ed. by Bernard S. Meyers.

CONTENTS: This one-volume work gives "an all-over picture of the outstanding painters, movements, styles, and techniques from most ancient times to the present day." Special features include sections on China, Japan, India, and Iran, and about 1,000 plates in color and black and white. The entries are biographical and descriptive and run anywhere from four lines (entry on the Hungarian artist Aba-Novak, Vilmos) to 115 lines (Michelangelo Buonarroti).

METHOD OF ORGANIZATION: Contains in one alphabetical arrangement about 4,000 entries for artists, famous galleries and museums, schools of painting, and terminology. Good cross references, but no index and no bibliography.

USEFULNESS: This book is neither complete nor exhaustive. What the reader will find are the basic facts—dates, biographical information, history, and a few remarks about style and influence.

An excellent feature is that one is told the location of all the illustrations.

EXAMPLES: The 4,000 entries include painters (A. Burgoyne Diller to Michelangelo), terms (diptych, disegno, etc.), museums (El Greco to the Louvre), schools and styles (Haitian painting, Coptic painting), movements (Constructivism, Dada), and techniques (enamel, engraving, etc.).

RELATED REFERENCE WORKS: *Everyman's Dictionary of Pictorial Art,* by William Gaunt (New York: Dutton, 1962), contains, in two volumes, biographies of about 1,200 artists, living and dead, descriptions of periods and schools, and definitions of terms. One thousand illustrations.

79] *Encyclopedia of World Art*

New York: McGraw-Hill, Inc., 1959.
15 vols. (12 completed.)

CONTENTS: Vast in scope, reliable in scholarship, highly detailed, and in great depth, with at least 800 pages of text and 800 pages of color, black and white plates in each volume, this comprehensive work covers architecture, sculpture, painting, and the decorative arts from pre-historic times to the present. All the entries are in the form of essays and run anywhere from half a page to 64 pages.

Each article has a selected and highly detailed bibliography appended to it as well as a list of major works, if the article is on an artist.

METHOD OF ORGANIZATION: All articles are arranged alphabetically no matter what their classification or category.

USEFULNESS: Factual, biographical, critical, bibliographical, historical, and geographical data written by some of the best scholars in the field. The excellent bibliographies and plates add to the usefulness of this work.

EXAMPLES: Here are some examples from Vol. XI to show the coverage: articles on Patronage, Peloponnesian Art, Perspective, Peru, Phidias, Phoenician-Punic Art, Picasso, Poland, Psychology of Art, Preservation of Art Works, Pre-Romanesque Art, Portraiture, and Polynesian Cultures.

RELATED REFERENCE WORKS: *Harper's Encyclopedia of Art,* rev. and ed. by J. Leroy Davidson and Philippa Gerry (New York: Harper and Row, 1937). Made up of short articles, bibliographies, and biographies. Living artists included. Original text based on Louis Hourtica's *Encyclopédie des Beaux-Arts.*

80] *Larousse Encyclopedia of Prehistoric and Ancient Art* (1962), *Byzantine and Medieval Art* (1963), *Modern Art* (1965)

New York: Prometheus Press. Translated from the French.

CONTENTS: These works not only summarize the history of art, from ancient times to the present, but also deal with the development of forms and aesthetic concepts and relate art "to the general evolution of ideas and customs, of culture and civilization, of humanity." The works contain facts as well as long essays by specialists on the art of a period and the philosophy of art.

Fully illustrated, with excellent black and white and color plates. Location of each illustration given whenever information is available.

METHOD OF ORGANIZATION: Chapters are arranged chronologically, with the facts about a period—dates, techniques, schools, artists, etc.—given concisely at the end of each chapter.

The main part of each chapter is made up of (1) a section called "Art Forms of Society," which deals with how art reflects man's material and spiritual conditions, and (2) essays by specialists on movements, influences, and trends.

USEFULNESS: A first-rate reference work for students interested in the history of art and the relationship of art to the culture out of which it develops. Don't come here merely for facts.

EXAMPLES: Interesting, well-developed, and informative essays from historical, geographic, and social points of view are here, on such topics as The First Asiatic Civilizations, Oceanic Art, The Aesthetics of India and China, The Later Byzantine Empire, The Romantic Period, and The Beginnings of Modern Art, to name just a few.

RELATED REFERENCE WORKS: *Encyclopedia of the Arts,* by D. D. Runes and Harry G. Schrickel (New York: Philosophical Library, 1946). You get definitions of terms as well as articles on schools of art, forms, and phases. Music and other arts included. No biographies.

81] *Bryan's Dictionary of Painters and Engravers*

London: G. Bell and Sons, Ltd., 1930–34.
Revised and enlarged 4th ed. 5 vols.

CONTENTS: One of the standard biographical dictionaries in English on painters and engravers from ancient times to the beginning of the twentieth century, this 5-vol. reference work, occasionally illustrated in half tones, gives "basic information on the facts and lives of those with whom it deals." The entries, well over 18,000, run from about 18 to 4,400 words, with many of the longer articles written and signed by specialists (the famous art critic, Roger E. Fry, wrote the article on Jacopo Bellini).

Entries are often accompanied by a list of the artist's works and the museums or galleries in which they hang.

METHOD OF ORGANIZATION: Alphabetical.

USEFULNESS: Good introductory source for basic, but often sketchy, biographical information. Long articles on famous artists are interesting and informative.

EXAMPLES: Here is an exact entry from vol. I. It is representative of the depth, scope, and precision given throughout the work.

Baldini, Pietro Paolo. According to TiTi, this artist was a native of Rome, and was a disciple of Pietro da Cortona. He flourished in the middle of the 17th century. He painted historical subjects, and several of his works in the public edifices at Rome were deservedly admired; among others, some pictures in the churches of San Nicolò da Tolentino, and Santa Maria di Loretto; but above all an altar-piece representing the "Crucifixion," in the church of Sant' Eustachio, finely composed, and designed with great care and correctness.

82] *History of Art*

Englewood Cliffs, N.J.: Prentice-Hall, Inc., 1962.
By H. W. Janson.

CONTENTS: Probably the best one-volume history of art in Europe and the Middle East, this work covers all important trends and movements from prehistoric man to the present. It presents a survey of art in the west from old stone age paintings to Jackson Pollock's *One*. Many black and white illustrations and some color. The location of illustrations is given whenever information is available.

Good bibliographies for each chapter appear at the end of the book.

METHOD OF ORGANIZATION: Divided into four parts:

Part I, The Ancient World, has 8 sections: Magic and Ritual, Egyptian Art, The Ancient Near East, Aegean Art, Greek Art, Etruscan Art, Roman Art, Early Christian and Byzantine Art;

Part II, The Middle Ages, has 4 sections: Islamic Art, Early Medieval Art, Romanesque Art, Gothic Art;

Part III, The Renaissance, has 9 sections: "Late Gothic" Painting, Sculpture, and the Graphic Arts, The Early Renaissance in Italy, The High Renaissance in Italy, Mannerism and Other Trends, The Renaissance in the North, The Baroque in Italy and Germany, The Baroque in Flanders, Holland, and Spain, The Baroque in France and England;

Part IV, The Modern World, has 5 sections: Neoclassicism and Romanticism, Realism and Impressionism, Twentieth-Century Painting and Sculpture, Twentieth-Century Architecture.

USEFULNESS: A first-rate introduction to western painting, sculpture, and architecture.

RELATED REFERENCE WORKS: *Pelican History of Art,* ed. by Nikolaus Pevsner (Baltimore: Penguin, 1953—). This is a series "covering world art and architecture of all periods, each written by a specialist and containing substantial bibliographies and many plates."

ECONOMICS AND BUSINESS

83] *International Bibliography of Economics/*
Bibliographie Internationale de
Science Economique

Paris: UNESCO, 1952–1959; Chicago: Aldine, 1960—.
Annual.

CONTENTS: A major bibliography in the field, this annual includes the most important books, articles in periodicals, pamphlets, and government publications listed in about 1,400 periodicals, from nearly every country and in almost every language in the world.

Titles in French remain in French; titles in English remain in English; titles in all other languages are translated into English.

METHOD OF ORGANIZATION: In fifteen sections: Preliminaries, Methods, General and Basic Works, History of Economic Thought, Economic History, Economic Activity, Organization of Production, Production (goods and services), Price and Markets, Money and Finance, Income and Income Distribution, Demand (use of income), Social Economics and Policy, Public Economy, International Economics. Authors in each section are listed alphabetically.

There is a detailed author and subject index either at the front or the back of each volume. There are no cumulations.

USEFULNESS: Indispensable for scholarly work in economics because it gives an international bibliographic guide to the latest and most important works.

EXAMPLES:

Jacobs, P. *The State of the Unions*. New York, Atheneum, 63, xiii + 303 P. (USA).

Julliard, J. "La CFTC Devant Son Avenir," *Esprit* 31 (9), Sept. 63: 290–302. (France)

Labor, L. "Il Ruolo Attuale Del Movimento Operaio Cristiano" (The Present Role of the Christian Labour Movement), *Quad. Azione Soc.* 13 (4–5), July–Oct. 62: 822–831. (Italy)

84] *Business Periodicals Index*

New York: H. W. Wilson Co., 1958—.
Monthly, with annual cumulations.

CONTENTS: This index to about 120 American business periodicals lists over 42,000 articles a year and covers such fields as management activities, marketing, accounting, advertising, distribution, promotion, insurance, taxation, banking and finance, and just about every other possible aspect of business.

The periodicals indexed and the articles listed are for the most part specialized, but not scholarly. They are for business people and for those interested in the business world.

METHOD OF ORGANIZATION: Arranged alphabetically by subject and then alphabetically by titles of articles under the subject.

USEFULNESS: Extremely useful for locating up-to-date information on happenings in the business world and fields related to it.

EXAMPLES: Here is a sample entry:

Automobiles
Ford runs wild with Mustang and Cobra.
R.R. Kay. il iron age 195:58 F 11 '65

The subject is *Automobiles*. The title of the article is "Ford runs wild with Mustang and Cobra," and the name of the author is R. R. Kay. The article is illustrated. It appeared in volume 195 of the periodical *Iron Age,* page 58, in the February 11, 1965, number.

RELATED REFERENCE WORKS: *Industrial Arts Index* (New York: H. W. Wilson, 1913–1957) is your index to business journals published from 1913–1957. Mostly American, but does include a few Canadian and British journals.

Index of Economic Journals, 5 vols. (Homewood, Illinois: Irwin, 1962), lists articles in English published in about 90 periodicals. Covers period from 1886–1959.

Funk and Scott Index of Corporations and Industries (Cleveland: Investment Index Company, 1960). Weekly with monthly and annual cumulations. "An index to periodical articles and other references (e.g., financial and corporation report findings) on industries as a whole, and on individual corporations. Approximately 100 serials are regularly indexed. Coverage includes United States, Canada, Great Britain, and Japan."

85] *Economic Abstracts*

The Hague: Martinus Nijhoff, 1953.
Semi-monthly.

CONTENTS: Prepared by the Library of the Economic Information Service with the collaboration of the Library of the Netherlands School of Economics and the Library of the Ministry of Social Affairs, this small reference work abstracts books and articles published in English, French, German, and Dutch, on economics, finance, trade and industry, management and labor. The abstracts, always unsigned, range from 8 to 150 words and are mostly in English.

METHOD OF ORGANIZATION: Each issue is divided into two major categories: (1) Social Sciences, and (2) Applied Sciences, Medicine, and Technology, with selected subjects under each category. Annual author and subject indexes are offered.

USEFULNESS: Good source for summaries of important books and articles published in English, French, German, and Dutch, and for a selected bibliographical guide to the field of your interest.

EXAMPLE: Here is a sample entry:

Grubel, H.G., and A.D. Scott. The Characteristics of Foreigners in the U.S. Economics Profession. 15 P. A5 (The American Economic Review, Evanston, No.1, March, 1967, P. 131. Bibliogr. Grafn. Tabn.).

By analyzing the characteristics of foreigners in the U.S. economics profession, an attempt is made to provide quantitative information relevant to the "quality" of the migrants and whether the "best" are drawn to the U.S.A. Some characteristics of U.S. and foreign-born economists. Analysis of the shares of foreign born supplied by individual countries and continents. Some information about foreign-born and foreign-trained U.S. economists. The data reveal that economists with European and Canadian training who stay on at U.S. universities earn a higher income than U.S. economists.

RELATED REFERENCE WORKS: *Journal of Economic Abstracts* (Cambridge: Harvard University Press, 1963). An international journal published quarterly, it contains lengthy abstracts selected from 35 contributing periodicals. Annual author index.

86] *Encyclopaedia of Banking and Finance*

Boston: The Bankers Publishing Co., 1962.
6th ed. Ed. by F. L. Garcia.

CONTENTS: Much more than a mere compilation of bare definitions of terms, this encyclopedia includes both short, succinct definitions of one-paragraph length and 2- to 15-page articles, well developed and often presenting a historical account of a term.

The authors give many examples to illustrate their definitions.

Good and often long bibliographies are given at the end of long articles.

METHOD OF ORGANIZATION: Alphabetically arranged. There is no index.

USEFULNESS: An excellent source for clear, concise, accurate, and developed definitions of economic and business terms.

It lists about 5,000 terms and is much more detailed and

comprehensive than the *McGraw-Hill Dictionary of Modern Economics* (our no. 87).

EXAMPLES: The work defines terms and has articles on money, credit, banking, law, accounting, trusts, finance, foreign exchange, investments, securities, business organizations, insurance, commodities, markets, brokerage.

RELATED REFERENCE SOURCES: *Financial Handbook*, ed. by Samuel S. Stripman (New York: Ronald, 1964), contains detailed information on business management from the financial point of view.

87] *McGraw-Hill Dictionary of Modern Economics*

New York: McGraw-Hill, 1965.

CONTENTS: This handbook of terms and organizations gives one-paragraph definitions of about 1,300 modern economic terms, descriptions of about 200 agencies, public and private, American and foreign, concerned with economics and marketing, plus a bibliography of sources.

METHOD OF ORGANIZATION: Divided into two sections, the first is devoted to terms and the second to organizations. Each is arranged alphabetically.

USEFULNESS: A handy, up-to-date, one-volume work for students with the most elementary economics background. Bibliographical references are extremely important because they indicate where to get information in depth and the pages to go to.

This handbook should be used in conjunction with *Encyclopaedia of Banking and Finance* (our no. 86).

EXAMPLES: The work contains definitions of such terms as Actuary, Balanced Budget, Credit, Depletion, Gold Standard, Marginal Cost, National Income, Union Shop, and descriptions of organizations such as American Bankers Association, Bureau of Labor Statistics, Council on Foreign Relations, Federal Aviation Agency, and National Association of Manufacturers.

Here is a sample term entry:

Bank Discount
The difference between the face amount of a bank loan and the amount credited to the borrower. It is the total amount of interest paid by a borrower to a bank in advance rather than at fixed intervals or at maturity. The interest is deducted at a fixed rate from the face amount of the loan, and the remaining balance is credited to the borrower.

RELATED REFERENCE SOURCES: *A Dictionary of Economics*, by Harold S. Sloan and Arnold J. Zurcher (New York: Barnes and Noble, 1961) contains definitions and explanations of terms used in economics, international trade, money and banking, and insurance. Also valuable because it has summaries of relevant United States laws about our economy.

88] *Sources of Business Information*

Berkeley; University of California Press, rev. ed., 1964.
By Edwin T. Coman, Jr.

CONTENTS: Accurate and detailed, simply and clearly written, this guide covers such fields as statistics, finance, real estate, insurance, accounting, automation, management, personal and industrial relations, marketing, sales management and advertising, public relations, and foreign trade.

It lists and briefly describes important bibliographies, one-volume works, authoritative handbooks, yearbooks, periodicals, trade magazines, supplementary bulletins, and books in each field.

METHOD OF ORGANIZATION: Arranged by fields. An author and subject index is at the back.

USEFULNESS: The careful selection of the works listed and the descriptions of most of these works make this a good book to help the reader locate the business information and the statistics he may need.

EXAMPLE: Here is an entry under Foreign Trade:

International Trade Reporter. Loose-leaf service published by The Bureau of National Affairs, Inc., Washington, D.C. This service provides comprehensive, well-organized information that is vital and useful. Weekly notification of trade developments and trends supplements the three looseleaf binders that are arranged and indexed by subject matter. The service furnishes working data on export and import controls imposed by the United States and overseas market, tariff and tax requirements, forms of export organization, sales policies and contracts, market exploration, patents and trade-marks, transport facilities, communication, packaging and shipping, and other subjects.

RELATED REFERENCE WORKS: *Business Periodicals Index* (our no. 84).

89] *Public Affairs Information Service. Bulletin*

New York: Public Affairs Information Service, 1915—.
Weekly bulletins with cumulations published five times a year.
The fifth cumulated issue becomes the permanent
annual volume.

CONTENTS: This weekly is an important index to current books, periodical articles, government documents, pamphlets, and other useful material in economics and public affairs.

Publications "from all English-speaking countries are included, as well as many printed in English in other countries. Emphasis is placed upon factual and statistical information. Works in foreign languages are not mentioned."

METHOD OF ORGANIZATION: Arranged alphabetically by subject.

USEFULNESS: An indispensable index for locating current works in political science, government, economics, and sociology.

A valuable feature is the very brief description, often only one line, of the contents of most works listed.

EXAMPLES: Here are two sample entries under the subject, "Western Europe":

Europe, Western

Economic union Jensen, Finn B. and Ingo Walter. The Common Market: economic integration in Europe. '65 vii + 278 p bibl tables charts $4.95; pa $1.95—Lippincott

Military policy Without France? the price of bringing the mixed-manned fleet into life may be high; let us be clear about the purposes that justify it. Economist 213: 671–2 N 14 '64

90] *Economic Almanac*

New York: National Industrial Conference Board, 1940—. Biennial.

CONTENTS: This annual almanac presents simply and concisely up-to-date, important, and accurate statistical data "wanted and used in connection with current economic and management questions." The information here is reliable and important "from the point of view of practical businessmen." There are no articles here and no maps.

METHOD OF ORGANIZATION: The first 565 pages are all statistical charts and the remaining 100 are devoted to a glossary of selected terms, a good general index, and a short Canadian index.

The charts are divided into 26 sections: Population, Material Resources, Labor, Productivity, Research and Development, Prices, National Income, Product and Wealth, American Enterprises—General, Agriculture, Mining, Construction and Housing, Manufacturing, Transportation, Utilities, Trade, Service, Banking and Finance, Statistics of Individual Industries, Personal Consumption and Savings, Public Finance, Public and Private Debt, United States Foreign Trade, International Financial Position of the United States, International Economic Statistics, and Canadian Statistics.

USEFULNESS: The almanac gives extensive, accurate, and up-to-date information about the economic condition of the

United States. It also gives the source of the information and any qualifications or limitations the reader should know for a correct interpretation of the statistical charts.

RELATED REFERENCE WORKS: *United States Council of Economic Advisers, Economic Indicators* (Washington: United States Government Printing Office, 1921—). Monthly with weekly statistical supplements. Gives basic statistics on "total output, income and spending, employment, unemployment, wages, production and business activity, prices, currency, credit, security market, and federal finance."

United States Bureau of Census: Census of Population (our no. 93).

91] *Commodity Year Book*

New York: Commodity Research Bureau, Inc., 1939—.
Annual.

CONTENTS: This yearbook describes briefly in short paragraphs and charts, but mostly in statistical tables, over 80 commodities of commerce (e.g. copper, cotton, gold, hogs, lard, rubber, sulphur, wheat and flour, zinc) in the United States as well as their physical characteristics, uses, prices, imports and exports, and types and grades.

Sources are supplied after each statistical table.

METHOD OF ORGANIZATION: Alphabetical.

USEFULNESS: A good, quick, reliable source for statistical data on commodities produced in the United States. Sources given enable the student to follow up his research in depth.

EXAMPLES: Here are the categories covered for eggs. One is given the same depth of treatment for all other commodities:

Eggs Laid per Hundred Layers in the United States; Average Price Received by Farmers for Eggs in the United States as of 15th of Month in Cents per Dozen; Average Wholesale Prices of Shell Eggs at Chicago in Cents per Dozen; Farm Parity Price of Eggs in the United States in Cents per Dozen; Cold Storage Holdings of Frozen Eggs in the United States, On First of Month in Thousands of Cases; Cold Storage Holdings of Shell Eggs in the United States, On First of Month in Thousands of Cases.

RELATED REFERENCE WORKS: *United States Bureau of the Census. Census of Business* (Washington: United States Government Printing Office, 1933—) contains just about every aspect of retail and wholesale trade statistics. Great detail.

92] *Foreign Commerce Yearbook*

Washington, D.C.: Government Printing Office, 1933–1939; 1948–1951. Annual.

CONTENTS: This annual presents in statistical tables the economic highlights of about 68 countries, especially the exports and imports to and from the United States.

"Statistical information in this volume reprints in the main a presentation, in highly condensed form, of official data published by the respective countries, supplemented by publications of international agencies and by information supplied by the United States Foreign Service and by other United States Government departments, derived generally from original foreign sources, sometimes unpublished."

METHOD OF ORGANIZATION: Arranged by geographical areas (European and Mediterranean areas, etc.) and then alphabetically by countries within each area. Only the volumes from 1933–1939 have indexes.

USEFULNESS: This is a good source for a quick, statistical economic profile of the countries of the world. The United States is not included.

EXAMPLES: The fields covered are Area and Population, Education, Agriculture (Wheat, Rye, Barley, Oats, etc.), Mining, Manufacturing, Industrial Production (Coal, Iron, Ore, Manganese Ore, etc.), Transportation and Communication, Postal, Telegraph, Telephone and Radio Statistics, and Foreign Trade.

RELATED REFERENCE WORKS: *Yearbook of International Trade Statistics* (New York: United Nations Statistical Office,

1950—) contains statistics from all nations on every aspect of trade and industry.

93] U.S. *Bureau of Census:*
Census of Population

Washington, D.C.: Government Printing Office, 1960.
Published every ten years.

CONTENTS: Probably the best known and most important publication of the government, this reference work presents detailed statistics, on maps and in charts, on the number of people living in the 50 states, and in the counties, urban and rural places, and other types of areas in the United States and its territories. It also gives statistics in great detail and depth on the general, social, and economic characteristics of the population.

METHOD OF ORGANIZATION: By categories, and then alphabetically by states and territories.

USEFULNESS: The *Census of Population* is an invaluable publication because it has detailed, massive, and accurate statistics on every aspect of the population of the United States. It is also excellent because it shows what changes take place in ten-year periods.

EXAMPLES: The range of the categories covered is astonishing. One will find figures here on sex, age, marital status, color or race, nativity and parentage, state of birth, country of origin of those of foreign stock, mother tongue, school enrollment, years of school completed, families and their composition, veteran status, occupation, and so many more, until one has a huge statistical portrait of the population of the United States.

EDUCATION

94] *Education Index*

New York: H. W. Wilson Co., 1929—.
Monthly with annual and triennial cumulations.

CONTENTS: This indispensable reference work in education indexes articles, book reviews, and some poems in about 160 American periodicals, bulletins, society proceedings, and a few books. The titles indexed are in English and range from the general (*Journal of General Education*) to the specialized (*Journal of Nursery Education*).

METHOD OF ORGANIZATION: Until June 1961, entries were arranged alphabetically under both author and subject. Now they are under subject only. Book reviews, however, appear under the subject heading "Book Reviews"; poems appear under the subject heading "Poems."

USEFULNESS: Absolutely essential if one wants to find articles and book reviews on every aspect of education.
The *Education Index* should be used with *Readers' Guide to Periodical Literature* (our no. 37).

EXAMPLES: Here is a sample entry:

Aspects of public school adult education. T. A. Van Sant. il Baltimore Bul Ed 33: 13–25 Je '56

The name of the article is "Aspects of Public School Adult Education" and the author is T. A. Van Sant. It has illustrations. The article appeared in June, 1956, in vol. 33 of the *Baltimore Bulletin of Education*, pages 13–25.

RELATED REFERENCE WORKS: *British Education Index* (London: Library Association, 1954) indexes about 50 British periodicals by subject only. Author index.

Education Abstracts (Paris: UNESCO, 1949–1965) contains abstracts of the literature on education published throughout the world. Separate volumes devoted to special topics, such as bibliographies, etc. No longer published.

95] *Cyclopedia of Education*

New York: The Macmillan Co., 1911–1913. 5 vols.
Ed. by Paul Monroe.

CONTENTS: Although dated in many of its articles (the one on Child Study is one of the most obvious), this work is still one of the best on education in all countries and all periods, with American subjects treated in greater detail and scope.

The articles were written and signed by some of the most eminent scholars (John Dewey, Franz Boas, Morris Raphael Cohen) from every field of knowledge (philosophy, anthropology, ecclesiastical history, botany, psychology, education, Greek, English, etc.). They are highly informative, well written, and accurate, ranging from a 5-line entry on John Quincy Adams to a 16-page article on art in schools. Excellent illustrations, some of them in color.

METHOD OF ORGANIZATION: Alphabetical. The index, in vol. V, classifies entries under broad subject headings.

USEFULNESS: Probably the best source to consult if the student wants to (1) do research in the history of education, (2) find out what subjects come under the discipline of education and how our notions of education and its functions differ from those held 50 years ago.

Many of the articles on individuals (Francis Bacon), institutions (Cambridge University), and historical events (Black Death) are still excellent today.

EXAMPLES: The subjects treated in the thousands of entries are from all fields of knowledge.

RELATED REFERENCE WORKS: *Encyclopedia of Modern Education*, ed. by Harry N. Rivlin (New York: Philosophical Library, 1943), contains signed articles, often by specialists, on trends in education. Has biographies of eminent men in education.

96] *Encyclopedia of Educational Research*

New York: The Macmillan Co., 3rd ed., 1960.
Ed. by Chester W. Harris.

CONTENTS: An important reference work in that each signed article (there are 185 and they range from 3 to 17 double-column pages) gives "a critical evaluation, synthesis, and interpretation of all pertinent research—early as well as recent." Highly selective and detailed bibliographies are appended to each article.

But this is not an encyclopedia in the usual sense. One will find nothing here about the function of primary, secondary, or higher education, about famous educators and institutions, about the history of secondary school education in the United States. Rather, the articles are selected from a specific point of view—the "characteristics and potentialities of man and their relevance to education."

METHOD OF ORGANIZATION: Articles are arranged alphabetically, with titles listed on pages xxvii to xxix. An index is supplied at the beginning of the volume.

USEFULNESS: This is a valuable reference work for knowing the subjects in education that scholars think important enough to research and to critically evaluate and synthesize.

The bibliographies are indispensable because they are the direct source for each article, often paragraph by paragraph, and because they tell exactly where to go should the student want to do any further reading.

EXAMPLES: Academic Freedom, Adolescence, Behavior Problems, Delinquency, Emotional Development, English, Family Life Education, Infancy and Early Childhood, Mass Media, Personality, Physically Handicapped Children, Religious Education, and Teacher Education are just a few of the subjects treated.

RELATED REFERENCE WORKS: *Handbook of Research on Teaching,* ed. by Nathaniel Lees Gage (Chicago: Rand McNally, 1963). This long, scholarly work is excellent for students who want to become teachers. Articles here are written by specialists and are on every aspect of education.

97] *Dictionary of Education*

> New York: McGraw-Hill Co., 2nd ed., 1959.
> Ed. by Carter V. Good.

CONTENTS: This dictionary defines about 20,000 technical and professional terms and concepts in the whole field of education. The names of persons, institutions, school systems, organizations, places, titles of periodicals, and "such purely content or subject-matter terms as *test tube* in science, *triangle* in mathematics, *voting* in civics" are excluded. Only words with "definite educational professional connotations" are included; the definitions range from 12 to 175 words.

METHOD OF ORGANIZATION: Definitions are arranged alphabetically. Terms used in foreign countries are grouped at the back of the book.

USEFULNESS: The *Dictionary of Education* is a good source for definitions of commonly accepted terms and concepts in education.

EXAMPLES: The entry below, exactly as it appears in the book, shows the kind of treatment given to each term defined:

Social Climate: that complex of tangible and intangible conditions which gives a group or situation its distinguishing atmosphere or stimulus value; the term is used with special reference to interpersonal relationships, attitudes, rules, and regulations which affect especially the tendency of the situation to be friendly and congenial or the opposite; those mores or interpersonal relationships which distinguish one group from another.

RELATED REFERENCE WORKS: *Cyclopedia of Education* (our no. 95).

Encyclopedia of Educational Research (our no. 96).

98] *Biennial Survey of Education in the United States*

Washington, D.C.: Government Printing Office, 1916–1958.

CONTENTS: One of the most important publications to come out of the United States Office of Education, the *Biennial Survey* gives, in clear, simple statistical charts, information on every significant aspect of public and non-public education in the United States, including such items as state and city school systems, vocational education, higher education, libraries, enrollment, expenditures, indebtedness, salaries, and per capita costs.

METHOD OF ORGANIZATION: Arranged by categories (there is a historical summary of public, elementary, and secondary school statistics in the United States; classroom teachers in public elementary and secondary day schools, by sex and level of instruction), by sections of the country (North Atlantic, Great Lakes and Plains, Southeast, West, Southwest, Outlying Parts), and by the various states alphabetically listed within these sections.

USEFULNESS: The *Biennial Survey* gives a thorough statistical profile of education in the United States for 1916 to 1958. The facts and figures for each state show the value people put on education and the value the states put on different parts of education (how many administrators a school has compared to its teachers and students, etc.).

EXAMPLES: Here is the kind of detail, depth, and scope to expect from this work. For example, the 1958 volume has, among other things, statistics on board members, professional staff, secretarial and clerical assistants, operation and maintenance staff, total school population (excluding armed forces overseas), school age population (5–17 years inclusive), high school graduates of full-time public secondary schools, by sex and by state, and percentage distribution of expenditures for public schools broken down by purpose—administration, instruction, plant operation, plant maintenance, etc.

99] *World Survey of Education*

Paris: UNESCO, 1955–Triennial.

CONTENTS: These four huge, highly detailed, up-to-date, accurate volumes, each about 1,400 pages, are the best reference source for an analysis, both in statistical charts and essays, of every aspect of education (general, primary, secondary, and higher) in every nation in the world. The work ranges from such topics as a world survey of education, a comparative description of educational systems, school-age and school-going population, the progress of primary education since 1930, and the trends of educational change to intellectual aspects of higher education, and the changing pattern of higher education.

Bibliographies for further reading are appended to each chapter.

METHOD OF ORGANIZATION: Each volume is arranged alphabetically by country.

Vol. 1, *Handbook of Educational Organization and Statistics,* deals with education throughout the world, from kindergarten to the university, including informal adult education; vol. 2, *Primary Education,* gives a detailed account of primary schooling in each country; vol. 3, *Secondary Education,* presents an analysis of the general, technical, vocational, and teacher training provided for students from 12–18 years of age; vol. 4, *Higher Education,* is an account of academic, professional, technological, artistic, and teacher education throughout the world. There is a general index.

USEFULNESS: The best source for information in the form of statistical tables and essays on every aspect of education throughout the world.

Glossary of terms for each non-English-speaking country.

EXAMPLES: Administration, finance, organization, teacher training, agricultural education, adult education, private schools, school buildings and supplies, education and status of teachers, compulsory education, curricula and methods, welfare service, scholarships, types of secondary education, vocational and technical schools, university institutions, and staff, student life and welfare, and teacher training institutions are some of the subjects treated.

RELATED REFERENCE WORKS: *International Yearbook of Education* (Paris: UNESCO, 1948—). This valuable annual surveys education in about 90 countries.

100] *Digest of Educational Statistics*

Washington, D.C.: Government Printing Office, 1962—. Annual.

CONTENTS: A continuation of the *Biennial Survey of Education in the United States* (our no. 98), the statistics in this annual, presented entirely in tables, have been gathered from governmental and private sources and cover the whole field of American education from kindergarten through graduate school.

METHOD OF ORGANIZATION: The *Digest* is divided into five chapters: (1) Elementary and Secondary Education, (2) Higher Education, (3) All Levels of Education, (4) Federal Programs of Education, and (5) Selected Statistics Related to Education in the United States.

An index is at the back of each volume.

USEFULNESS: Extremely useful for obtaining facts and figures on the nature and scope of education in the United States, the annual is also important because a good many of the statistical tables go back ten years or more. A glance at these will show the trends in American education today.

EXAMPLES: Among the many statistics to be found in this work are: enrollment in special education programs for exceptional children; number of science and mathematics teachers in public secondary day schools; number of high school graduates compared with population seventeen years ago; average annual expenditure per pupil in public school systems; enrollment in junior colleges, 1917/18–1963; property of institutions of higher education, 1870–1960; United States college students abroad.

HISTORY

101] *Guide to Historical Literature*

New York: Macmillan, 1961. Also known as *The American Historical Association's Guide to Historical Literature*. Ed. by George F. Howe, *et al.*

CONTENTS: A comprehensive, annotated bibliography of historical literature, that covers the whole field—ancient, medieval, modern; American, European, and non-European—of works, in English and foreign languages. Over 20,000 items are listed, briefly described, and evaluated.

METHOD OF ORGANIZATION: The *Guide* is divided into 9 main parts by general region or era. Each main part is divided into a number of subsections, usually by country. Each subsection is further divided by types, e.g., bibliographies, atlases, specialized histories, government publications, etc. Items are then listed alphabetically by authors.

Consult the detailed table of contents to locate the subsection of particular interest. Consult the index for specific items; references are to item numbers, not to pages.

USEFULNESS: This annotated bibliography is meant for the student who wishes to acquaint himself with the major historical sources available in his special area. Good coverage of American, European, and non-European history.

EXAMPLES: The following information is given for each work listed: author's name, title of work, number of volumes, city and date of publication (but not publisher's name), followed by a brief description of contents and scope, and evaluative or comparative comment. Here is a short sample entry:

X 251. Trotskii, Lev. *The History of the Russian Revolution.* 3 v. N.Y., 1936. The highly subjective account of one of the main actors.

RELATED REFERENCE WORKS: *International Bibliography of Historical Sciences* (our no. 102). Advanced students might also want to consult the various specialized bibliographies dealing with the history of a particular country or region or with specific historical periods.

102] *International Bibliography of Historical Sciences*

Paris: International Committee of Historical Sciences, 1930—. Annual; covers 1926—.

CONTENTS: Annual descriptive bibliographies of books and periodical articles on world history that were published during each year. Annual volumes for each year since 1926 except 1940–1946. A comprehensive yet selective listing of noteworthy publications in English and foreign languages, in the field of history, European and non-European, ancient and modern. The latest annual volume lists close to 8,000 books and articles.

METHOD OF ORGANIZATION: Divided into major sections by topic (e.g., Pre-History; History of the Middle Ages; Modern Religious History) or region (e.g., Asia; Africa; America; Oceania). Then further divided into subtopics and sub-subtopics within each major section (e.g., major section: Modern History —General Works; subtopic: History by Countries; sub-subtopic: France). Within each subdivision or part of subdivision, items are listed alphabetically by authors. Slavic, Japanese, Chinese, Hebraic, and Arabic names are transcribed into our alphabet.

Consult the detailed table of contents to locate the subsection of particular interest. The annual indexes are divided into two parts: an index of names and a geographical index. References are to item numbers, not pages. Note that alphabetization of countries follows the French form of the names of the countries; thus one will find Germany under A, and the United States under E.

USEFULNESS: A valuable listing of current publications throughout the world dealing with all phases of history. Note that there is a slight time gap between the year covered and the publication of the bibliography, e.g., the volume for 1964 was published in 1967.

This work is meant for advanced students. Introductory matter and descriptions are often given in a foreign language.

EXAMPLES: Here are two sample entries; the first a book, the second an article. "CR" stands for criticism; references following this symbol are to major critical reviews of the book; abbreviations of the names of periodicals are explained in the beginning of each annual volume.

4558. **Footman (David).** Civil war in Russia. New York, Frederick A. Praeger, 62, 328 p. (Praeger publs. in russian history a. world communism, no 114).—CR: J. S. Curtiss, *Am. hist. R.*, 63, vol. 68, no 3, p. 749–750.

4557. **Florovsky (George).** The problem of old russian culture. *Slavic R.*, 62, vol. 21, no 1, p. 1–15.

RELATED REFERENCE WORKS: *International Bibliography of Political Science* (our no. 164). Also see the various specialized bibliographies in the field, e.g., *Writings on American History* (our no. 105); *Writings on British History* (London: Jonathan Cape, 1934—).

103] *Historical Abstracts 1775–1945*

Santa Barbara: American Bibliographical Center, Clio Press, 1955—. Quarterly. Ed. by Eric H. Boehm.

CONTENTS: A quarterly publication of abstracts—short, objective summaries—of articles on world history appearing in current periodicals. Some 1,300 journals in thirty languages (English and foreign) are examined for pertinent articles in the field of modern history, 1775–1945.

METHOD OF ORGANIZATION: Summaries of articles are grouped by subject classifications, in three major sections, and then into subsections: I. "General" (subsection, e.g., "Historiography"); II. "Topics" (subsections, e.g., "Political History"; "World War II"); III. "Area or Country" (subsection, e.g., "Latin America"; "Russian Empire & USSR"). The abstracts in each subsection or part of subsection are arranged alphabetically by authors.

Consult the table of contents in each issue to locate the subsection of particular interest. Cumulative indexes are published annually and every five years.

USEFULNESS: A quick way to check on whether or not it's worth one's time to read a particular article. Also good for getting a general idea of what is currently being published in periodicals the world over about a particular aspect of history.

Warning: abstracts are extremely brief; be sure to read the full article if interest is aroused.

EXAMPLES: The following information is given for each article listed: volume and abstract number; "cues" to identify topic, geographic area, and time period covered by article (see "List of Cues" for explanations); author's name; title of article, in caps (with translation if required); journal in which it appeared (underlined); year; volume (with number), and pages; abstract; name of abstracter.

Here is a sample entry:

12:3213   LAW: Courts   RUS   1865–1908

Williams, D.S.M. NATIVE COURTS IN TSARIST CENTRAL ASIA. Central Asian R. 1966 14(1): 6–19. Based on contemporary czarist materials. Bribery and corruption were so frequent that the organization and functioning of the native courts of Turkistan were unsatisfactory from the point of view of both the rulers and the ruled.

G. Robina Quale.

RELATED REFERENCE WORKS: An extremely valuable directory of U.S. and foreign periodicals is Boehm and Adolphus' *Historical Periodicals: An Annotated World List of Historical & Related Serial Publications* (Santa Barbara: Clio Press, 1961), which lists more than 4,500 current journals.

See the various specialized abstracts, e.g., *America: History and Life* (our no. 106); *Current Digest of the Soviet Press* (New York: Joint Committee on Slavic Studies, 1949—); *African Abstracts* (London: International African Institute, 1950—).

American

104] *Harvard Guide to American History*

Cambridge: Harvard University Press, 1954.
Compiled by Oscar Handlin, *et al.*

CONTENTS: A guide book for the study and reading of American history, containing essays on "method, resources and materials," and selected bibliographies of books and periodical articles on the various historical periods. The bibliographies are not annotated.

METHOD OF ORGANIZATION: Divided into three parts: I. (chapts. 1–2) essays on the methods and study of American history; II. (chapts. 3–5) essays on the resources and materials for the study of American history, plus bibliographies of general historical reference works; III. (chapts. 6–30) reading list, arranged chronologically by historical periods, divided into 25 chapters, e.g., 6. "From Prehistoric Times to 1660"; 10. "The Revolutionary Era"; 18. "The Civil War"; 24. "Social & Economic Conditions, 1900–1920"; 30. "War & Its Aftermath, 1941–1952."
The index lists authors, titles of works, and subjects.

EXAMPLES: Bibliographical citations are very brief. Here are two examples; the first is a book, the second an article:

J. H. Franklin, *From Slavery to Freedom: A History of American Negroes,* N.Y., 1947.
F. A. Golder, "Purchase of Alaska," *Amer. Hist. Rev.*, XXV (1920), 411.

USEFULNESS: A widely used manual for students of American history; a good introduction to research. The bibliographical entries are somewhat awkward to use (they encourage eyestrain and discourage browsing) because they are lumped together in paragraph form.

RELATED REFERENCE WORKS: *Guide to Historical Literature* (our no. 101); *A Guide to the Study of the United States of America* (our no. 189); *Writings on American History* (our no. 105).

105] *Writings on American History*

Washington, D.C.: Government Printing Office, 1904—.
Annual; covers 1902—. (Also listed as being "vol. II of the Annual Report of the American Historical Association.")

CONTENTS: An annual descriptive bibliography of books and articles in English and foreign languages on the history of America; the latest volume lists close to 10,000 items.

Through 1935 this bibliography also covered Canadian and Latin American history.

Volumes for 1904–1905 and 1941–1947 have not been published. Some volumes cover a two-year period.

METHOD OF ORGANIZATION: Divided into three main sections: (1) "The Historical Profession," listing writings on methods, materials, historians, etc.; (2) "National History"; (3) "Regional, State, and Local History." Section 3 is subdivided geographically. Sections 1 and 2 are subdivided by topics. Within each subdivision or part of subdivision, items are listed chronologically or alphabetically. Consult the detailed table of contents to locate the subsection of particular interest.

There is an index in each annual volume; also, *Index to the Writings on American History, 1902–1940* (Washington, D.C.: American Historical Association, 1956) provides a cumulative index of subjects, names, places, and authors through 1940.

USEFULNESS: A valuable descriptive bibliography that provides an easy way of finding out what has been published in each area of American history.

Note, though, that there is a considerable time lapse between the year covered and the publication of the bibliography; e.g., the volume for "1957" was published in 1964.

EXAMPLES: The following information is given for each book listed: author's name; title of book; city of publication, publisher, and date; number of pages; additional material (maps, portraits, bibliography); very brief descriptive annotation; The item number is at bottom right of entry. Here is a sample:

Roy Meredith. Storm over Sumter: the opening engagement of the Civil War. N.W.: Simon and Schuster, 1957. [8], 214 [1] p. map, ports. (1 double), views. bibliog. (p. 208–10). On the bombardment of Fort Sumter, Charleston Harbor, commanded by Maj. Robert Anderson, by Confederate forces, Apr. 1861.   [3556

RELATED REFERENCE WORKS: *Guide to Historical Literature* (our no. 101); *America: History and Life* (our no. 106).

106] *America: History and Life, A Guide to Periodical Literature*

Santa Barbara: American Bibliographical Center, Clio Press, 1964—. Quarterly. Ed. by Eric H. Boehm.

CONTENTS: A quarterly publication of abstracts (short, objective summaries) of articles on American and Canadian history and life appearing in current periodicals. Some 1,300 journals (American and foreign) are examined, and approximately 3,000 articles are abstracted each year.

METHOD OF ORGANIZATION: Summaries of articles are grouped by subjects, in six major sections: I. North America; II. Canada; III. U.S.A., National History to 1945; IV. U.S.A., 1945 to Present; V. U.S.A., Regional, State, & Local History; VI. History, The Humanities & Social Sciences. Each major section is divided into appropriate subsections, and the abstracts in each subsection are arranged alphabetically by the subjects of the articles, indicated by a system of "cues" (i.e., subject headings in abbreviated form, such as "FOR" for foreign relations).

Consult the detailed table of contents in each issue to locate the subsection of particular interest. The fourth issue of each year contains an annual index. (References are to item numbers, not to pages.)

USEFULNESS: A quick way to check on whether or not it's worth one's time to read a particular article. Also good for getting a general idea on what is currently being published in periodicals about a particular aspect of American history.

Warning: an abstract is not the equivalent of an article; be sure to read the full article if an abstract arouses interest.

EXAMPLES: The following information is given for each article listed: volume and abstract number; "cues" to identify topic, geographic area, and time period covered by article; author's name; title of article, in caps (with translation if required); journal in which it appeared (underlined); year; volume (with number), and pages; abstract; name of abstracter ("A" means the abstract was prepared by author of article).

Here is a sample entry:

3:2146   **AMR IND**   **US Gt. Britain**   **1775–77**

Sosin, Jack M. THE USE OF INDIANS IN THE WAR OF THE AMERICAN REVOLUTION: A REASSESSMENT OF RESPONSIBILITY. Can. Hist. R. 1965 46(2): 101–121. Examines American and British actions concerning the use of Indians. The decision to use them was precipitated on both sides by local groups. Due to a distaste for savage warfare by certain British officials, Indians were not used until relatively late and then with little effect. Based primarily on unpublished manuscripts in the Clements Library and the Public Archives of Canada. A.

RELATED REFERENCE WORKS: *Writings on American History* (our no. 105); *Historical Abstracts 1775–1945* (our no. 103).

ENCYCLOPEDIAS, HANDBOOKS, HISTORIES, etc.

American

107] *Dictionary of American History*

New York: Scribner's, 1940; Supplement, 1961.
5 vols., index plus supplement. Ed. by James T. Adams.

CONTENTS: A multivolume encyclopedia of American history, from its beginnings to 1940 in the original volumes, brought up to 1960 by the *Supplement*. The work contains more than 6,000 brief articles, written and signed by specialists, with very brief, selected bibliographies for further study.

Articles cover political, economic, social, and cultural history. No biographical articles. (For biographies, see the *Dictionary of American Biography*, our no. 27.)

Most articles are brief, from a paragraph to a page in length; however, the work includes a number of longer "covering articles" on broad subjects, e.g., the American Revolution; the Civil War; international law; slavery.

METHOD OF ORGANIZATION: Vols. I–V are alphabetical, from "A.B. Plot," to "Zwaanendael Colony." The *Index* volume covers the first 5 vols., listing subjects and names.

Supplement I (vol. VI), alphabetical; no index. This volume contains new topics and replacements and supplements of articles in the original volumes. It is indexed in the 1963 *New Revised Index*.

Many cross references are given to related articles.

USEFULNESS: The dictionary provides clear and compact information on "specific facts, events, trends or policies in our American past." Useful for beginners.

RELATED REFERENCE WORKS: *Album of American History*, by the same editor and publisher (5 vols. plus Index, 1944–1960), presents a pictorial record of America from the colonial days to the present, "a panorama of the common life." Fascinating browsing.

For rapid consultation, see the *Concise Dictionary of American History*, ed. by Thomas C. Cochran and Wayne Andrews

(New York: Scribner's, 1962), a one-volume condensation of the parent work.

There are, of course, numerous histories-cum-textbooks on the subject, e.g., Samuel E. Morison's one-volume *Oxford History of the American People* (New York: Oxford Univ. Press, 1965). Also of interest are the forty individual volumes in *The New American Nation Series,* Henry Steele Commager and Richard B. Morris, general eds. (New York: Harper, 1954—), e.g., *The American Revolution,* John R. Adler; *The U.S. and World War II,* A. Russell Buchanan, etc.

108] *Encyclopedia of American History*

New York: Harper, rev. ed., 1965. Ed. by Richard B. Morris.

CONTENTS: A one-volume outline of American history in chronological form, giving brief summaries of pertinent facts, definitions, and identifications. The work "covers American historical events from the era of discovery and exploration" to 1965.

METHOD OF ORGANIZATION: The two main sections are arranged chronologically, giving a year-by-year (and sometimes day-by-day) account of the events. Section I, "Basic Chronology," presents the major political and military events. Section II presents the nonpolitical events, arranged by topics, with a chronological treatment of each topic. Section III offers brief biographies of representative American notables, arranged alphabetically. A detailed subject and name index facilitates the use of the work.

USEFULNESS: The work lives up to its aim: "to provide in a single handy volume the essential facts about American life and institutions." The year-by-year approach helps dramatize the history presented.

EXAMPLES: Here is a typical short entry from section I:

22 Mar. [1765] Stamp Act, the first direct tax levied by Parliament upon America, was designed to raise £60,000 annually, which, together with the return from the 1764 imposts,

would produce an American return equal to about one third the £300,000 upkeep of the colonial military establishment. The act (passed the Commons, 27 Feb., the Lords, 8 Mar., to become effective 1 Nov.) placed a tax upon newspapers, almanacs, pamphlets and broadsides, legal documents of all types, insurance policies, ship's papers, licenses, and even dice and playing cards. The receipts were to be paid into the royal exchequer for the defense of the colonies. With the sensibilities of the colonists in mind Greenville appointed Americans to be the stamp agents. Penalties for infringements could be imposed by courts of vice-admiralty (which had no jury) as well as by colonial common-law courts.

RELATED REFERENCE WORKS: A similar work is Gorton Carruth's *The Encyclopedia of American Facts and Dates* (New York: Crowell, 1966). Also see such specialized works as Mark M. Boatner's *Civil War Dictionary* and *Encyclopedia of the American Revolution* (New York: David McKay, 1959; 1966).

109] *Documents of American History*

New York: Appleton-Century-Crofts, 7th ed., 1963.
Ed. by Henry Steele Commager.

CONTENTS: A collection of over 650 selected documents of importance to students of American history, including proclamations, acts, treaties, ordinances, charters, supreme court decisions, presidential messages, etc., from the colonial days to the present. Limited mainly to "documents of an official or quasi-official character."

The reprints of these original documents are introduced by brief editorial notes, which also contain bibliographies suggesting steps for further research and study.

METHOD OF ORGANIZATION: Chronological, from "Privileges and Prerogatives Granted to Columbus. April 30, 1492" to a presidential proclamation of 1962. The subject, name, and title index makes it possible to easily locate the documents included.

USEFULNESS: An extremely valuable source book that puts primary sources into the hands of students.

EXAMPLES: Here is a brief sampling of the documents reproduced: Mayflower Compact, 1620; Maryland Toleration Act, 1649; Stamp Act, 1765; Proclamation of Rebellion, 1775; Declaration of Independence, 1776; Constitution of the United States, 1787; Jay Treaty, 1794; Jefferson's First Inaugural Address, 1801; The Missouri Compromise, 1819–1821; Monroe Doctrine, 1823; Jackson's Veto of the Bank Bill, 1832; Trial of Mrs. Douglas for Teaching Colored Children to Read, 1853; Lincoln's House Divided Speech, 1858; Mississippi Resolutions on Secession, 1860; Homestead Act, 1862; Civil Rights Act, 1866; Impeachment of President Johnson, 1868; Fourteenth Amendment, 1868; Chinese Exclusion Act, 1882; Sherman Anti-Trust Act, 1890; Wilson's Appeal for Neutrality, 1914; Espionage Act, 1918; Balzac v. Porto Rico, 1922; La Follette Platform, 1924; Vanzetti's Last Statement in Court, 1927; The Atlantic Charter, 1941; The Truman Doctrine, 1947; Civil Rights Act of 1957; Gomillion v. Lightfoot, 1960.

RELATED REFERENCE WORKS: For a listing of other primary sources dealing with American history, past and present, check the *Monthly Catalog of United States Government Publications* (our no. 65). *English Historical Documents* (our no. 112).

English

110] *Oxford History of England*

Oxford: Clarendon Press, 1936—. 14 vols.
Ed. by George Clark.

CONTENTS: A modern, detailed history of England from Roman times to 1914. Each volume, written by a noted scholar, provides facts and interpretations dealing with political, military, social, economic, and cultural history. "Each volume is an independent book, but the whole series forms a continuous history." Many of the volumes are in their second, revised edition.

METHOD OF ORGANIZATION: Chronological from vol. I, *Roman Britain & the English Settlement,* to vol. XIV, *England, 1870–1914.*

Each volume (of approximately 800 pages) has a detailed table of contents and specific running-titles at the top of each page of text; a detailed index of names and subjects; and an extensive, annotated bibliography for its period.

USEFULNESS: The extended essay form of these volumes makes the work best suited for full reading, rather than for quick reference. However, these important volumes can be used for locating specific points of information through the individual volumes' detailed indexes, tables of contents, and specific, pointed running-titles. The annotated bibliographies (especially in the volumes that have recently been revised) are valuable guides for further study.

RELATED REFERENCE WORKS: Another multivolume history of recent vintage, although not so detailed, is the 8-vol. *Pelican History of England* (Harmondsworth: Penguin Books, 1950–1955). There are, of course, numerous one-volume general histories-cum-textbooks on the subject, as well as numerous histories on special periods, areas, and topics of English history.

For a dictionary of facts, see *A New Dictionary of British History* (our no. 111).

111] *A New Dictionary of British History*

New York: St. Martin's Press, 1963.
Ed. by S. H. Steinberg, *et al.*

CONTENTS: A one-volume dictionary of British history from its beginnings to the present. The work contains brief entries, written and initialed by experts, on political, constitutional, administrative, legal, ecclesiastical, and economic history.

The dictionary contains no purely biographical entries (see *Dictionary of National Biography,* our no. 31, for this information); nor does it deal with cultural, philosophical, or scientific history. Items on the history of England's overseas possessions are included "as long as their British connections lasted" (e.g., coverage of Calais ends in 1564, of the U.S. in 1783, of Burma in 1947).

METHOD OF ORGANIZATION: Alphabetical, from "Aachen, peace of" to "Zulu war." Many cross references, indicated by words printed in SMALL CAPS. (No index.)

USEFULNESS: Valuable for quick reference; concise, clear presentation of material; wide scope. However, the lack of an index makes it somewhat difficult to locate information if one has only a name, e.g., Thomas à Becket or Queen Victoria, to start with.

EXAMPLES: Most entries are short, from a paragraph to one page in length. Here is a brief sample list of items, chosen at random: Abjuration Oath; Balaclava, battle of; Bedchamber Crisis; Black Death; Chartism; Corn Laws; Divine Right of Kings; Domesday Book; East India Co., Egypt; Glorious Revolution; Hastings, battle of; Hue and Cry; Independent Labour Party; India Act; Jutes; Kilkenny, statutes of; Lambeth Conferences; Lollard Rising; Magna Carta; Merchant Adventurers; Merciless Parliament; Parnell Commission; Reform Acts; Roses, wars of the; Roundheads; Scottish Church; Templars; Tudors; Virginia Co.; Yalta Conference; York, treaty of.

112] *English Historical Documents*

London: Eyre & Spottiswoode, 1953—. 13 vols., in progress. Ed. by David C. Douglas.

CONTENTS: A 13-volume collection of selected English historical documents from 500 to 1914. A wide selection of representative primary-source material—political, judicial, military, ecclesiastical, and civil—is given for each historical period. Each of the volumes is approximately 1,000 pages long.

The reprints of these original documents are accompanied by brief editorial introductions, footnotes, and critical bibliographies to assist further investigation. Anglo-Saxon, Latin, or Old French texts are translated into English.

METHOD OF ORGANIZATION: The 13 volumes are arranged chronologically. Documents in the individual volumes are arranged by categories (regionally or topically, e.g., a section of material dealing with the murder of Thomas à Becket) and then chronologically within each category. Detailed tables of contents in each volume facilitate the location of documents, as do the indexes at the end of each volume (figures refer to document numbers, not pages).

USEFULNESS: Extremely valuable source books that make "the fundamental sources of English history" readily accessible.

EXAMPLES: Among the various kinds of original documents reprinted are the following: treaties (e.g., King Ethelred's treaty with the Viking Army), judicial rulings, trial records, petitions, resolutions, laws (e.g., Reform Bill of 1859), acts (e.g., Married Women's Property Act), writs, rules (e.g., Rules of Kendal Workhouse 1797), decrees, charters, reports of commissions, accounts, financial records, memorandums, debates, speeches, surveys (e.g., The Domesday Book), chronicles (e.g., The Anglo-Saxon Chronicle), guild regulations, tables (e.g., Occupations: 1841 Census), manumissions, wills, marriage settlements, letters (e.g., of popes, kings, archbishops, monks), sermons, papal bulls (e.g., Laudabiliter), church reports, etc.

RELATED REFERENCE WORKS: *Documents of American History* (our no .109).

European

113] *Cambridge Ancient History*

Cambridge: Cambridge University Press, 1923–1939.
12 vols. plus 5 vols. of plates. Ed. by John B. Bury, *et al.*

CONTENTS: A detailed history of the western world (principally Europe) from "the remote and dim beginnings to the victory of Constantine the Great in A.D. 324." All aspects of history are covered—political, military, economic, social, cultural, and religious. The various chapters are written by specialists;

extensive (but somewhat dated) bibliographies are given at the end of each volume.

METHOD OF ORGANIZATION: Chronological and regional: vol. I, *Egypt & Babylonia to 1500 B.C.*: vol. II, *The Egyptian & Hittite Empires to ca. 1000 B.C.*: vol. III, *The Assyrian Empire;* vol. IV, *The Persian Empire & the West;* vol. V, *Athens, 478–401 B.C.;* vol. VI, *Macedon, 401–301 B.C.;* vol. VII, *The Hellenistic Monarchies & the Rise of Rome;* vol. VIII, *Rome & the Mediterranean, 218–133 B.C.;* vol. IX, *The Roman Republic, 133–44 B.C.;* vol. X, *The Augustan Empire, 44 B.C.–A.D. 70;* vol. XI, *The Imperial Peace,* A.D. *70–192;* vol. XII, *The Imperial Crisis & Recovery,* A.D. *193–324.*

Each volume has a detailed table of contents and specific running-titles at the top of each page of text; a detailed index of names and subjects (but there is no general index for all twelve volumes); extensive bibliographies; and appendixes, which contain chronological charts, lists of rulers, etc.

Illustrations are issued in five separate volumes, *Plates,* each of which has a table of contents but no index.

USEFULNESS: The standard detailed history of the period, scholarly and thorough.

ALSO NOTE: The *Cambridge Ancient History* is currently being issued in a new revised edition (1961—). For the time being, individual chapters of this new work are published in pamphlet form ("fascicles") so that they may be consulted now; they show the result of the latest scholarship and contain up-to-date bibliographies.

RELATED REFERENCE WORKS: A one-volume work on the subject is the *Larousse Encyclopedia of Ancient and Medieval History,* ed. by Marcel Dunan (New York: Harper & Row, 1963; translated from the French). Also see *New Century Classical Handbook* (our no. 140); *Oxford Classical Dictionary* (our no. 139).

114] *Cambridge Medieval History*

Cambridge: Cambridge University Press, 1911–1936. 8 vols.
Ed. by Henry M. Gwatkin, *et al.*

CONTENTS: A detailed history of the entire field of European
medieval history. All aspects of history are covered—political,
military, economic, social, cultural, and religious. The various
chapters are written by specialists; extensive (but somewhat
dated) bibliographies are given at the end of each volume. Illustrative maps.

METHOD OF ORGANIZATION: Chronological and regional: vol. I,
*The Christian Roman Empire & the Foundation of the Teutonic
Kingdoms;* vol. II, *The Rise of the Saracens & the Foundation
of the Western Empire;* vol. III, *Germany & the Western Empire;* vol. IV *Eastern Roman Empire* (now issued in a new revised edition. *The Byzantine Empire,* in two parts—Part 1, *By-
zantium & Its Neighbours,* 1966; Part 2, *Government, Church
& Civilization,* 1967); vol. V, *The Contest of Empire & Papacy;*
vol. VI, *The Victory of the Papacy;* vol. VII, *The Decline of
Empire & Papacy;* vol. VIII, *The Close of the Middle Ages.*

Each volume has a detailed table of contents and specific
running-titles at the top of each page of text; a detailed index
of names and subjects (but there is no general index for all
eight volumes); extensive bibliographies; and "Chronological
Tables of Leading Events." Portfolios of illustrative maps are
appended to each volume.

USEFULNESS: The standard detailed history of the period,
scholarly and thorough.

RELATED REFERENCE WORKS: A 2-volume abridgment of the
parent work is *The Shorter Cambridge Medieval History,* ed.
by C. W. Previté-Orton (Cambridge Univ. Press, 1962). These
volumes contain the essence of the larger work. No bibliographies, but a detailed index of names and subjects, plus maps,
genealogical tables, illustrations, and a "Chronological Table of
Leading Events" from A.D. 284–1492. A very handy reference
tool.

Basic Documents in Medieval History, ed. by Norton Downs
(Princeton, N.J.: D. Van Nostrand Co., 1959).

115] *New Cambridge Modern History*

Cambridge: Cambridge University Press, 1957—.
14 vols. plus atlas. Ed. by George Clark, *et al.*

CONTENTS: A detailed history of Europe and her colonies from the Renaissance to the present.

All aspects of history are treated—political, military, economic, social, cultural, and religious. The various chapters are written by specialists. There are no bibliographies.

METHOD OF ORGANIZATION: Chronological and by subjects: vol. I, *The Renaissance, ca. 1493–1520;* vol. II, *The Reformation, ca. 1520–1559;* vol. III, *The Counter-Reformation & Price-Revolution, 1559–1610;* vol. IV, *The Decline of Spain & the Thirty Years War, 1610–1648/59;* vol. V, *The Ascendancy of France, 1648/59–1688;* vol. VI, *The Decline of Louis XIV & the Great Northern War, 1688–1715/21;* vol. VII, *The Old Regime, 1713–1763;* vol. VIII, *The Revolutions in America & Europe, 1763–1793;* vol. IX, *The New Regimes & the Industrial Revolution, 1793–1830/32;* vol. X, *The Zenith of European Power, 1830/32–1870;* vol. XI, *Material Progress & World-Wide Problems, 1870–1898/1901;* vol. XII, *The Era of Violence, 1898/1901–1945;* vol. XIII, *1945—;* vol. XIV, *Atlas.*

Each volume has a detailed table of contents, and a detailed index of names and subjects (but there is no general index for all volumes).

USEFULNESS: A modern treatment of modern history, showing the result of the latest scholarship; detailed and thorough. This is the successor to the *Cambridge Modern History* (1902–1912), which used to be the standard history of the period.

General and Others

116] *An Encyclopedia of World History*

Boston: Houghton, 3rd ed., 1952.
Compiled and ed. by William L. Langer.

CONTENTS: A chronology of world history, ancient, medieval, and modern, European and non-European, from the Paleolithic Period to 1952. This chronological handbook presents concise summaries of the principal events, stressing political, military, and diplomatic history (although social, cultural, religious, and scientific history is also touched upon).

METHOD OF ORGANIZATION: Divided into seven large chronological periods, as per the table of contents: I, The Prehistoric Period; II, Ancient History; III, The Middle Ages; IV, The Early Modern Period; V, The Nineteenth Century; VI, Two World Wars & the Inter-War Period; VII, The Post-War Period. Then further subdivided by countries or topics.

The detailed index of names, historical events, and subjects is in two parts: the main index covers events to 1945; the supplementary index covers events from 1946 to 1952. An appendix contains lists of heads of states—emperors, popes, prime ministers, presidents, etc. and the years of their rule.

USEFULNESS: Excellent for quick identification and precise dating of historical events in world history. Historical events can be located by dates (consult table of contents first) or by subject or name (consult index first). Good coverage of European and non-European history.

EXAMPLES: Here is a typical entry from section VII, The Post-War Period; F. Asia; 2. India:

Aug. 15 [1947]. The INDEPENDENCE OF INDIA went into effect. The process of partition was accompanied by terrible acts of violence, notably in the Punjab region, between Moslems and Hindus. By the end of September, close to two million refugees had been exchanged between India and Pakistan.

RELATED REFERENCE WORKS: *Concise Encyclopedia of World History*, ed. by John Bowle (London: Hutchinson, 1958). *Newnes Dictionary of Dates,* compiled by Robert L. Collison (London: Newnes, 1962); *Everyman's Dictionary of Dates,* comp. by C. Arnold Baker and Arnold Dent (London: Dent, 1954); *Historical Tables: 58 B.C.–A.D. 1965* (our no. 117).

117] *Historical Tables: 58* B.C.–A.D. *1965*

New York: St. Martin's Press, 8th ed., 1966.
Compiled by Sigfrid H. Steinberg.

CONTENTS: A chronological list of events from world history, 58 B.C. to A.D. 1965, arranged in tabular form. Major occurrences are enumerated without explanations or comments. Although the tables' coverage is worldwide, the history of the British Commonwealth and of the U.S.A. is given in greater detail.

METHOD OF ORGANIZATION: Chronological. Double pages are divided into six columns, thus listing the events for each year in six categories.

For the greater part of the book, these columns list events of political and military history in:
   I, Western & Southern Europe;
   II, Central, Northern, & Eastern Europe;
   III, Non-European Countries;
   IV, Ecclesiastical History;
   V, Constitutional & Economic History;
   VI, Cultural Life.

USEFULNESS: Good for quick checks, to see what major events were occurring in the different parts of the world during a particular year.

The bones of history are laid bare; dates and events stand out clearly.

RELATED REFERENCE WORKS: *An Encyclopedia of World History* (our no. 116).

118] *Survey of International Affairs*

London: Oxford University Press for the Royal Institute of
International Affairs, 1925—. Annual; covers 1920—.
Ed. by Arnold J. Toynbee, *et al.*

CONTENTS: An annual summary in essay form of selected
major political, military, and diplomatic events of each year,
starting with 1920. Some volumes cover more than one year,
and the war years, 1939–46, are covered in 11 vols. arranged by
topics.

The volumes are constructed around "salient points," concen-
trating on the important historical events that came to a head
in the year under review. Illustrated with historical maps.

Footnotes to the essays provide some bibliography.

METHOD OF ORGANIZATION: Each volume is divided into a
number of main sections according to geographical areas or
topics. E.g., the volume for 1951 is divided into the following
seven sections: The North Atlantic Alliance; Western Europe
& Germany; The U.S.S.R. & Central & Eastern Europe; Yugo-
slavia; The Middle East; China & Japan; Far Eastern Wars &
Security.

Each volume contains a detailed table of contents and an
index, which lists subjects, events, and names. Early volumes
have appendixes with chronologies of events.

A *Consolidated Index* serves as a cumulative index of events,
subjects, and names for the years 1920–1938. There is no cumulative index for the years since 1938.

USEFULNESS: The *Surveys* provide informative, well-docu-
mented summaries of contemporary world history from 1920
to the present. Especially useful for obtaining background information on current topics, e.g., for the prelude to the current
Vietnam tragedy, see the accounts of the revolution against the
French in Indochina, 1946—.

Note that there is a time gap between the year covered and
the date of publication; e.g., the 1961 volume was published in
1965.

RELATED REFERENCE WORKS: The annual volumes of *Documents on International Affairs* (our no. 119) are meant to accompany and supplement the *Survey*.

119] *Documents of International Affairs*

London: Oxford University Press for the Royal Institute of
International Affairs, 1929—. Annual; covers 1928—.

CONTENTS: A selective collection of documents of international diplomacy, from 1928 to the present. The annual volumes present "in a compact and handy form all the more important pronouncements, verbal and written, which have appeared during the twelve months under review."
Some volumes cover more than one year. Foreign documents are translated into English.

METHOD OF ORGANIZATION: The documents are arranged according to geographical areas or topics. For instance, the volume for 1959 is divided into the following sections: East-West Negotiations; Trouble Spots in Asia; The Middle East; Latin America; The Western Powers; The Communist Powers. Within these sections, documents are grouped in related clusters, e.g., a section of items dealing with the suspension of nuclear weapon tests.

There is no index, but the table of contents lists each document. The documents are also listed by dates, from January through December, in the "Chronological List of Documents" found at the end of each volume. The *Consolidated Index* (1967) serves as a cumulative index for the years 1928–1938.

USEFULNESS: Important primary sources are made easily available.

EXAMPLES: Among the various kinds of documents reprinted are the following; treaties, government statements, communiqués, declarations, proposals, resolutions, memorandums, messages, reports, speeches, discussions (radio and T.V.), white papers, letters, and notes.

Wherever possible the full text of a document is reproduced, but in some cases only pertinent extracts are given.

RELATED REFERENCE WORKS: *Survey of International Affairs* (our no. 118). For other collections of historical documents, see *English Historical Documents* (our no. 112); *Documents of American History* (our no. 109); *Basic Documents in Medieval*

History, ed. by Norton Downs (Princeton, N.J.: D. Van Nostrand Co., 1959).

120] *The Concise Encyclopedia of Archaeology*

New York: Hawthorn, 1960. Ed. by Leonard Cottrell.

CONTENTS: A compilation of brief articles on archaeological topics: civilizations, cities, tombs, customs, discoveries, ancient languages, terms, methodology, biographies of famous archaeologists, etc. Coverage is worldwide, "ranging from the antiquity of the Far East, Europe and the Middle East to the Pre-Columbian cultures of South America," but there are few references to classical Greece and Rome.

There are illustrations, and a brief, selected bibliography for further reading is offered at the end of the volume.

METHOD OF ORGANIZATION: Alphabetical. The numerous cross references are indicated by **bold type.**

"Classified List of Topics" (pp. 7–13) lists titles of articles arranged by areas and topics, e.g., "Africa, America, Archaeologists & Historians, Early Man & Geological Periods, Egypt, India, The Middle East." These lists are valuable as study guides.

USEFULNESS: Concise and accurate information for the general reader as well as the student.

EXAMPLES: Here is a brief sample list of entries, chosen at random:

Abbevillian; Assyrians; Beaker People; Breuil, Abbé Henri; Champollion, Jean-François; Coptic Language; Cro-magnon; Dong-son; Etruscans; Evans, Sir Arthur; Ideograms; Incas; Iran; Iron Age; Knossos; Maya; Minoan Scripts; Miocene Epoch; Nineveh; Papyrus; Piltdown Skull; Pottery; Rosetta Stone; Scarabs; Schliemann, Heinrich; Shaft Graves; Shih Chai Shan; Stone Tools; Sutton Hoo; Thalos Tombs; Ur-Nammu; Valley of the Kings; Ziwigè.

121] *Handbook of Oriental History*

London: Offices of the Royal Historical Society, 1951.
Ed. by Cyril H. Philips.

CONTENTS: A companion to Oriental historical studies, this handbook gives brief explanations of: (1) the transliteration and pronunciation of Oriental languages; (2) personal names and titles; (3) place names; (4) "the main political, economic, social, and religious terms" (i.e., a glossary); (5) calendars and systems of dating; (6) lists of dynasties and rulers.

METHOD OF ORGANIZATION: The handbook is divided into five sections: I, Near & Middle East; II, India & Pakistan; III, Southeast Asia & the Archipelago; IV, China; V, Japan.

USEFULNESS: A valuable little book which provides simple and concise explanations of the elementary difficulties which confront the general student who comes to study Oriental history.

EXAMPLES: Here is a brief sample list of terms defined, chosen at random and taken from part 4, "the glossary," of section II, "India & Pakistan":

Adalat, Akhbar, Avatar, Begum, Bira, Caste, Chit, Currency, Dharma; Indigo, Karma, Khan, Kisan, Kos, Maharani, Measures, Mir, Nirvana, Pandit, Pariahs, Rama, Sahib, Sari, Sati, Shri, Swami, Tahsil, Zanana, Zoroastrianism.

RELATED REFERENCE WORKS: *An Encyclopedia of World History* (our no. 116).

122] *McGraw-Hill Encyclopedia of Russia and the Soviet Union*

New York: McGraw-Hill, 1961.
Ed. by Michael T. Florinsky.

CONTENTS: A compilation of brief articles on all aspects of Russian life from medieval times to the present. More than 3,500 entries on Russian history, economics, science, and culture. Many biographical sketches. Principal articles are signed by specialists, mostly American, in Soviet affairs, and have brief bibliographies attached. Numerous illustrations, maps, and charts.

METHOD OF ORGANIZATION: Alphabetical. Note that "all dates in this book are given in accordance with the calendar in force in Russia at the time the event occurred," i.e., Old Style prior to February 14, 1918; New Style thereafter.

USEFULNESS: The most comprehensive and up-to-date—and extremely readable, general encyclopedia on Russia available in the English language. Useful to students of history to supplement textbooks and for quick consultations on specific questions (e.g., a synopsis of the February Revolution, or a brief biography of Khrushchev). However, the user should be aware of the book's general western slant.

RELATED REFERENCE WORKS: We have described here just one of the many reference works that specialize in a particular nation or region. There are many other such encyclopedias, dictionaries, and handbooks. To name just a few: *An Encyclopedia of Southern Africa*, ed. by Eric Rosenthal (London: Warne, 1964); *Africa: A Handbook to the Continent*, ed. by Colin Legum (London: Blond, 1961); *Encyclopedia Canadiana* (Ottawa: Canadiana Co., 1957–58); *Japan: Its Land, People & Culture* (Tokyo: Japanese National Commission for UNESCO, 1958); *Concise Encyclopaedia of Arabic Civilization*, ed. by Stephen and Nandy Ronart (New York: Praeger, 1960, 1966); *An Encyclopedia of Latin-American History*, ed. by Michael R. Martin, *et al.* (Indianapolis: Bobbs-Merrill, 1967); *Handbook of Oriental History* (our no. 121).

Also note the various specialized histories, e.g., *Cambridge History of India*, ed. by Edward J. Rapson, *et al.* (Cambridge: Univ. Press, 1922–37, 1960); *Cambridge History of the British Empire* (Cambridge: Univ. Press, 1929–36, 1963); and the volumes on France, Germany, Italy, the Near East, the Far East, Latin America, etc., in *The University of Michigan History of the Modern World* series, ed. by Allan Nevins and Howard Ehrmann (Ann Arbor: Univ. of Michigan, 1958—).

See the *Guide to Historical Literature* (our no. 101).

LITERATURE

BIBLIOGRAPHIES and INDEXES

123] *MLA International Bibliography*

New York: Modern Language Association of America, 1922—.
Annual; covers 1921—. Title varies: "American Bibliography"
1921–1955; "Annual Bibliography" 1956–1962;
"MLA [or PMLA] International Bibliography" 1963—.

CONTENTS: An annual, comprehensive bibliography of current critical works—books, periodical articles, monographs, collections, and dissertations dealing with the modern languages and literatures. Each volume attempts to cover all the secondary studies (in various languages, although most are written in English) published in the previous year. It aims to make a listing of "over ninety per cent of the important material of scholarship available annually on schedule." The entries are not annotated.

The latest volume has close to 20,000 entries.

There is no general index, only an index of critics.

METHOD OF ORGANIZATION: Each annual bibliography is divided into a number of main sections, principally by nationality: Collections, General and Miscellaneous, English, American, French, Italian, Spanish (including Spanish America), Portuguese (including Brazilian), Rumanian, Germanic (including German, Yiddish, Netherlandic, Frisian, Afrikaans), Scandinavian (including Danish, Icelandic, Norwegian, Swedish), East European (Russian, Czech, Polish, etc.).

Each national section is in turn subdivided into a number of sections, mainly chronological; e.g., the "English Language & Literature" section is subdivided as follows: I, Linguistics; II,

General; III, Themes, Types & Special Topics; IV, Old English; V, Middle English; VI, Renaissance & Elizabethan; VII, Seventeenth Century; VIII, Eighteenth Century; IX, Nineteenth Century; X, Twentieth Century; XI, Canada, Australia, etc. The items within each subsection are arranged alphabetically according to the authors about whom the secondary studies have been written.

Since there is no index (except an index of critics whose works are included in the bibliography), a reader looking for a list of the scholarship about a particular author must first know his nationality and the century in which he lived. E.g., for a list of critical works on Hawthorne, look (1) in the "American Literature" section, (2) in the "Nineteenth Century, 1800–1870" subsection, and (3) alphabetically under "H" in this subsection.

USEFULNESS: The major annual listing of current scholarly publications in English and the modern languages. The student of literature will find this reference tool invaluable for locating recent scholarship (1921—). This bibliography is of special interest to students of comparative literature since its coverage of European languages and literatures is excellent, especially since 1955.

Note, however, that annotations and evaluative comments are not included.

EXAMPLES: Here are two sample entries from the bibliography, one referring to a book, the other to an article in a scholarly journal. Author or subject headings are in heavy print.

Camus.
9595. Brée, Germaine. *Albert Camus*. New York, London: Columbia Univ. Press.

Item number is followed by author's name; title of book; city of publication; publisher's name.

Hawthorne.
6767. Warren, Austin. *"The Scarlet Letter:* A Literary Exercise in Moral Theology." *So R*, I, 22–45.

Item number is followed by author's name; title of article; journal in which it appeared (*So R = Southern Review;* see key to abbreviations at front of bibliography); volume number; pages of journal.

RELATED REFERENCE WORKS: *Annual Bibliography of English Language and Literature* (our no. 125). *Bibliography of Comparative Literature* (our no. 129).

Annotations and evaluative comments are usually found in the bibliographies of specialized journals (e.g., for the Renaissance see *Studies in Philology*, for Shakespeare see the *Shakespeare Quarterly*, for American literature see *American Literature*, etc.) and in such specialized bibliographical works as *Year's Work in English Studies* (our no. 126), *Abstracts of English Studies* (our no. 127), *Year's Work in Modern Language Studies* (our no. 128).

124] *Cambridge Bibliography of English Literature*

Cambridge: Cambridge University Press, 1941, 1957.
5 vols. (3 vols., plus index, plus supplement).
Ed. by F .W. Bateson.

CONTENTS: A basic bibliography of *English* literature (American literature is *not* included) from the Anglo-Saxon period to the end of the nineteenth century. The bibliography lists both primary sources, i.e., works *by* the authors, and secondary sources, i.e., important works *about* the authors and about the authors' works.

The entries are not annotated.

METHOD OF ORGANIZATION: Chronological. Vol. I covers the years 600–1660 (divided into three major periods: Anglo-Saxon 600–1100; Middle English 1100–1500; the Renaissance to the Restoration 1500–1660). Vol. II covers the years 1660–1800 (the Restoration to the Romantic Revival). Vol. III covers the years 1800–1900 (the nineteenth century).

Vol. IV contains the index to vols. I–III, and should be consulted first for speedy and efficient use of the bibliography. The index is arranged alphabetically, listing authors, subjects (e.g.,

Ballads), and names of magazines (e.g., *The Tatler*). Titles of works are not included unless they are anonymous.

Vol. V is a supplement, listing publications of scholarly interest "which have appeared since the original bibliography was prepared," thus bringing the bibliography of *secondary* material up to 1955. Remember, though, that this reference work is still concerned only with authors who were prominent between 600 and 1900. Vol. V has no index; therefore users must find their author by consulting the table of contents and then turning to the appropriate section. (E.g., to find works about Thomas Hardy, look in the section which deals with the nineteenth century, then under "Prose Fiction," then under "Late Nineteenth-Century Novelists.")

USEFULNESS: The standard bibliography for English (but not American) literature, comprehensive and relatively easy to use, especially the first four volumes. *The* source to check for a complete list of works by a British author who wrote between 600 and 1900. An excellent place to check for selected (but not annotated) lists of criticism, both book-length studies and articles, *about* these authors. (However, more complete lists of twentieth century critical works, 1921—, can be found by consulting the annual volumes of our no. 123 and our no. 125.)

EXAMPLES: A student interested in the poet Blake will find him listed in his alphabetical place in vol. IV, the index volume, "Blake, William (1757–1827), II, 347 f." Turning to vol. II, pages 347–350, he will find (1) a list of Blake bibliographies, (2) a list of manuscripts and first editions of Blake's works, (3) a list of recent editions of Blake's works, (4) a chronological list of biographical and critical studies about Blake from 1806 to 1938. Then turning to the supplement, vol .V, he will find an additional three pages on Blake (pp. 425–28), mainly secondary studies, arranged chronologically, bringing the bibliography up to 1953.

For books, the following bibliographical information is given: author, title, city of publication, year of publication. For articles, the following information is given: author, title, name of journal (abbreviated—see the key to abbreviations at the front of each volume), volume number, year.

ALSO NOTE: The *Concise Cambridge Bibliography of English Literature, 1600–1950* (Cambridge: Cambridge Univ. Press, 2nd ed., 1965) is a one-volume abridgment of the *Cambridge Bibliography*. Like its parent work, it is arranged chronologically and lists both works *by* and *about* each author. But note that a new section has been added, "The Early Twentieth Century," thus bringing its coverage of British authors up to 1950. A comprehensive index at the end of the book makes this concise bibliography suitable for quick reference. This bibliography is extremely useful for beginners who need a basic list of works by and about a British author. (Obviously, though, it is not as complete as the full five-volume parent work; e.g., the *CBEL* devotes six pages to Blake, while the concise work devotes only one page to Blake.)

RELATED REFERENCE WORKS: For fuller bibliographies of recent secondary studies, 1920—, see *Annual Bibliography of English Language and Literature* (our no. 125) and *MLA International Bibliography* (our no. 123). For the best annotated bibliography of American literature, see vol. 2 of the *Literary History of the United States* (our no. 130).

125] *Annual Bibliography of English Language and Literature*

Cambridge: Cambridge University Press, for the Modern Humanities Research Association, 1921—.
Annual; covers 1920—.

CONTENTS: An annual, comprehensive bibliography of current critical works from 1920 on. The latest volume lists over 9,000 items. Books, periodical articles, monographs, collections, and dissertations dealing with English and American language and literature are listed. Each volume attempts to cover all the secondary studies completed in the previous year.

The entries are not annotated. Each volume is indexed.

Although there have been some time gaps between volumes, the editors have now caught up and volumes "will in the future appear annually" on schedule.

METHOD OF ORGANIZATION: Each annual volume is divided into a number of main sections, and the items within each main section are arranged alphabetically by author and subject.

Each annual volume is provided with two indexes: one lists authors and subjects *about* which critical works have been published; the other lists authors of the secondary studies included in the bibliography.

The numbers in the index refer to entry numbers, not to page numbers.

USEFULNESS: One of the best and most complete bibliographies of recent work (1920—) about English and American literature and language. This work is especially useful to the student who is on his way toward becoming an expert on a particular writer. It is also useful for the general student who is searching for a list of articles on a specific work of an author (e.g., Shakespeare's *Measure for Measure*).

EXAMPLES: Here are two sample entries from the bibliography, one referring to a book, the other to an article in a scholarly journal. Author or subject headings are in heavy print.

Thomas, Dylan:
    6717. Maud, Ralph. Entrances to Dylan Thomas' Poetry. Pittsburgh: Univ. of Pittsburgh Press. pp. 175.
Shakespeare, William, *Measure for Measure:*
    3438. Hyman, Lawrence W. Mariana and Shakespeare's Theme in 'Measure for Measure'. UR., Dec., xxxi, 123–7.

The numbers 6717 and 3438 are item numbers. UR is *University Review*, in which Hyman's article appeared—see the key to abbreviations at front of volume.

RELATED REFERENCE WORKS: *MLA International Bibliography* (our no. 123). For less comprehensive but annotated bibliographies, see *Year's Work in English Studies* (our no. 126) and *Abstracts of English Studies* (our no. 127).

126] *Year's Work in English Studies*

New York: Humanities Press, for the English Association
(Oxford), 1921—. Annual; covers 1919/20—.

CONTENTS: An annual, selective bibliography of critical works
(books and periodical articles, monographs, and dissertations)
dealing with English and American language and literature,
with annotations and evaluative comments. Recent volumes
contain about 1,500 entries of approximately 150 words each.

METHOD OF ORGANIZATION: Usually in fifteen sections, beginning with I, Literary History & Criticism, General Works, and
II, English Language, then moving chronologically from III,
Old English Literature, to XIV, Twentieth Century Literature,
and finally to XV, American Literature.

Each section is organized in subdivisions (e.g., Eighteenth
Century Literature: a. general studies; b. poetry; c. prose, non-
fiction; d. the novel; e. drama and theatre). Within each subdivision the items are grouped by author.

Each volume includes two indexes: (1) an index of critics
whose works are summarized (useful if one wants a summary
of or comment on a particular article or book of criticism); and
(2) an index of "Authors & Subjects Treated" in the critical
works summarized (useful if one wants to find the section in
the book in which the year's scholarly works on a particular
author are treated).

USEFULNESS: More informative than bibliographies that simply list items, this work can help students decide whether or
not to read a particular critical item.

EXAMPLES: The bibliography is in essay form. Books and articles included are briefly (and sometimes superficially) summarized.

RELATED REFERENCE WORKS: *Abstracts of English Studies* (our
no. 127), *Year's Work in Modern Language Studies* (our no.
128).

127] *Abstracts of English Studies*

Chicago: University of Illinois, 1958—.

CONTENTS: Short summaries of current articles in periodicals dealing with English and American language and literature. The more than 400 periodicals examined include not only the scholarly and critical ones, but also high-quality general circulation magazines and foreign journals that carry relevant articles.

Published since 1958; now ten times a year, with annual accumulations.

METHOD OF ORGANIZATION: Summaries of articles are grouped by the periodicals in which they were printed; the periodicals are listed alphabetically in each issue of *AES*.

Two annual indexes are provided: (1) an index of periodical titles, and (2) a subject and author index. The numbers in the index refer to the abstract numbers, not page numbers.

USEFULNESS: A quick way to check on whether or not it is worth one's time to read a particular article. Also good for checking on the current work being done on a specific author.

Warning: abstracts are necessarily brief, they are skeletal, and, thus, may distort. Be sure to read the full article if the abstract arouses interest.

EXAMPLES: Here is a typical abstract. The article appeared in *Nineteenth-Century Fiction*. Reference to the abstract appears in two places in the index: one, under the author of the works of literature treated, i.e., "James, Henry . . . *Ambassadors*"; two, under the name of the author of the critical article.

2242. Kaye, Julian B. *"The Awkward Age, The Sacred Fount, and The Ambassadors:* Another Figure in the Carpet," pp. 339–351. Henry James's *The Awkward Age* (1899) and *The Sacred Fount* (1901) may be read as preliminary sketches of *The Ambassadors* (1903). The central figure in each, an unmarried man in later middle age, is an outsider who theorizes about the values of the society he observes. A fortyish woman, predatory and egoistic in her love of a younger man, represents the society observed. However, the later novel resolves the central conflict of the earlier two, as Strether triumphs over "the predatory world."

RELATED REFERENCE WORKS: *Year's Work in English Studies* (our no. 126), *Year's Work in Modern Language Studies* (our no. 128), *Dissertation Abstracts,* 1938—, a collection of abstracts of doctoral dissertations.

128] *Year's Work in Modern Language Studies*

Cambridge: Cambridge University Press, for the Modern Humanities Research Association, 1932—.
Annual; covers 1929/30—.

CONTENTS: An annual, selective bibliography of critical works since 1929 (books and periodical articles) dealing with modern European languages and literature exclusive of English, with summaries and evaluative comments. Annual except for 1940–1949, which are in one volume. The latest volume lists close to 7,000 works.

METHOD OF ORGANIZATION: Now divided into four main divisions: (1) Medieval Latin; (2) Romance Languages (Linguistics, French, Provençal, Spanish, Catalan, Portuguese, Latin-American, Italian, Rumanian); (3) Germanic Languages (German, Netherlandic, Danish, Norwegian, Swedish); (4) Slavic Languages (Czech, Slovak, Polish, Russian, Ukrainian, White-Russian, Serbo-Croat). And further subdivided within each division, principally chronologically, then by subjects, and finally alphabetically by authors.

Consult the index first, which lists subjects (e.g., Arabic influence, Anthologies), titles (e.g., *Faust*), and authors (e.g., Gogol, Rabelais) treated in the critical works summarized, as well as the names of the authors of the critical works.

The key to abbreviations is at the back of book, preceding the index.

USEFULNESS: A good annotated bibliography, this provides a quick yet comprehensive survey of the year's work in modern language studies. (It does not include English studies; see our no. 125 for this coverage.)

EXAMPLES: The bibliography is in essay form. Comments on books and articles included are very brief (a sentence or two on each item), but give a good idea of the items' contents.

RELATED REFERENCE WORKS: *MLA International Bibliography* (our no. 123), *Bibliography of Comparative Literature* (our no. 129).

129] *Bibliography of Comparative Literature*

Chapel Hill: University of North Carolina Press, 1950.
Compiled by Fernand Baldensperger and
Werner P. Friederich.

CONTENTS: A comprehensive bibliography of critical works written in various languages (books and periodical articles) dealing with comparative literature, especially with the interrelationships among the literatures of the world.

The emphasis of this 33,000-item bibliography (most items listed were published between 1850 and 1950) is on "the influence of one country upon another . . . ; second, of an individual author upon a foreign country or author . . . ; and, third, the general influence of a country upon an individual foreign author."

The entries are not annotated. There is no index.

METHOD OF ORGANIZATION: The bibliography must be used through its detailed table of contents. The items are arranged according to the "emitter" of an influence, and not according to the receiver—e.g., works dealing with the influence of the Bible on the works of Heine or Calderon are listed in the section on the Bible.

The bibliography is divided into four main sections: (1) general works; (2) the influence of the Orient, antiquity, Judaism, early Christianity, and Mohammedanism; (3) the influence of modern Christianity, literary currents, international literary relations, and collective influences; (4) influences of various modern cultures and modern national literatures upon the literatures of other nations.

USEFULNESS: An important and extensive bibliography of critical works dealing with comparative literature (although somewhat difficult to use because of the lack of an index).

RELATED REFERENCE WORKS: For a list of scholarly works in this field published since 1949, see the "Annual Bibliography of Comparative Literature" printed in the *Yearbook of Comparative and General Literature,* 1952—, which serves as an annual supplement, and uses the same system of arranging the bibliographical items (again, no index).

Year's Work in Modern Language Studies (our no. 128). Also see the various specialized bibliographies that deal with the literature of one country only, e.g., D.C. Cabeen, *Critical Bibliography of French Literature* (Syracuse: Syracuse Univ. Press, 1947—).

HANDBOOKS, DICTIONARIES, HISTORIES, etc.

American

130] *Literary History of the United States*

New York: Macmillan, new ed., 1963 (1st ed., 1948).
2 vols. Ed. by Robert E. Spiller, *et al.*

CONTENTS: A comprehensive and detailed history volume (1,511 pages of signed essays) of American literature from colonial times to the present; the second volume has more than 1,000 pages of bibliographical essays, giving annotated lists of primary and secondary works.

Indexed.

METHOD OF ORGANIZATION: Vol. 1, the history, is arranged chronologically. Its use is facilitated by a detailed author, title, and subject index. This volume also contains a 36-page bibliography for the general reader.

Vol. 2, the 1,000-page bibliography, is divided into two parts: part one lists works published through 1946; part two lists works published through 1957. Each part has four sections:

Guide to Resources; Literature and Culture; Movements and Influences; Individual Authors. The "Individual Authors" sections contain bibliographical essays on 207 American authors, listing both primary works and secondary works. The bibliographies are selective yet full; and they provide valuable critical and evaluative comments on the works listed.

One must consult both parts to find the complete coverage on an author or subject. But the volume has an author and subject index which refers the user to both parts of the volume. (Lightface page numbers refer to part one; **boldface** page numbers refer to part two.)

USEFULNESS: Vol. 1 is by now considered the standard modern history of American literature. It views the literary history of the United States from a mid-twentieth-century viewpoint; the critical opinions given are judicious; its scope is wide. Although students may wish to use this work for quick introductory consultation (via the index), the work is best suited for more leisurely reference since the individual chapters are cohesive essays which should be read in their entirety. The first volume's bibliography-in-miniature is an excellent source for the general student seeking a list of critical books for the next step in his research project.

Vol. 2 is the best available annotated bibliography of American literature.

EXAMPLES: Here are some representative chapter titles from vol. 1: The European Background, Benjamin Franklin, The Beginnings of Fiction and Drama, The American Dream, Washington Irving, Democratic Values, Ralph Waldo Emerson, Nathaniel Hawthorne, A House Divided and Rejoined, The Orators, Literary Culture on the Frontier, Humor, The West as Seen from the East, Experiments in Poetry: Sidney Lanier and Emily Dickinson, Toward Naturalism in Fiction, Henry James, Henry Adams, The "New" Poetry, Eugene O'Neill, Between Wars.

RELATED REFERENCE WORKS: *Cambridge History of American Literature* (our no. 131).

131] *Cambridge History of American Literature*

Cambridge: Cambridge University Press, 1917–1924. 4 vols.
Ed. by William P. Trent, *et al.*

CONTENTS: A detailed, multivolume history of American literature from colonial times to the beginning of the twentieth century. The work deals with both major and minor writers. Indexes and bibliographies are provided.

METHOD OF ORGANIZATION: Chronological, divided into three main sections (but four volumes): (a) Colonial and Revolutionary Literature, (b) Early National Literature, (c) Later National Literature and General Topics.

An author and title index and bibliographies of primary and secondary works for each chapter are found at the end of vols. 1, 2, and 4. (Index and bibliographies in vol. 4 are for both vols. 3 and 4.) The bibliographies are full, but are, of course, limited by the publication dates of the history, thus giving little coverage of the twentieth century.

EXAMPLES: Major writers are treated in separate chapters (e.g., Jonathan Edwards, Washington Irving, Franklin, Emerson, Thoreau, Hawthorne, Poe, Whitman, Twain, Henry James). Other chapters are organized by subjects (e.g., The Puritan Divines; Early Humorists; Newspapers, 1775–1860; Dialect Writers; The Short Story; The Drama, 1860–1918; Scholars; Book Publishers and Publishing; Non-English Writing: German, French, Yiddish, Aboriginal).

USEFULNESS: A famous work on American literature, especially thorough on the early period. Although still useful, the history as a whole is somewhat dated in its critical attitudes and interpretations.

RELATED REFERENCE WORKS: The *Cambridge History of American Literature* has been reprinted in a one-volume edition (New York: Macmillan, 1967), which is identical with the original edition except that the outdated bibliographies have been omitted.

For a more up-to-date history of American literature see the *Literary History of the United States* (our no. 130).

132] *Oxford Companion to American Literature*

New York: Oxford University Press, 4th ed., 1965.
Ed. by James D. Hart.

CONTENTS: A handbook in dictionary form, containing concise articles on American authors; more than one thousand summaries of important American novels, stories, poems, plays, and essays; definitions and outlines of literary movements; information on literary awards, societies, magazines, anthologies, etc.; as well as entries on "major non-literary aspects of the American scene as they are reflected in and influenced by American literature."

METHOD OF ORGANIZATION: Alphabetical. An appended chronology gives a year-by-year outline in parallel columns of the social and literary history of the U.S.

USEFULNESS: A ready reference work, good for quick identifications and checking on facts. Gives a broad coverage of American literature. No critical judgments are made; the work concentrates on presenting facts.

EXAMPLES: Here is a brief sample list of entries, chosen at random: Henry Adams, Edward Albee, Billy Budd, Anne Bradstreet, Columbus, Dime Novel, The Enormous Room, Erie Canal, The Fall of the House of Usher, The Great Gatsby, O. Henry, Hemingway, Little Theatre, Local Color, Minstrel Show, Miss Lonelyhearts, Moby-Dick, Thomas Paine, Poor Richard's Almanack, The Raven, Rip Van Winkle, Salem Witchcraft Trials, Saturday Review, The Sound and the Fury, Transcendentalism, When Lilacs Last in the Dooryard Bloom'd, William Carlos Williams, Richard Wright, Young Goodman Brown, Zuni Indians.

RELATED REFERENCE WORKS: Max J. Herzberg, *et al.*, *Reader's Encyclopedia of American Literature* (New York: Crowell, 1962). William J. Burke and Will D. Howe, *American Authors and Books, 1640–1940*, (New York: Crown, 1962).

For comparable handbooks on British literature, see *Oxford Companion to English Literature* (our no. 136) and *New Century Handbook of English Literature* (our no. 137).

133] *Cambridge History of English Literature*

Cambridge: Cambridge University Press, 1907–1916, 1927.
15 vols. Ed. by A. W. Ward and A. R. Waller.

CONTENTS: A detailed, multivolume history of English literature from its beginnings to the end of the nineteenth century. Each volume is written by a noted scholar who provides a general literary and cultural history of the period as well as detailed treatments of individual authors and their works.
Indexes and bibliographies are provided.

METHOD OF ORGANIZATION: Chronological, from vol. I, *From the Beginnings to the Cycles of Romance*, to vols. XII–XIV, *The Nineteenth Century;* vol. XV is a general index.

Each of the fourteen volumes of text is provided with a detailed table of contents, an index, a brief table of important dates, plus bibliographies. However, the reader is advised to use the general index, vol. XV, which will refer him to the correct volume and exact pages.

USEFULNESS: The standard history of English literature, good for ascertaining the generally accepted critical evaluation of an author or period. Noted for its scholarly sanity and thoroughness. Although it devotes a good deal of space to major authors (e.g., 42 pages to Chaucer) and literary movements, it also provides a wide coverage of minor figures, giving information not easily available elsewhere.

The bibliographies (not included in the 1932 "cheap edition" reprint) are out of date; for bibliography, use the *Cambridge Bibliography of English Literature* (our no. 124).

RELATED REFERENCE WORKS: The *Concise Cambridge History of English Literature*, ed. by George Sampson (Cambridge Univ. Press, 1941) is a one-volume abridgment of the full work. A chapter, "Late Victorian and Post Victorian Literature," has been added to bring the history up to the 1930's. The coverage given to each author is brief (e.g., 6 pages to Chaucer), but the book is useful for quick checks on facts, and summaries of judgments. Its treatment of twentieth century literature is poor and often misleading. There are a detailed table of contents and an index of authors and anonymous works, but no bibliographies.

Oxford History of English Literature (our no. 134).

134] *Oxford History of English Literature*

Oxford: Clarendon Press, 1945—. 12 vols. in 14 books.
Ed. by Frank P. Wilson and Bonamy Dobrée.

CONTENTS: A modern, detailed, multivolume history of English literature from its beginnings to the first half of the twentieth century. Each section is written by a noted scholar, who provides a general literary and cultural history of the period as well as detailed treatments of individual authors and their works.

Indexes and bibliographies are provided.

METHOD OF ORGANIZATION: Chronological, from vol. I, part 1, *English Literature Before the Norman Conquest*, to vol. XI, *The Mid-Nineteenth Century*, and vol. XII, *Eight Modern Writers* (*Hardy, James, Shaw, Conrad, Kipling, Yeats, Joyce, Lawrence*).

Each volume has an index—author, title, and subject; full bibliographies of primary and secondary materials; and a chronological table, a year-by-year list of important public and literary events and publications.

USEFULNESS: The individual volumes provide excellent and detailed introductions to the various periods with which they deal. The opinions presented, although generally cautious, are valuable since they reflect modern trends in literary criticism. Though the style and coverage vary from volume to volume, all the books in the series are well written, and they often give fuller and more scholarly treatment of authors than the *Cambridge History*.

Bibliographies of primary and secondary works are adequate and up to date.

RELATED REFERENCE WORKS: *Cambridge History of English Literature* (our no. 133).

Those particularly interested in literary criticism, its theories and history, will want to consult René Wellek, *A History of Modern Criticism: 1750–1950* (New Haven: Yale Univ. Press, 1955), and J. W. H. Atkins, *English Literary Criticism* (London: Cambridge Univ. Press, 1943–1951).

135] *A Literary History of England*

New York: Appleton-Century-Crofts, 2nd ed., 1967.
Ed. by Albert C. Baugh, *et al.*

CONTENTS: A comprehensive (1673 pages) one-volume history of English literature from its beginnings to the first half of the twentieth century. Bibliographical references and a thorough index are provided.

METHOD OF ORGANIZATION: Chronological. Divided into the following main sections: The Old English Period (to 1100); The Middle English Period (1100–1500); The Renaissance (1485–1660); The Restoration and Eighteenth Century (1660–1789); The Nineteenth Century and After (1789–1939).

Pages are provided with marginal headings, very helpful for quick consultation.

The work has an exhaustive index—author, title, subject. Bibliographical references are given in footnotes. Note that the bibliographies are thoroughly updated in the "Bibliographical Supplement" included in the second edition.

USEFULNESS: A one-volume history of English literature, (often assigned as a text or as supplementary reading in English literature survey courses), providing accurate, scholarly information and safe, acceptable judgments.

RELATED REFERENCE WORKS: *Concise Cambridge History of English Literature* (listed along with our no. 133). *A History of English Literature* by William V. Moody and Robert M. Lovett (New York: Scribner's, 1964) is a well-known shorter and less detailed one-volume work.

136] *Oxford Companion to English Literature*

Oxford: Clarendon Press. 3rd ed., 1946.
Ed. by Sir Paul Harvey.

CONTENTS: A handbook in dictionary form, containing approximately 10,000 concise articles on British authors, literary works, fictitious characters, and on allusions commonly made in English literature, such as to places, mythological figures, and statesmen.

METHOD OF ORGANIZATION: Alphabetical.

USEFULNESS: The *Oxford Companion* is good for quick identifications and checking on facts. It gives a broad coverage of English literature.

No judgments are given: "original literary appreciation is not attempted."

EXAMPLES: Most articles are only one paragraph long.

Here is a sample list of items identified, chosen at random:

Babylon, Beowulf, Canterbury Tales, Chaucer, Cheapside, Chekhov, Conrad, David Copperfield, Dickens, Doggerel verse, Dog-Latin, Dog-star, Dryden, George Eliot, Falstaff, Fielding, Frankenstein, Gladstone, Globe Theatre, Lady Godiva, Grendel, Grub Street, Hamlet, Leigh Hunt, The Idler, Ben Jonson, Kubla Khan, Thomas Kyd, Lycidas, Mars, Mermaid Tavern, Old Bailey, Orpheus, Othello, Paradise Lost, Parnell, Saint Patrick, Rasputin, Scrooge, Tennyson, Tiresias, Titanic, Tom Jones, Tristram, Venus, Wife of Bath, Wife of Usher's Well, Wordsworth, The Yellow Book, Zola.

The information given for an author consists of facts bearing on his life and literary works. The information given for a literary work consists of its date and a concise indication of its nature; for an important work, a brief sketch of its contents is added.

RELATED REFERENCE WORKS: The *New Century Handbook of English Literature* (our no. 137) is very similar in form, scope, and information given.

137] *New Century Handbook of English Literature*

New York: Appleton-Century-Crofts, 1956.
Ed. by Clarence L. Barnhart.

CONTENTS: A handbook in dictionary form, containing more than 14,000 concise articles on British authors, literary works, fictitious characters, and on allusions commonly made in English literature such as to places, mythological figures, and statesmen. (This work is in part based upon the *New Century Cyclopedia of Names;* see our no. 6).

METHOD OF ORGANIZATION: Alphabetical. Numerous cross references.

USEFULNESS: The *New Century Handbook* is good for quick identifications and checking on facts.

It gives a broad coverage of English literature. No judgments are given, only identifications.

EXAMPLES: Most articles are only one paragraph long.

To illustrate the coverage offered, here are a few examples, chosen at random, from the various categories; *authors:* Chaucer, Donne, Hardy, Heine, Shelley, Tennyson; *works:* Canterbury Tales, Doctor Faustus, Frankenstein, Hamlet, Pride and Prejudice, The Seafarer, Sea-Fever, Vanity Fair, Wife of Bath's Tale; *characters:* Molly Bloom, Don Juan, Falstaff, Iago, Lancelot, Romeo, Scrooge, Sheriff of Nottingham, Herr Teufelsdröckh; *place-names:* Babylon, Cheapside, Globe Theatre, Grub Street; *literary terms:* catastrophe, doggerel, elegy, Gothic novel; *mythology, history, etc.:* Bacchus, King Canute, Dark Lady, El Dorado, Eleanor of Aquitaine, Helen of Troy, Hermes, Mary Magdalen, Niebelungs, Tower of Babel, Venus.

The information given for an author consists of facts bearing on his life and literary works. The information given for a literary work consists of its date and concise indication of its nature; for an important work, a brief sketch of its contents is added.

RELATED REFERENCE WORKS: The *Oxford Companion to English Literature* (our no. 136) is very similar in form, scope, and information given.

138] *Annals of English Literature: 1475–1950*

Oxford: Clarendon Press. 2nd ed., 1961.
Ed. by Jyotish C. Ghosh, *et al.*

CONTENTS: A year-by-year listing of the titles of the outstanding works of English literature published from 1475 to 1950.
The works of all major and some influential minor authors of the English-speaking world are included.

METHOD OF ORGANIZATION: Chronological.

Pages are divided into two columns: the main column lists authors and titles of their books published that year; the side column records births and deaths of authors, publications of periodicals and newspapers, as well as selected relevant foreign events.

Running page headings give reigning British monarchs.

A detailed index lists authors (with titles and dates of major works), anonymous and collective publications.

USEFULNESS: A practical small reference work. "The purpose of this book is to give the student of English literature, at a glance, the main literary output of any year; to show what books people were likely to be reading at any time, and with what rivals a candidate for literary fame had to reckon."

Classical and Mythology

139] *Oxford Classical Dictionary*

Oxford: Clarendon Press, 1949. Ed. by M. Cary, *et al.*

CONTENTS: A dictionary of classical Greek and Roman literature and civilization. Brief articles cover literature, mythology, art, history, philosophy, science, geography, and other topics relevant to the world of ancient Greece and Rome.

The entries are signed; brief bibliographies are appended to most articles.

METHOD OF ORGANIZATION: Alphabetical, from Abacus to Zosimus (writer on alchemy of third or fourth century A.D.).

Works of literature are not given separate articles; thus, one will not find an entry on *The Aeneid,* but will find articles on Aeneas and Virgil.

There are numerous cross references.

USEFULNESS: A reliable and scholarly dictionary, presenting comprehensive coverage of all aspects of classical literature and civilization.

EXAMPLES: Most articles are brief, but the dictionary also contains longer survey articles (e.g., 5 pages on medicine, 8 on music, 10 on Rome, 5 on tragedy). To illustrate the comprehensive range of the work, here is a brief sample list of subjects defined or discussed: Academy, Achaean League, Achilles, Aeschylus, Alexander the Great, Aristotle, Assonance, Botany, Bronze, Catullus, Circe, Colonization, Creon, Disposal of Dead, Discus, Dithyramb, Epicurus, Eros, Festivals, Galen, Gymnasium, Hades, Hannibal, Helicon, Herodotus, Hiatus, Homer, Horse and Chariot Races, Io, Justinian, Leda, Lex, Lighting, Livius, Macedonia, Medea, Neoplatonism, Odysseus, Pan, Pastoral Poetry, Pericles, Phoenicians, Pisistratus, Psyche, Punic Wars, Romulus and Remus, Scylla, Spartacus, Tantalus, Tragedy, Virgil, Xerxes, Zeus.

RELATED REFERENCE WORKS: *New Century Classical Handbook* (our no. 140).

140] *New Century Classical Handbook*

New York: Appleton-Century-Crofts, 1962.
Ed. by Catherine A. Avery.

CONTENTS: A dictionary of classical Greek and Roman literature and civilization. Brief articles cover literature, mythology, art, history, philosophy, science, geography, and other topics relevant to the world of ancient Greece and Rome. There are no bibliographies.

METHOD OF ORGANIZATION: Alphabetical, from Abacus to Zosteria (an epithet of Athena).

USEFULNESS: A reliable dictionary on the classical age and its literature for the general reader and student. Useful for succinct introductory information and for checking on facts.

EXAMPLES: To illustrate the comprehensive range of the handbook, here is a brief sample list of entries, chosen at random: Achilles, Aeneas, Aeneid, Aeolus, Alexander the Great, Ambrosia, Apollo, Ares, Bacchanalia, Cassandra, Julius Caesar, Carthage, Circe, Colossus of Rhodes, Corinth, Delphi, Dido, Diogenes, Drama, Erinyes, Euripides, Gallic Wars, Hades, Hadrian, Hecuba, Horace, Horn of Plenty, Iliad, Jason, Leda, Lyceum, Medea, Metamorphoses, Minos, Nymphs, Oedipus Rex, Odysseus, Odyssey, Orestes, Ovid, Paris, Pegasus, Pericles, Phidias, Pindar, Pisistratus, Prometheus, Sabines, Sappho, Senate, Sol, Tiberius, Troy, Vestal Virgins, Zeno.

RELATED REFERENCE WORKS: *Oxford Classical Dictionary* (our no. 139); *Oxford Companion to Classical Literature* (Oxford: Clarendon Press, 1937). Also of interest are a number of more specialized handbooks, such as Philip W. Harsh, *A Handbook of Classical Drama* (Stanford: Stanford Univ. Press, 1956), and H. J. Rose, *A Handbook of Greek Literature* (New York: Dutton, 1942) and *A Handbook of Latin Literature* (London: Methuen, 1936).

141] *Mythology of All Races*

Boston: Marshall Jones, 1916–1932 (reprinted by Macmillan). 13 vols. Ed. by Louis H. Grey, John A. MacCulloch, *et al.*

CONTENTS: A comprehensive collection of the major mythologies of the world, written by competent scholars and copiously illustrated with aboriginal pictures. Aiming to present a "readable" retelling of the typical myths of the various cultures, the work stresses facts, not theories. Bibliographies are provided, and vol. XIII is an index.

METHOD OF ORGANIZATION: Arranged by cultures: vol. I, *Greek and Roman* (354 pages of text, 63 plates of illustrations); vol. II, *Eddic;* vol. III, *Celtic, Slavic;* vol. IV, *Finno-*

Ugric, Siberian; vol. V, *Semitic;* vol. VI, *Indian, Iranian;* vol. VII, *Armenian, African;* vol. VIII, *Chinese, Japanese;* vol. IX, *Oceanic;* vol. X, *North American;* vol. XI, *Latin American;* vol. XII, *Egypt, Far East;* vol. XIII is an index. Each of the first twelve volumes has a detailed table of contents and a bibliography.

Since the individual volumes do not have indexes, the student is advised to consult vol. XIII, the *Index,* first, for rapid location of the pertinent pages. The *Index* lists names and subjects.

USEFULNESS: The most comprehensive reference work in the field of mythology in English. The analytical index facilitates "the comparative study of myths among different and widely remote peoples." However, the bibliographies are obviously out of date.

EXAMPLES: Here are some sample chapter titles from vol. I, *Greek & Roman Mythology:* The Creation of the World, Myths of Crete and Attike, Herakles, The Voyage of the Argo, The Tale of Troy, The Afterworld, Dionysos, The Lesser Gods of Water, Wind, and Wild, The Element of Chance, Etruscan Mythology, Mars.

RELATED REFERENCE WORKS: *Larousse Encyclopedia of Mythology* (our no. 142); *Funk & Wagnalls Standard Dictionary of Folklore, Mythology & Legend* (our no. 72); *The Golden Bough* (our no. 73).

There are, of course, numerous reference works dealing with the mythology of a particular culture, e.g., Robert Graves, *The Greek Myths* (London: Penguin, 1955).

142] *Larousse Encyclopedia of Mythology*

London: Batchworth Press, 1959.
Translated from the French.

CONTENTS: A one-volume encyclopedia of the major mythologies of the world. Each section is copiously illustrated with photographs and reproductions of aboriginal works of art.

METHOD OF ORGANIZATION: Arranged by cultures—divided into the following chapters: Prehistoric Mythology; Egyptian; Assyro-Babylonian; Phoenician; Greek; Roman; Celtic; Teutonic; Slavonic; Finno-Ugric; Ancient Persia; India, Chinese; Japanese; The Two Americas; Oceania; Black Africa.

Index of names, but not of subjects.

USEFULNESS: A handy one-volume compendium meant for introductory reading; also useful as a dictionary for checking allusions, although the lack of a subject index is a handicap.

EXAMPLES: As an example of the contents, here are the major subdivisions of the chapter on the Mythology of India: Mythology of the Brahmanic Dharma, Mythology of the Warrior Caste, Mythology of the Priestly Caste, Popular Mythology: The Demons, Abstract Mythology of the Brahmanas, Mythology of the Heretical Dharmas, Jainism, Buddhism, Legend of Buddha, Mythology of Hinduism, Religion of Vishnu, Religion of Siva, The Descendants of Siva and Pârvati; Expansion of Hindu Mythology.

RELATED REFERENCE WORKS: *Mythology of All Races* (our no. 141); *Funk & Wagnalls Standard Dictionary of Folklore, Mythology & Legend* (our no. 72). Also see *Eastman Index to Fairy Tales.*

A favorite old work, *Bulfinch's Mythology,* has recently been reissued (New York: Crowell, 1959) and made somewhat more useable as a reference work by a new combination index-dictionary. This book is mainly concerned with the mythologies of the western world and tends to be more of a story book than a reference work; yet it is a classic and should not be ignored since it was the introduction to mythology for most western writers.

143] *Cassell's Encyclopaedia of World Literature*

London: Cassell & Co., 1953. 2 vols.
Ed. by S. H. Steinberg.

CONTENTS: A handbook in dictionary form, containing concise articles on world literature, both western and Oriental, from ancient times to the twentieth century. The encyclopedia includes articles on individual authors, anonymous works, the various literatures of the world, and general literary topics, such as movements, style, and genres. Each article is signed, and short bibliographies are supplied.

METHOD OF ORGANIZATION: Alphabetically, within three parts: Histories of the Literatures of the World and General Subjects, Biographies of Authors Who Died Before 1 August 1914, Biographies of Authors Who Were Living on 1 August 1914 or Who Were Born After that Date.

EXAMPLES: Articles in part I deal with the histories of the various major literatures of the world, as well as the lesser known literatures and regional literatures. Short bibliographies are supplied in each case. Also included in part I are articles on general subjects: schools and movements, form and style (rhetoric), genres, anonymous and general works, and miscellaneous matters (e.g., censorship, humor and wit, printing, textual criticism).

Articles in parts II and III deal with individual authors, giving brief sketches of each writer's life and literary career, a list of his publications, plus a short bibliography of secondary studies. The writers of some eighty literatures are represented. ("Care has been taken not to give undue space to writers in English.") To illustrate the coverage here are a few names, chosen at random: Aarestrup, Calderon, Catullus, Cellini, Chand Bardai, Confucius, Dante, Donne, Emerson, Goethe, Gogol, Hauptman, Heraclitus, Hölderlin, Homer, Ibsen, I-ching, Jnanesvar, Joyce, Kafka, Kan'ami, Lu Chi, Montaigne, Novalis, Ovid, Pushkin, Rabelais, Racine, Tagore, Urfi, Zweig.

USEFULNESS: The work provides excellent coverage of world literature. Useful for brief introductory information and for checking on facts.

RELATED REFERENCE WORKS: *Columbia Dictionary of Modern European Literature* (our no. 144); Lillian Hornstein, *et al.*, *The Reader's Companion to World Literature* (New York: Dryden Press, 1956).

144] *Columbia Dictionary of Modern European Literature*

New York: Columbia University Press, 1947.
Ed. by Horace Smith.

CONTENTS: A handbook in dictionary form, containing 1,167 brief articles on continental European literature. The dictionary includes articles (brief biographical sketches and critical evaluations) on all important European literary artists of the second half of the nineteenth and first half of the twentieth century. Also included are "survey articles, with bibliographies, of the thirty-one literatures of the Continent." Each article is signed, and short bibliographies are supplied.

METHOD OF ORGANIZATION: Alphabetical, by author and country, from Aakjaer, Jeppe (Danish novelist and poet, 1866–1930) to Zweig, Stefan (Austrian writer, 1881–1942); from Albanian literature to Yugoslav literature.

USEFULNESS: A reliable source for brief introductory information. Also good for quick identifications and checking on facts.

EXAMPLES: Articles on authors list the writer's publications (both in the original language and in English translation) with dates; a synopsis of his life and literary career; critical comments on themes, importance, influence; and a short bibliography of secondary studies. Among the more than one thousand authors listed are such important figures as Camus, Čapek, and Cocteau, as well as many lesser known writers (approximately 40 Czech, 200 French, 150 German, 100 Italian, 50 Polish, 100 Russian, 100 Spanish).

Articles on countries present short histories of modern literature. A number of articles deal with subjects.

RELATED REFERENCE WORKS: *Cassell's Encyclopaedia of World
Literature* (our no. 143). There are also a number of handbooks which specialize in the literature of a particular country,
e.g., *The Oxford Companion to French Literature,* ed. by Paul
Harvey and J. E. Heseltine (Oxford: Clarendon Press, 1959);
Dictionary of Russian Literature, ed. by William E. Harkins
(London: Allen & Unwin, 1957); *Dictionary of Spanish Literature,* ed. by Maxim Newmark (New York: Philosophical Library, 1956).

145] *Encyclopedia of Poetry and Poetics*

Princeton: Princeton University Press, 1965.
Ed. by Alex Preminger, *et al.*

CONTENTS: A dictionary of literary terms, literary movements,
and the "theory, technique, and criticism of poetry from earliest times to the present." Approximately 1,000 entries (varying
from paragraph to essay length) written and signed by experts.
Many articles are illustrated by examples and supplemented by
bibliographies.
Poets and poems are not listed.

METHOD OF ORGANIZATION: Alphabetical, from an entry on
Abstract Poem to one on Zeugma. Numerous cross references.

EXAMPLES: The scope of this encyclopedia is wide; the editors
have attempted to include all terms and subjects of interest to
students of poetry. Consider the following sample list of topics
treated, chosen at random: Acrostic, Albanian Poetry, Alliteration, Ambiguity, Anacreontic, Apollonian-Dionysian, Arche-
type, Ballad, Bathos, Blank Verse, Bucolic, Bulgarian Poetry,
Canzone, Carpe Diem, Catharsis, Cavalier Poets, Chinese Poetry, Closet Drama, Conceit, Enjambement, Epic, Fabliau,
Foot, Haiku, Idyl, Inscape, Irish Literary Renaissance, Irony,
Limerick, Litotes, Madrigal, Metaphor, Music and Poetry,
Naturalism, New Criticism, Octave, Old Norse Poetry, Objec-

tive Correlative, Parody, Poetic Diction, Pun, Romanticism, Science and Poetry, Sentimentality, Sonnet, Strophe, Subjective and Objective, Symbolism, Terza Rima, Touchstone, Tribe of Ben, Vers Libre.

USEFULNESS: An excellent source for succinct and coherent definitions of literary terms, as well as for summaries and explanations of literary movements and critical theories.

RELATED REFERENCE WORKS: Note that the *Encyclopedia of Poetry and Poetics* is mainly concerned with poetry. The following dictionaries cover all aspects of literature: William F. Thrall and A. Hibbard, *A Handbook to Literature*, revised by C. H. Holman (N.Y.: Odyssey Press, 1960); Karl Beckson and Arthur Ganz, *A Reader's Guide to Literary Terms* (N.Y.: Noonday Press, 1960).

146] *Library of Literary Criticism: Modern British Literature*

New York: Ungar, 1966. 3 vols.
Ed. by Ruth Z. Temple and M. Tucker.

CONTENTS: A selection of excerpts from critical studies on over 400 important British authors who have lived or won recognition in the twentieth century. Authors about whom critical opinions are cited include poets, novelists, dramatists, essayists, as well as selected famous non-belletrists (e.g., critics, philosophers, psychologists). "For each author included, excerpts from criticism have been chosen to describe his qualities and define his status."

Indexes and bibliographies are supplied.

METHOD OF ORGANIZATION: Alphabetical. Bibliographies of the authors' works are given at the end of each volume. Vol. III also contains a "Cross-Reference Index to Authors," and an "Index to Critics."

EXAMPLES: The space for each author varies from a half page for minor figures to over 10 pages for major figures (e.g.,

Yeats, 10 pages; Joyce, 11 pages; Eliot, 15 pages; Lawrence, 20 pages). The individual excerpts from the various critical studies (book reviews, periodical articles, book-length studies) are brief, a paragraph or two from each.

USEFULNESS: A handy survey of critical opinions about an author. Excerpts are well chosen to present the range of opinion and "are arranged in chronological order to show the rise and sometimes fall of fame and favor." Useful as a possible introductory step between literary histories or dictionaries and the actual critical articles and books.

Caution: these excerpts are not meant to serve as a substitute for the full-length critical works. Hopefully, they will introduce the student to the range of critical opinion and whet his appetite for further research.

RELATED REFERENCE WORKS: Dorothy Nyren, *A Library of Literary Criticism: Modern American Literature* (New York: Ungar, 1960, soon to be printed in a revised edition, co-edited by Maurice Kramer); Charles W. Moulton, *Library of Literary Criticism of English and American Authors: 1680 to 1904*, 8 vols. (Buffalo, Moulton Publishing Co., 1901–1905).

147] *The Reader's Encyclopedia*

New York: Crowell, 2nd ed., 1965.
Ed. by William R. Benet.

CONTENTS: A gathering of miscellaneous information about or connected with literature. The dictionary includes entries on famous authors and books from all nations and all times; famous characters in legend, fiction, drama, opera, and poetry; literary terms and allusions; and various miscellaneous entries on such topics as history, philosophy, art, music, superstitions, and phrases. Individual entries are brief, many not more than a paragraph long.

METHOD OF ORGANIZATION: Alphabetical. Numerous cross references.

EXAMPLES: To illustrate the comprehensive scope of this dictionary, here are a few examples from the various categories, found listed under the first letter of the alphabet:

Authors(entries give dates, titles of principal works, and a brief critical comment): Adamov, Adams, A. E. (George Russell), Aelfric Grammaticus, Aristotle, St. Augustine. *Titles* (entries give author, date, and a summary of contents): Absalom, Absalom!, Absalom and Achitophel, The Adding Machine, Adonais, Against the Grain (A Rebours), Aida. *Characters:* Achates, Nick Adams, Aeneas, Aladdin, Anna Karenina, Anna Livia Plurabelle, Ariel, L'Avare. *Mythological & Biblical Figures:* Aaron, Acheron, Actaeon, Adonis, Aeolus, Ajax, Amazons, Aphrodite. *Literary Terms:* accent, meter, acrostic, allegory. *Historical Information:* Act of Union, John Adams, Alamo, Appian Way. *Words and Phrases* (entries give origin and definition): abomination of desolation, Abraham's bosom. *Miscellaneous:* Abbey Theatre, absurd, agnostic, All Saints' Day, The American Mercury, animals in heaven, apple of discord, Augean stables.

USEFULNESS: A valuable desk book for tracing literary allusions, as well as non-literary allusions. Most of the information included here can, of course, be found by looking in various other reference works, but this book brings the facts together and makes them readily available in one alphabetical listing.

RELATED REFERENCE WORKS: An older work similar to the above is Ebenezer C. Brewer's *Dictionary of Phrase and Fable,* first published in 1870 and now in its 8th revised edition (New York: Harper & Bros., 1963). Brewer's work is similar in scope to the *Reader's Encyclopedia,* yet includes many more entries dealing with words and phrases. It is on the whole a more general reference tool, rather than one intended mainly for students of literature.

148] *Twentieth Century Authors: A Biographical Dictionary of Modern Literature*

New York: H. W. Wilson Co., 1942. First Supplement, 1955. Ed. by Stanley J. Kunitz and Howard Haycraft.

CONTENTS: Approximately 2,550 biographical sketches (1,850 in the original volume, 700 in the supplement) of living and dead authors "of this century, of all nations, whose books are familiar to readers of English."
Bibliographies are supplied.

METHOD OF ORGANIZATION: Alphabetical, from Abbott, Eleanor Hallowell (American short story writer and novelist) to Zweig, Stefan (Austrian biographer and novelist). In order to obtain the complete information available on an author, be sure to consult the supplement volume first, since it lists all the authors covered in both volumes, bringing the biographies of the original volume up to date as well as adding "sketches of authors who have come to prominence since 1942."
Unfortunately there is no title index.

EXAMPLES: The sketches vary from a half page to one and a half pages. Each gives a summary of the subject's life and accomplishments, a photograph, a brief critical evaluation, a list of his principal publications, and a list of biographical and critical works about the author.
Many times, authors themselves have supplied the needed biographical data; some wrote their own sketches (shown by quotation marks).

USEFULNESS: One of the best-known specialized biographical dictionaries, the work should be consulted if a student is seeking introductory information about a twentieth-century author. The bibliographies of secondary sources about each writer are useful as a guide to further study.

RELATED REFERENCE WORKS: Among the many other specialized bibliographical dictionaries dealing with literary figures, the following are particularly useful: S. J. Kunitz and H. Haycraft, *American Authors: 1600–1900* (New York: H. W. Wilson

Co., 1938); and by the same editors and publishers *British Authors Before 1800* (1952), *British Authors of the Nineteenth Century* (1936); *Contemporary Authors* (Detroit: Gale Research Co., 1962—). Frank N. Magill, *et al., Cyclopedia of World Authors* (New York: Harper, 1958). Also see our section I.C., where the major standard biographical dictionaries are described.

149] *A History of the Theatre*

New York: Crown, 2nd ed., 1955.
By George Freedley and John A. Reeves.

CONTENTS: A chronicle of the main trends and principal events of the theater, all over the world, from its beginnings to the mid-twentieth century. The history deals not only with the dramatic literature and the playwrights, but also with the playhouse and the actors. Motion pictures and television are not included.

A bibliography and indexes are supplied. Many illustrations.

METHOD OF ORGANIZATION: The thirty-two chapters in the main section are arranged chronologically and by national areas. The "Supplementary Section, 1940–1954" contains short survey articles arranged by countries, bringing the history up to mid-century.

The index is in two parts, the first for the main section, the second for the supplement; each lists titles, names, and subjects.

USEFULNESS: A useful one-volume history of world theater, in essay form, yet simple and concise. The chapters are well organized and the index is detailed.

EXAMPLES: Here are some chapter titles from the main section: I, Egypt, the Beginning of the Theatre; II, The Glory that was Greece; III, Roman Grandeur; IX, Neo-Classic France (1550–1700); XII, The Legendary East; XIII, America's Age of Actors (1815–1905); XXVI, Nationalist Italy (1815–1940); XXXII, America Takes Its Place (1906–1940).

150] *Oxford Companion to the Theatre*

New York: Oxford University Press, 2nd ed., 1957.
Ed. by Phyllis Hartnoll.

CONTENTS: A one-volume dictionary of the theater, emphasizing the non-literary aspects, i.e., the actors, the playhouse, and minor "popular" works and writers. It deals with the theater "in all ages and in all countries," but concentrates on that which will "interest the English-speaking reader."

Motion pictures and television are not covered; related areas such as opera and ballet are included, but not in detail. Full bibliography of secondary sources. Many illustrations.

METHOD OF ORGANIZATION: Alphabetical, from Aasen, Ivar (author of a nineteenth-century Norwegian musical play) to Zuckmayer, Carl (twentieth-century German dramatist). Many cross references.

Appendixes: "Bibliography" of more than 1,000 books on the theater and related subjects; "Supplement," a short section, arranged alphabetically; "Illustrations," 154 plates.

USEFULNESS: Information about the stage; especially good for those interested in "the popular rather than the literary theatre."

EXAMPLES: The work contains entries on actors, producers, directors, dramatists, famous theaters, the architecture of the stage, scenery, costumes, theatrical terms, and the history of the theater in various countries. The length of the items varies from paragraph-long identifications and definitions to essay-length survey and history articles (e.g., 6 pages on the theater in Scandinavia, 8 pages on theatrical scenery).

RELATED REFERENCE WORKS: Students doing research in specific genres or types of literature should acquaint themselves with the specialized reference works that apply, e.g.,—criticism: René Welleck, *A History of Modern Criticism* (New Haven: Yale Univ. Press, 1955—); —proverbs: William G. Smith, *Oxford Dictionary of English Proverbs* (Oxford: Clarendon Press, 2nd ed., 1948); and the many works that deal with the novel, short stories, poetry, etc.

MUSIC

151] *Music Index*

Detroit: Information Service, Inc., 1949—.
Monthly with annual cumulations.

CONTENTS: This monthly indexes articles on all phases of music in about 200 outstanding American and foreign periodicals.

Periodicals completely devoted to music are fully indexed; periodicals with coverage broader than music are indexed only for material relevant to music.

METHOD OF ORGANIZATION: In dictionary form, with authors of articles, proper names and subjects (composers, instrumentalists, names of countries, operas, The Beatles, phonograph record, etc.) all together in one alphabetical listing. But this is primarily a subject index.

There is a special section for review of books called *Book Reviews;* books chosen are listed under the author's name in one alphabetical listing. Musical compositions are listed under the name of the composer. Performance reviews are listed under the name of the performer or organization.

USEFULNESS: This is the reference work for looking up articles or book reviews dealing with music or almost anything connected with music.

EXAMPLES: Each annual indexes about 45,000 articles, so that the range of subjects is enormous. The 1963 volume, for example, indexes articles on Acoustics, Alberini String Quartet, Appreciation of Music, Auditoriums and Concert Halls, The

Beatles, Civil Rights, Debussy, Finland, History, Jazz Musicians, London Philharmonic Orchestra, Thelonius Monk, Popular Combos, Royal Ballet, Theory, Woodwind Instruments, among other topics.

RELATED REFERENCE WORKS: *Guide to the Performing Arts,* compiled by S. Yancey Belknap (New York: Scarecrow, 1957—), indexes articles in about 40 periodicals, most of them in English. *The History of Music,* by Ernst C. Krohn (St. Louis: Washington University, 1952), indexes literature on the history of music appearing in about 40 periodicals, mainly English and German. *Music Reference and Research Materials,* by Vincent Duckles (New York: The Free Press, 1964) (our no. 152).

152] *Music Reference and Research Materials*

New York: The Free Press, 1964. By Vincent Duckles.

CONTENTS: This annotated bibliography lists and describes over 1,100 important books, most of them in English, concerned directly with music (there is nothing here, for example, on theater arts or the dance).

Descriptions of the books are short, usually two to ten lines; often, book reviews are cited.

METHOD OF ORGANIZATION: Organized under the following categories and in this order: Dictionaries and Encyclopedias, Histories and Chronologies, Guides to Systematic and Historical Musicology, Bibliographies of Music Literature, Bibliographies of Music, Catalogs of Music Libraries and Collections, Catalogs of Musical Instrument Collections, Histories and Bibliographies of Music Printing and Publishing, Discographies, Yearbooks, Miscellaneous Bibliographical Tools. An index of authors, editors, and reviewers; index of subjects; and index of titles, follow.

USEFULNESS: A good bibliography of music bibliographies. Gives brief descriptions of works. No entries for biographies.

EXAMPLES: Here is a sample entry:

Westrup, Jack A. and F. L. Harrison. The new college encyclopedia of music. New York, Norton (1960) 739 p.
  Pub. in England, 1959, under the title *Collins Encyclopedia of Music.*
  A popular "student" dictionary. Detailed summaries of works for major composers, fields of activity for minor ones. References to early works republished in standard historical editions or anthologies. Technical articles with musical illustrations. Title entries for repertory works, instrumental and vocal, selected bibliography, primarily English. British pronunciations.
  Review by James B. Coover in *Notes,* 17 (1960) p. 564–66.

153] *International Cyclopedia of Music and Musicians*

New York: Dodd, Mead & Co., 9th ed., 1964.
Ed. by Robert Sabin.

CONTENTS: Probably the best one-volume cyclopedia of music and musicians in English. International in scope but with strong emphasis on America, this 2,467-page work has biographical entries on musicians, definitions of terms, and long signed articles by authorities on such special subjects as American Music, Music Criticism, Song, Ballet and Music, etc.
  The biographical entries range from a 13-word description of Étienne Briard, a French music engraver, to a 6,000-word entry on Beethoven. The signed articles range anywhere from a few thousand words to a 17,000-word article on Folk Music.
  Long articles on composers and special subjects are always followed by detailed bibliographies and a chronological list of works, broken down into categories (Chamber Music, Orchestra Music, Piano Music, Songs, etc.), with date of composition and publication.

METHOD OF ORGANIZATION: Alphabetical.

USEFULNESS: Accurate and precise information on music and musicians, written by some of the best authorities, in a clear and interesting manner.

The entries serve as excellent introductory material; but they should never be used in place of detailed studies.

EXAMPLES: To illustrate the variety, scope, and depth of this cyclopedia, here are some sample entries: A Chula, Acoustics, Aeolian Piano, American Indian Music, Bach, Bardini, Bote and Bock, Consecutive, Dirge, Discant, Guidonian Hand, Harmonica, Mode, Nationalism in Music, Psalmody, and Steinway & Sons, to name just 16 out of more than 36,000.

RELATED REFERENCE WORKS: *The New College Encyclopedia of Music*, ed. by J. A. Westrup and F. Harrison (New York: W. W. Norton, 1950) contains entries on composers, their works, performers, and musical terms.

154] *Baker's Biographical Dictionary of Musicians*

New York: G. Schirmer, 5th ed., 1958, with 1965 supplement, completely rev. by Nicolas Slonimsky.

CONTENTS: Although primarily a dictionary of musicians (composers, singers, instrumentalists, conductors) from the western world, from the middle ages to the present, hundreds of individuals associated with music such as librettists, publishers, impresarios, music historians, and choreographers, are also included.

There are close to 14,000 entries, most of them with bibliographies appended. Entries vary in length from 20 to about 2,700 words each.

Biographical sketches of composers include titles of major compositions with dates of first performance.

METHOD OF ORGANIZATION: Alphabetical.

USEFULNESS: Probably the most comprehensive biographical reference work on musicians and individuals associated with them, from the obscure to the giants of music. Information is usually brief and factual, with some comments about style, influence, and historical importance.

EXAMPLES: The range here is large and varied, with entries, for example, on:

Hermann Abert, German music scholar; Girolamo Abos, Maltese composer; Max Abraham, German publisher; Alexander Étienne Choron, French music editor and theorist; Boris Christoff, Bulgarian bass-baritone; Antonine Kontski, Polish pianist; Paul-Marie Masson, French musicologist; Carl Gottlieb Röder, German printer of music; William Shakespeare, English tenor and singing teacher; Henry Willis, English organ builder. All major figures are, of course, represented.

RELATED REFERENCE WORKS: *Everyman's Dictionary of Music,* 4th edition, revised by Jack Westrup (New York: Dutton, 1962). A good popular dictionary "for quick reference, but not for the specialist." Deals with western music of the Christian era. Includes terms, works, places, and biographical sketches but omits living performers.

155] *Grove's Dictionary of Music and Musicians*

New York: St. Martin's Press, 5th ed., 1955.
Ed. by Eric Blom. 9 vols. and supplement in 1961.

CONTENTS: Much more of an encyclopedia than a dictionary, this comprehensive work is made up of signed articles that range in length from a 33-word entry on Joseph Becker, a Hungarian baritone, to a 58,000-word detailed account of Beethoven's life and works. It covers every aspect of music from the middle of the fifteenth century to the present.

Precise, accurate, and authoritative, the well over 40,000 entries deal with musical terms, musical history, theory, musicians, instruments, songs, operas, symphonies, quartets, and anything else directly associated with music.

There is strong emphasis on English music and musicians and their relationship to foreign composers and their works.

Bibliographies appended to most entries. Articles on composers are always accompanied by a catalogue of works—

Opera, Choral, Orchestral, Solo Instrument and Orchestra, Voice and Orchestra, Chamber, etc.

METHOD OF ORGANIZATION: Arranged alphabetically, with cross references.

Volume X, the supplement, contains material published from 1955 to 1961 that, in the opinion of the editors, would increase the accuracy and scholarship in Volumes I to IX.

USEFULNESS: This is the work to consult for encyclopedic articles on music. The scholarship is reliable and the treatment of subjects for the most part detailed and extensive.

EXAMPLES: The work begins with:
A, A.B.A., A Basso Porto, A Battuta, A Capella, A Capriccio, A Due, and then continues through the alphabet.

RELATED REFERENCE WORKS: *The Oxford Companion to Music,* 9th edition, ed. by Percy A. Scholes (New York: Oxford University Press, 1955). "A comprehensive, alphabetical dictionary on all phases of music containing long, encyclopedic articles." About 1,500 biographic sketches. Pronouncing glossary of foreign terms and names.

156] *Harvard Dictionary of Music*

Cambridge: Harvard University Press, 1951. By Willi Apel.

CONTENTS: The dictionary's well over 5,700 entries, varying from about 10 to 1,600 words long, give concise and accurate information on musical topics, except biography.

Every entry is divided "into two paragraphs, one of which treats the subject from the present day point of view, the other, from that of a historian."

Good bibliographies of books and periodicals. Some illustrations.

METHOD OF ORGANIZATION: Alphabetical.

USEFULNESS: Excellent source for accurate definitions of all subjects associated directly with music. All entries are based on sound, thorough scholarship.

EXAMPLES: Here is a sample list of entries, chosen at random: Ab, Abbellimenti, Added Sixth, Ambrosian Hymns, Arpeggio, Ballet in Opera, Buffo, Clavichord, Functional Harmony, Harmonic Analysis, Lay, Masculine-Feminine Cadence, Neumes, Oratorio, Refrain, Scale, Spanish Music, Timbre, Variations, Znamenny.

Note that the dictionary does *not* contain entries on composers, organizations, orchestras, or publishers.

RELATED REFERENCE WORKS: *The Harvard Brief Dictionary of Music*, by Willi Apel and Ralph T. Daniel (Cambridge: Harvard University Press, 1960), contains short articles for the nonspecialist on opera plots, songs, and compositions. No composers here.

157] *Handbook of World Opera*

London: Arthur Barker Ltd., 1961.
Compiled by Frank Ledlie Moore.

CONTENTS: "This comprehensive guide will supply the music lover with the answer to a vast number of questions about the opera—the background, plot, and the cast of operas; biographies of composers, musicians, conductors, etc.; characters with role and name of opera; first lines and titles of famous numbers; a chronology; a glossary; themes of famous numbers and recordings of complete operas."

METHOD OF ORGANIZATION: Arranged by the following categories: The Operas; The People in Opera; The Characters in Opera; First Lines and Titles of Famous Musical Numbers; Chronology of Opera; Glossary; Themes of the Most Famous Musical Numbers; Recordings of Complete Operas; Special Index.

USEFULNESS: This work is of enormous help in tracking down "nearly any reference (identity of an opera from its nickname, full name of a character and the role he plays in the opera, the singer who first sang a certain role, etc.) that may cross your mind in the course of reading about or listening to opera."

RELATED REFERENCE WORKS: *Encyclopedia of the Opera,* by Davis Ewen (New York: Hill and Wang, 1963) is one of the best source books on opera, in English. It covers plots, characters, biographies (composers, librettists, singers, conductors), the history of opera, opera houses and technical terms.

158] New Oxford History of Music

New York: Oxford University Press, 1954–1960. 3 vols.
Vol. I, ed. by Egon Wellesz; Vol. II, ed. by Anselm Hughes;
Vol. III, ed. by Anselm Hughes and Gerald Abraham.
Vols. IV–XI in preparation.

CONTENTS: Undertaken specifically to take the place of *The Oxford History of Music,* this immense work was planned in 10 volumes, with volume 11 devoted to chronological tables and a general index.

The first 3 volumes present a history of music from ancient and oriental music to the music of the Renaissance.

Excellent bibliographies and index at the back of each volume. Black and white illustrations.

METHOD OF ORGANIZATION: Arranged by chapters, chronologically and by categories.

Vol. I: Primitive Music; The Music of Far Eastern Asia-China; The Music of Far Eastern Asia—Other Countries; The Music of India; The Music of Ancient Mesopotamia: The Music of Ancient Egypt; Music in the Bible; The Music of Post-Biblical Judaism; Ancient Greek Music; Roman Music; The Music of Islam.

Vol. II: Early Christian Music; Music of the Eastern Churches; Latin Chant Before St. Gregory; Gregorian Chant; Trope, Sequence, and Conductus; Liturgical Drama; Medieval Song; The Birth of Polyphony; Music in the Twelfth Century; Music in Fixed Rhythm; The Motet and Allied Forms.

Vol. III: Ars Nova in France; The Fourteenth Century in Italy; English Church Music in the Fourteenth Century; Popular and Secular Music in England to 1470; The Transition on the Continent; English Church Music of the Fifteenth Century;

Dufoy and His School; The Age of Ockeghem and Josquin; English Polyphony; European Song; Secular Vocal Music in Italy; The Instrumental Music of the Middle Ages and Early Sixteenth Century; Musical Instruments.

USEFULNESS: Detailed, scholarly, and lucid history of music from ancient times to the sixteenth century, this is for advanced music students, but could be used to great advantage by those just past their introductory courses.

RELATED REFERENCE WORKS: *Oxford History of Music* (New York: Oxford University Press, 1931–38). The great standard history of music from ancient times to 1900. *Music Since 1900*, by Nicolas Slonimsky (New York: Coleman-Ross, 1949) contains history of stylistic trends in music from 1900 to 1948.

159] *Great Composers: 1300–1900*

New York: H. W. Wilson Co., 1966. Ed. by David Ewen.

CONTENTS: This one-volume dictionary gives short (Bach, Beethoven, and Mozart get a few pages at most) but fairly complete biographical sketches of about 200 composers, including many relatively unknown (the Irish John Dowland and John Field), from 18 countries of the west: America, Austria, Czechoslovakia, Denmark, England, France, Germany, Hungary, Ireland, Italy, Belgium, Holland, Norway, Poland, Russia, Spain, Sweden, Switzerland.

"Each sketch . . . includes the principal works of the composer and a bibliography."

Black and white portraits of most of the composers.

METHOD OF ORGANIZATION: Alphabetical. "Appendixes provide a chronological listing of the composers . . . and a listing by nationality."

USEFULNESS: Probably the best one-volume source for detailed biographical, historical, analytical, critical, and personal information, especially about minor composers. Information, however, is merely introductory, and should never replace a biography.

EXAMPLES: John Dunstable, Giovanni Pierluigi da Palestrina, Claudio Monteverdi, Dietrich Buxtehude, Arcangelo Corelli, Domenico Scarlatti, Joseph Haydn, Giacomo Meyerbeer, Vincenzo Bellini, Bedřich Smetana, Léo Delibes, and Gustav Mahler are some of the composers listed in this volume.

RELATED REFERENCE WORKS: *Baker's Biographical Dictionary of Musicians.* (See our no. 154).

PHILOSOPHY

160] *The Concise Encyclopedia of Western Philosophy and Philosophers*

New York: Hawthorn Books, Inc., 1960. Ed. by J. O. Urmson.

CONTENTS: Short, concise, and concerned only with the immediate discipline of philosophy, this handy one-volume work describes in brief, unsigned articles, the key technical terms (analytic, category, universal) and philosophical positions (realism, idealism, rationalism, pragmatism). It also describes the works of individual philosophers and the main fields in philosophy (logic, metaphysics, ethics, aesthetics, epistemology).

Some of the contributors are well known and respected scholars in the field—A. J. Ayer, Ernest Nagel, Gilbert Ryle.

There are black and white and color plates of famous philosophers from Aristotle to Bertrand Russell.

Short, selected bibliographies appear at the back.

METHOD OF ORGANIZATION: Arranged alphabetically, from ancient Greece to the present.

USEFULNESS: Don't expect more than a few short paragraphs or a few pages at most for any subject.

Useful for a brief introduction to and explanation of important technical terms, figures, movements, and fields in western philosophy. Good short biographical sketches.

RELATED REFERENCE WORKS: For a full treatment of the subject, see *The Encyclopedia of Philosophy*. (our no. 161).

161] *Encyclopedia of Philosophy*

New York: Macmillan, 1967. 8 vols.
Ed. by Paul Edwards.

CONTENTS: This work covers the whole of philosophy—ancient, medieval, renaissance, modern, eastern, western—as well as the "theories of mathematicians, physicists, biologists, sociologists, psychologists, moral reformers, and religious thinkers where these have an impact on philosophy."

Clear, authoritative, comprehensive, and well-written, the nearly 1,500 articles (900 are devoted to individuals), signed by some of the best scholars in the field, range from a half page on Albert of Saxony to a 52-page, detailed treatment of the history of logic.

Excellent bibliographies appear at the end of each article.

METHOD OF ORGANIZATION: Arranged alphabetically from Abbagnano, Nicola, to Zubiri, Xavier.

Volume 8 has a 157-page index, extremely detailed yet easy to use.

USEFULNESS: The best encyclopedia on the subject in English, it supplies information in a clear and authoritative manner on every aspect of philosophy, from individuals to movements.

The bibliographies are of immense help for further reading.

EXAMPLES: The range of the subjects chosen is vast. To show the scope, here are some article titles, chosen at random:

The History of Aesthetics, Alienation, Analogy in Theology, Any and All, Pierre Bayle, Being, British Philosophy, Greek Drama, Humanism, Indexical Signs, Egocentric Particulars, Suicide, Teleological Argument for the Existence of God.

162] *Dictionary of Philosophy and Psychology*

New York: The Macmillan Co., 1901–1905. 3 vols.
Ed. by James M. Baldwin.

CONTENTS: Much more of an encyclopedia than a dictionary, this work, so obviously dated, contains brief, interesting, and informative articles. Most of them are about 300 words long, but a few special articles on movements range from 1,000 to 5,000 words; they cover philosophy, logic, ethics, psychology, philology, biology, economics, law, philosophy of religion, education, and aesthetics.

All articles are signed, some of them by such eminent philosophers as Charles Peirce, G. E. Moore, and John Dewey.

METHOD OF ORGANIZATION: Arranged alphabetically.

Vols. 1 and 2 make up the dictionary itself. Vol. 3, divided into two parts, is devoted to bibliography and glossaries of philosophical terms in English, French, German, and Italian.

USEFULNESS: A major reference work for those interested in the development of philosophical terms, schools, movements, and fields, from the historical point of view.

Short, factual biographical sketches are included.

Two excellent features of this work are: (1) a detailed account of the etymology of every entry, and (2) a comprehensive bibliography of the works of philosophers up to the date of publication. Also contains bibliographies of works in all the fields covered in the volumes.

163] *A History of Philosophy*

New York: Image Books, Doubleday & Co., 1960–1964.
7 vols. By Frederick Copleston, S. J.

CONTENTS: Scholarly, accurate, and well-written, this work traces the history of western philosophy from the earliest Greek philosophers, the Ionians, to Friedrich Nietzsche.

Short bibliographies appear at the end of each volume.

METHOD OF ORGANIZATION: In seven volumes:

Vol. I, Greece and Rome; vol. II, Medieval Philosophy, Augustine to Scotus; vol. III, Late Medieval and Renaissance Philosophy, Ockham to Suárez; vol. IV, Modern Philosophy, Descartes to Leibniz; vol. V, Modern Philosophers—The British Philosophers, Hobbes to Hume; vol. VI, Modern Philosophy. The French Enlightenment and Kant; vol. VII, Modern Philosophy, Fichte to Nietzsche.

USEFULNESS: One of the most detailed and comprehensive histories of philosophy available in English. Especially good on Plato, Aristotle, the medieval philosophers, continental rationalism in the seventeenth century, and Kant.

Do, however, keep in mind the point of view maintained throughout—"the interplay of philosophical currents in Christian thought for over fifteen centuries."

EXAMPLES: Professor Copleston's treatment of Plato will show the kind of detail, scope, and depth the reader can expect in all seven volumes.

Out of the 517 pages in the volume on Greece and Rome, 136 are devoted to Plato, to an account of his life, his work (genuineness, chronology, Socratic period, middle period, transition period, period of maturity, works of old age), his theory of knowledge, psychology, and the doctrine of forms, his moral theory, and his theory of the state of physics and of art. There is also a short note on his influence.

164] *International Bibliography of Political Science/Bibliographie Internationale de Science Politique*

Paris: UNESCO, 1953—. Annual.

CONTENTS: One of the four major publications by UNESCO for the social science disciplines (the other three are *International Bibliography of Sociology* [our no. 187], *International Bibliography of Economics* [our no. 83], *International Bibliography of Social and Cultural Anthropology* [our no. 69]), this extensive yet selective annual bibliography lists between 4,000 and 5,000 books, magazine articles, and national and international documents on political science and fields related to it (e.g. law, history) published in most of the languages of the world.

Titles other than in English or French are translated into English only.

METHOD OF ORGANIZATION: Each annual is divided into six categories: Political Science; Political Thought; Government and Public Administration; Government Process; International Relations; Area Studies.

Entries under each category are arranged alphabetically by author.

Author and subject index at the back.

There are no cumulations.

USEFULNESS: An invaluable source for tracking down books, reviews, articles, and documents in political science and disciplines related to it.

EXAMPLES:

Heald (M.M.). *A free society: an evaluation of contemporary society.* New York, Philosophical Library, 53, 546 p.
Czerny (W.F.). "Der Parlamentarismus der ersten und zweiten Republik" (Parliamentarism in the first and second republics), Österr. M.H. [name of magazine] Apr. 53:219–224.

RELATED REFERENCE WORKS: For brief summaries of many of the articles listed in this bibliography, consult *International Political Science Abstracts* (our no. 165), a quarterly printed in English and French, where English articles are summarized in English, those of other languages in French.

165] *International Political Science Abstracts/ Documentation Politique Internationale*

Oxford: Basil Blackwell, 1951—. Prepared by the
International Political Science Association in cooperation
with UNESCO and the International Committee for
Social Science Documentation. Quarterly with annual vols.

CONTENTS: This quarterly abstracts articles selected from over 90 periodicals published in about 15 countries in Europe, South America, and Asia. The abstracts vary in length from 50 to 250 words, and are printed in either English or French. In the 1951 volume, articles in English are always abstracted in French; articles in any other language are abstracted in English. In all other volumes, all articles in English are abstracted in English; articles in other languages are abstracted in French.

Titles in English remain in English; titles in French remain in French; titles in all other languages are translated into English and French.

There are annual accumulations.

METHOD OF ORGANIZATION: In six large sections: Political Science; Political Theory; Government and Public Administration; Government Process; International Relations; Area Studies. Each section is arranged alphabetically by author. Cumulative annual author and subject index at the back of each volume.

EXAMPLES:

Hurwicz (E.)—*Zur Psychologie und Problematik des Russischen Judentums* (On the Psychology and Problems of Russian Judaism/ Psychologie et Problematique du Judaïsme en Russie). Z Polit. [Name of Periodical] 8 (3), 1961:256–270.

L'Histoire des Juifs en Russie passe par des hautes et des bas. De 1860, qui marque l'origine des rêves vite déçus d'émancipation, jusqu'à 1917, ou s'annonce une ère nouvelle, le judaïsme russe est remarquable par sa vitalité et une résistance exceptionnelle à l'assimilation. Le sionisme n'a pas pu contribuer à rendre leur dignité à des hommes destinés à n'être que des citoyens de second ordre, sans pour autant les détacher de la Russie et de sa culture. A partir de 1917, l'assimilation fit des progrès, et l'on vit peu à peu disparaître le judaïsme russe, si important pour la culture juive.

USEFULNESS: Extremely valuable reference work because it enables readers to keep up with periodical scholarship throughout the world. Therefore indispensable if one wants (1) a summary of important articles and (2) a bibliographical guide to the field of your interest.

166] *U.S. Congress: Official Congressional Directory*

Washington, D.C.: Government Printing Office, 1809—. Biennial.

CONTENTS: These detailed volumes include, among the thousands and thousands of entries, "biographical sketches of members of Congress arranged by state; state delegations; terms of service; committees and commissions; sessions of Congress; governors of states; votes cast for congressmen; biographical sketches of cabinet members and a list of officials in each department; biographies of members of the Supreme Court and a list of courts; officials of independent agencies; international organization delegations; foreign and U.S. diplomatic officers;

press galleries; maps of congressional districts; and an index of individuals."

METHOD OF ORGANIZATION: Detailed table of contents and individual index, alphabetically arranged.

USEFULNESS: Indispensable for detailed information about Congress and the names of individuals and organizations, either governmental or private, associated with it.

RELATED REFERENCE WORKS: *Congressional Staff Directory*, ed. by Charles B. Brownson (Washington: Government Printing Office, 1959—), contains listing of Congressional staffs, committees, subcommittees, and names of important officials of major cities. Biographical sketches included.

United States Government Organization Manual (Washington: Government Printing Office, 1935—) contains information on the organization, activities, and employees of different department and agencies in Washington. Good descriptions of selected international organizations.

167] *United States National Archives: Federal Register*

Washington, D.C.: Government Printing Office, 1936—.

CONTENTS: This is the most important reference source for U.S. Government regulations "having the force of law." It contains all presidential proclamations, all executive orders, and the rules and regulations of the various bureaus and departments of the three branches of the government.

METHOD OF ORGANIZATION: Arranged chronologically. Issued daily except Sunday, Monday, and days following holidays, with monthly indexes cumulating every three months and annually.

USEFULNESS: Best source for full text of presidential proclamations and executive orders.

RELATED REFERENCE WORKS: *United States Laws, Statutes, etc.* (New York: Edward Thompson Company, 1942—) contains most public laws (complete texts), executive orders, presidential proclamations, administrative regulations, presidential messages. Latest issues carry digest of bills passed.

United States Laws, Statutes, etc. Index to the Federal Statutes [1789–1873, 1874–1931] general and permanent law. (Washington: U. S. Government Printing Office). All federal legislation of importance to the public is indexed in two volumes.

168] *United States Congress: Congressional Record*

Washington, D.C.: Government Printing Office, 1873—.
Daily.

CONTENTS: "Issued daily while Congress is in session," revised and issued in permanent form at the end of each congressional session, this indispensable publication contains all presidential messages, all speeches made in Congress, all debates in full, and the voting record of every congressman and senator. Only the texts of bills are excluded.

METHOD OF ORGANIZATION: Arranged chronologically from the first to the last day of each session, and paged continuously though bound in many volumes. Bi-weekly index plus final index volume to the permanent edition.

The index is divided into two parts: (1) alphabetical index of names and subjects; (2) history of each bill arranged by bill number. Part two of this index "is the best source for full information about a bill because it gives you page references to everything in the *Record* about the bill from its introduction to its final passage and signing."

USEFULNESS: This is the work to consult for (1) an accurate, detailed account of the everyday happenings in Congress, and (2) the history of a bill or a particular piece of legislation.

RELATED REFERENCE WORKS: For material before 1873 consult the following works: *Annals of Congress*, 1789–1824; *Register of Debates*, 1824–1837; *Congressional Globe*, 1833–1873.

169] *Municipal Year Book*

Chicago: International City Managers Association, 1934—.
Annual.

CONTENTS: This annual is an accurate, highly detailed account, sometimes in essays but most often in the form of statistical tables, of the "current activities and practices of cities throughout the United States. Although the emphasis is on statistics for individual city programs, considerable attention also is given to developments in urban counties and metropolitan areas. Bibliographies in subject fields and comprehensive directories of officials provide additional reference information."

METHOD OF ORGANIZATION: Divided into five parts: Governmental Units, Municipal Personnel, Municipal Finance, Municipal Activities, Directories of Officials.

USEFULNESS: This provides information on the current problems of cities, with facts and statistics on individual city activities, and with analyses of trends by population groups.

EXAMPLES: The five parts in the 1966 volume cover such subjects as population change in American cities, 1960–1965; federal–city relations in 1965; governmental data for cities over 5,000 population for every state; salaries of municipal officials; municipal personnel data (education, union affiliation, grievance procedure); public purchasing; trends in municipal finance; planning and zoning; public health; police administration; schools and education; and municipal law courts.

RELATED REFERENCE WORKS: *Municipal Year Book and Public Utilities Directory* (London: Municipal Journal, 1897—) is the English equivalent of our *Municipal Year Book*. Among other things it includes articles on all phases of English local government: finance, power, roads, education, parks, public health, town planning, water supply; a list of associations and societies concerned with local government; information about municipal corporations with lists of offices, county and district councils, etc.

Book of the States (Chicago: Council of State Governments, 1935—). (See our no. 170).

170] *Book of the States*

Chicago: Council of State Governments, 1935—. Biennial.

CONTENTS: Issued in the spring of even-numbered years, with supplements in odd-numbered years, this manual provides information in the form of general articles, signed and unsigned, and statistical charts, on every important aspect of state government—constitutions and elections, legislatures and legislation, the judiciary, administrative organization, finance, intergovernmental relations, and major state services.

METHOD OF ORGANIZATION: Arranged by categories.
Supplements between issues list all state officials and members of the legislatures.

USEFULNESS: Extremely useful for "comprehensive information on the work of the state governments and convenient current directories of the men and women, both elected and appointed, who comprise them."

EXAMPLES: The material here is detailed, accurate, and of immense variety. One can find information on polling hours during elections; the use of voting machines; names of governors and party affiliations; length of term and number of previous terms; breakdown of state revenues; major state services including detailed account of education, highways, health and welfare, corrections, defense and public protection; and the nickname, motto, flower, bird, song, and date of entry into the Union of all 50 states.

171] *An Encyclopaedia of Parliament*

London: Cassell and Co., Ltd., 1958.
Ed. by Norman Wilding and Laundy Philip.

CONTENTS: This is a reliable, well-written book with over 1,800 entries, ranging from a few lines to a 9,500-word article entitled *Parliament,* on the history and function of the English Parliament and most terms associated with it, from the thirteenth century to the present. It does not include biographical entries under the names of statesmen and politicians, "which are readily available in other works of reference. Where the activities of such people concern parliamentary history they are dealt with in the historical articles. Personal entries are confined to those individuals who have in some way been directly concerned with the creation and growth of the powers, privileges, and precedents of Parliament or who have influenced its customs and procedure." The student will, therefore, find nothing on Churchill, but a good deal on Oliver Cromwell.

METHOD OF ORGANIZATION: Arranged alphabetically. No index.

USEFULNESS: This is the work to consult for brief descriptions of any aspect of Parliament; that is, its history, procedure, function, and administration. It also has a good bibliography and an appendix that includes such useful items as the "Parliaments of England, Great Britain, and the United Kingdom from 1213 to 1955, Lord Chancellors and Keepers of the Great Seal, Presiding Officers and Speakers of the House of Commons, Secretaries of State for Air, for the Colonies, and for War."

EXAMPLES: One will find entries here for Big Ben, Cabinet, Catching the Speaker's Eye, Coalition, Fourth Clerk-At-The-Table, Gentleman Usher of the Black Rod, George III (1738–1820) and Parliament, Kitchen Committee, Mace, Mad Parliament, Point of Order, Protest Book, Running Parliament, Speaker, Strangers, Ten O'Clock Rule, and Zinoviev Letter, among the many others.

172] *Yearbook of the United Nations*

New York: United Nations and Columbia University Press, 1946/47—. Annual.

CONTENTS: This annual provides a continuing historical account of the complex and numerous endeavors of the United

Nations by giving the reader, concisely and conveniently, a record of activities of its 13 specialized agencies during the year covered. The various subjects in each volume "—political and security questions, economic and social questions, trusteeship, legal questions, administrative questions—are treated in detailed essays to which are appended documentary references and in many cases the test of and the vote on the relevant resolutions. Information of a more general nature is provided for the specialized agencies." The yearbook also has a roster of the members, the charter and structure of the U.N., the matters considered by the principal bodies of the U.N., the delegations to the General Assembly and the Councils, and a list of U.N. information centers and offices.

METHOD OF ORGANIZATION: Divided into two parts. Part one deals with the United Nations; part two deals with the intergovernmental organizations related to the U.N.

There is a detailed index of persons, countries, and subjects.

USEFULNESS: An excellent source to consult for a survey of the main activities of the U.N. and its 13 specialized agencies for a particular year.

EXAMPLES: The 1965 volume treats such subjects as:

The Peaceful Uses of Outer Space; Questions Concerning the Uses of Atomic Energy; The Situation in Cypress; Questions Relating to the Middle East; Narcotic Drugs; Territories Under Portuguese Administration; Treaties and Multilateral Conventions; Development of Private International Law to Promote International Trade; and others.

RELATED REFERENCE WORKS: *Everyman's United Nations,* 7th edition (New York: United Nations Department of Public Information, 1964), contains sections on the organization of the United Nations, its work in political, economic, social, and administrative areas, and the specialized agencies which make up the United Nations and UNESCO.

II. J.
PSYCHOLOGY

173] *The Index of Psychoanalytic Writings*

New York: International University Press, 1956–1966. 9 vols.
Ed. by Alexander Grinstead.

CONTENTS: This is a 9-volume revision and a bringing up to
date of John Rickman's *Index Psychoanalyticus 1900–1926.*

Lists close to 50,000 articles, books, monographs, and reviews on psychoanalysis and selected subjects related to it,
published from 1900–1959 in English, German, French, Spanish, Italian, Norwegian, Swedish, Danish, Finnish, Dutch,
Czech, Hungarian, Polish, Russian, Hebrew, Portugese, Greek,
Japanese, Hindi, and Arabic. Titles are printed in the original
language and followed by the English translation.

All of Freud's works, known or available at present, including the non-psychological writings, have been included.

METHOD OF ORGANIZATION: Vols. 1–4 and 6–8 are arranged alphabetically by author. Vols. 5 and 9, each over 500 pages, are
a detailed subject index.

USEFULNESS: Indispensable for locating writings on psychoanalysis—articles, books, monographs, reviews, abstracts—and
subjects related to it.

EXAMPLES: The scope of this index is great. The student will
find literature not only on every aspect of psychoanalysis itself,
but on such related subjects as Balzac's love life, Baudelaire's
incest complex, Beethoven and his nephew, the *Mona Lisa* and
feminine beauty, black magic, civilian defense and psychiatry,
Fascism in France, ritual defloration and virginity, and countless other subjects related to psychoanalysis.

RELATED REFERENCE WORKS: For abstracts of many works listed here see *Psychological Abstracts* (our no. 175).

174] *Psychological Index*

Princeton, N.J.: The Psychological Review Co., 1894–1935. 42 vols. Annual.

CONTENTS: This annual index listed "original publications in all languages, both books and periodical articles, together with translations and new editions in English, French, German, and Italian. . . ." About 5,000 titles each year were listed, and about 350 periodicals indexed.

The *Psychological Index* ceased publication in 1935; its work is carried on by *Psychological Abstracts* (our no. 175).

METHOD OF ORGANIZATION: Each volume is classified by subject (for instance, General; Nervous System; Sensation and Perception; Feeling and Emotion; Attention, Memory, and Thought, etc.).

An author index appears at the back of each volume. There is no subject index.

The list of the principal periodicals indexed, with abbreviations used, is given in volume 30.

USEFULNESS: This is the work to consult for an index to writings in psychology found in books and periodicals from 1894–1935. Unlike *Psychological Abstracts,* however, it does not give abstracts of the works listed. Should the reader want abstracts of entries in volumes 1–35 of the *Index,* he must consult H. L. Ansbacher's 2-vol. *Psychological Index: Abstract References* (Columbus, Ohio: American Psychological Association, 1940–1941).

EXAMPLES:

General Textbooks and Systematic Treatises
1. Allers, R. The New Psychologies. New York: Sheed & Ward, 1933. Pp. xx + 81.
2. Bechterev, V. M. General Principles of Human Reflexology: An Introduction to the Objective Study of Per-

sonality. (Trans. by E. & W. Murphy.) New York: Int. Publishers, 1933. Pp. 467.

175] *Psychological Abstracts*

Lancaster, Pa.: American Psychological Association, 1927—. Monthly, with annual cumulations.

CONTENTS: This monthly is one of the truly important reference works in psychology (it is absolutely indispensable after 1935 because the *Psychological Index* [our no. 174] ceased publication in that year).

It lists new books and articles in English and foreign languages with signed abstracts in English (descriptive summaries without any evaluation), usually about 100 words long, of each work listed.

There are annual accumulations.

METHOD OF ORGANIZATION: Each monthly issue is organized by subjects—General, Methodology and Research Technology, Experimental Psychology, Animal Psychology, Social Psychology, for instance.

A subject and author index appears at the back. For the subject index for 1927–1960, see the 2-vol. *Cumulated Subject Index to Psychological Abstracts 1927–1960* (Boston: G. K. Hall & Co., 1966).

USEFULNESS: This is the work the reader should consult if he wants to know what books and articles on psychology are being published each month and what these books and articles are about.

EXAMPLES: Here is a sample entry:

Bluestone, Harvey; O'Malley, Edward P., & Connell, Sydney. Homosexuals in Prison. Corrective Psychiatry & Journal of Social Therapy, 1966, 13–24.—The male and female homosexual in prison cannot be treated with a view toward conversion to heterosexuality but rather with a view toward abstinence from criminal behavior, improvement in interpersonal relationship, increase in work capacity, treatment for drug addiction, and reduction in overt psychiatric symptoms. Post-institutional programs to complement short-term municipal correctional settings should be instituted. 5 female case histories and demographic data on 31 male cases are presented.—C.T. Gaza.

176] A Comprehensive Dictionary of Psychological and Psychoanalytical Terms

London: Longmans, Green and Co., 1958.
Ed. by Horace B. and Ava C. English.

CONTENTS: This dictionary includes over 11,000 terms and concepts used in a special or technical sense by psychologists, psychoanalysts, and psychiatrists.

The definitions are always brief (this is a defining dictionary, not an encyclopedic compilation of facts) and strictly current. No illustrative quotations here, no definitions from the historical point of view, and no derivations.

METHOD OF ORGANIZATION: Alphabetical.

USEFULNESS: A good dictionary for brief, accurate, current terms used in psychology. Many of the definitions range from 10 to 20 words.

EXAMPLES: Many of the terms and concepts in the *Psychiatric Dictionary* (our no. 177) are here, but the student will also find thousands particular to psychology and psychoanalysis, such as: child development; childhood; child marriage; conditioned response; feeding problem; gestalt; group dynamics; learning curve; personnel; readability—and countless others.

RELATED REFERENCE WORKS: A *Dictionary of Psychology* by James Drever, revised by Harvey Wallerstein (Baltimore: Penguin, 1964), is a good, small dictionary with concise definitions of about 4,000 terms.

177] *Psychiatric Dictionary*

New York: Oxford University Press, 3rd ed., 1960.
Ed. by L. E. Hinsie and R. J. Campbell.

CONTENTS:　This dictionary defines about 8,000 important psychiatric "terms and concepts used during the span of time approximately since Hippocrates up to our own days."
Authoritative, usually brief (most of the definitions are no more than a few hundred words long; many, however, are encyclopedic in length and detail), and with illustrative quotations used to add vital meaning and give historical perspective to a term, this reference work includes not only psychiatric but also terms "in allied fields—clinical neurology, constitutional medicine, genetics and eugenics, mental deficiency, forensic psychiatry, social service, nursing and occupational therapy."
Each term is accompanied by its derivation.

METHOD OF ORGANIZATION:　Alphabetical.

USEFULNESS:　One of the best of the psychiatric dictionaries because the scholarship, presentation, and perspective have made "it possible for the reader to gain appreciation of the historical development of psychiatric nomenclature and to grasp more clearly the meaning of old and new scientific achievements in the field."

EXAMPLES:　There is good variety, scope, and depth in this dictionary: aggression; aichmophobia; anal character; birth trauma; compulsion; constitutional; autopsychic delusion; dream; echopraxia; hypertonia; insanity, neologism; paranoia; psychosis; sexuality; symptom; transference; unconscious wish —are some of the terms here.

RELATED REFERENCE WORKS:　*A Psychiatric Glossary*, 2nd edition (Washington: American Psychiatric Association, 1964), contains close to 700 terms. Definitions are clear and concise.

178] *Mental Health Book Review Index*

Flushing, New York: Queens College, 1956—. Annual.

CONTENTS: An annual index to signed book reviews in the field of mental health in about 235 periodicals in the English language.

Each yearly volume lists about 300 books, some translated from foreign languages, "with references to three or more reviews; at least one of the reviews cited is from a journal in the psychological sciences: psychology, psychiatry, and psychoanalysis."

METHOD OF ORGANIZATION: Arranged alphabetically by author. No subject index.

There are no cumulations.

USEFULNESS: Extremely useful for finding reviews of important books in the psychological sciences, and of related books in the humanities (e.g., Arthur Koestler's *The Act of Creation*).

EXAMPLES: Here is a sample entry—the reviews of the book *Beyond All Reason:*

Coate, Morag, pseud. *Beyond All Reason.*
[An Autobiographical Account of the Illness and Recovery of a Schizophrenic Patient.] With an Introduction by R. D. Laing. London, Constable, 1964; Philadelphia, Lippincott, 1965, c 1964. 227 p. 4.95; 215
Aust. J. Psychol., 1965
Brit. J. Med. Psychol., 1965
Brit. J. Psychiat., 1965
Case Comf., 1964/65
Ment. Hlth. Lond., 1964

II. K.

RELIGION

179] *Encyclopaedia of Religion and Ethics*

New York: Scribner's, 1908–1927. 13 vols.
Ed. by James Hastings, *et al.*

CONTENTS: A comprehensive encyclopedia; signed articles
dealing with "all the religions of the world and all the great
systems of ethics," and a variety of subjects related to the fields
of theology and philosophy.

Extensive but dated bibliographies are appended to most articles. The last volume is an index.

METHOD OF ORGANIZATION: Alphabetical. Besides relatively
short articles defining terms or identifying names or places, the
encyclopedia contains many long sections on general subjects,
which contain clusters of subarticles in which the same subject
is treated as it applies to the various religions or cultural re-
gions.

Vol. XIII, the index, contains a list of article titles and an
exhaustive subject index. This is useful not only as a means
of quickly locating a specific reference, but also as a reading
and study guide.

USEFULNESS: A thorough and extremely scholarly work. Excellent for comparative study of the world's religions; also good
for philosophical subjects. Although the work could be used for
quick consultations, it is best suited for more exhaustive study.

EXAMPLES: Here are a few of the article titles, chosen at random, found listed under the first letter of the alphabet: Aban-
donment and Exposure; Abbot (Christian); Abbot (Tibetan);

Abiogenesis; Aborigines; Achaemenians; Achilles; Adoption; Adultery; Aeschylus; Aesthetics; Agape; Agnosticism; Ahiqar, Story of; Air and Gods of the Air; Akbar; Albigenses; Alchemy; Algonquins; Ambrose of Milan; Anabaptism; Anger (Psychological and Ethical); Anger (Wrath) of God; Anthropomorphism; Arthurian Cycle; Arya Samaj; Assassins; Atavism; Atomic Theory; St. Augustine; Avesta; Axiom. The individual articles are relatively long; most run to two or three pages; some run to chapter-length.

RELATED REFERENCE WORKS: *An Encyclopedia of Religion* (our no. 180). Those interested in non-Christian religions might want to consult the specialized encyclopedias or dictionaries in those areas, e.g., *The Encyclopaedia of Islam,* ed. by B. Lewis, *et al.* (Leiden: Brill, 1959); *A Dictionary of Chinese Buddhist Terms,* ed. by W. E. Soothill and L. Hodus (London: Kegan, 1937). Also see *Mythology of All Races* (our no. 141). J. G. Barrow's *Bibliography of Bibliographies in Religion* is an exhaustive index, useful for specialists.

180] *An Encyclopedia of Religion*

New York: Philosophical Library, 1945.
Ed. by Vergilius Ferm.

CONTENTS: A one-volume, desk-size dictionary with brief articles on the major religions of the world—Christianity, Judaism, Mohammedanism, Confucianism, Taoism, and others—"with special attention to Biblical literature and Christian theology."

Signed articles deal with the theologies of the major religions, denominations and cults, ecclesiastical history, customs, sacred books, related topics, and biographies of important religious figures. There are brief, selected bibliographies for further study.

METHOD OF ORGANIZATION: Alphabetical. Generous cross references.

USEFULNESS: A ready reference work for quick identifications and concise, simple definitions.

EXAMPLES: To show the wide range of the dictionary, here is a sample list of article titles, chosen at random: Abbess, Allah, All Soul's Day, American Lutheranism, Ancestor Worship, Babylonian Captivity, Baptism, Buddhahood, Catherine of Sienna, Charity, Child Marriage, Chinese Religions, Christmas, Church of England, Confession, Confucius, Crusades, Dante, Darwin, Death and Burial Practices, Deism, Eastern Orthodox Churches, Fatalism, Father Divine, Fish as Symbol, Freemasonry, Hinduism, Human Sacrifices, Hume, Imprimatur, Infallibility, Inquisition, Kant, Koran, Lent, Logos, Loki, Lord's Prayer, Mahdi, Methodism, Midrash, Mutilation, Omniscience, Parochial Schools, Passover, Paul the Apostle, Peter the Hermit, Predestination, Presbyterian Church, Puritanism, Ramadan, Satan, Socialism, Swedenborg, Theosophy, Torah, Tower of Babel, Vedas, Virgin Birth, Vishnu, Zoroastrianism. Most articles are short, paragraph-length to one page.

RELATED REFERENCE WORKS: For a more scholarly and thorough treatment of the subject, see the *Encyclopaedia of Religion and Ethics* (our no. 179).

181] *New Schaff-Herzog Encyclopedia of Religious Knowledge*

New York: Funk, 1908–1912. 12 vols. Ed. by Philip Schaff and Samuel M. Jackson, *et al.* (Vol. XIII, *Index*, by George W. Gilmore; Grand Rapids, Mich.: Baker Book House, 1950.)

CONTENTS: A compilation of articles dealing principally with every aspect of the Christian religion, from a Protestant point of view. Signed articles by scholars and specialists deal with church history, ritual, religious philosophy and theory (not only of the various Protestant sects, but also of the Catholic and other western religions), major Biblical figures, church notables, and related topics, such as social and cultural background. Bibliographies and indexes are supplied.

METHOD OF ORGANIZATION: Alphabetical, from "Aachen, Synods of" to "Zwingli." Scholarly, though dated, bibliographies are appended to most articles in the original 12 volumes.

Readers are advised to consult vol. XIII the *Index,* first, in order to quickly and fully utilize the first 12 volumes of the encyclopedia.

The original volumes of the work are brought up to date by two supplementary volumes, *Twentieth Century Encyclopedia of Religious Knowledge,* ed. by Lefferts A. Loetscher (Grand Rapids, Mich.: Baker Book House, 1950 and 1955). These books contain articles, arranged alphabetically, supplementing the basic articles of the same titles in the original volumes, adding twentieth century developments, plus articles on new subjects, and bibliographies of recent studies, mainly of American origin. They are not indexed.

USEFULNESS: The best-known and most authoritative encyclopedia of Christianity, written from a Protestant point of view. The main volumes, based on a famous nineteenth century German work, emphasize subjects dealing with the continent of Europe. The supplementary volumes bring the encyclopedia up to date and provide modern bibliographies for further study.

EXAMPLES: Here are a few of the article titles, chosen at random, found listed under the first letter of the alphabet: Aaron; Abbey; Ablutions of the Mass; Abrasax; Acta Martyrum; Acta Sanctorum; Adam; Adamites; Adoptionism; Adrian; Advent; Agenda; Agnosticism; Agricola, Johann; Alsace-Lorraine; Altar; Amarna Tablets; Amulet; Amyrant, Moise; Anabaptists; Angel; Animals; Annihilationism; Antinomianism; Antitrinitarianism; Apocrypha; Apologetics; Asylum, Rights of; Athanasian Creed; Atonement; Augsburg Confession and its Apology. The individual articles vary in length from paragraph-long items to chapter-length articles (e.g., 20 pages on Africa).

182] *New Catholic Encyclopedia*

New York: McGraw-Hill, 1967. 15 vols. Prepared by
an editorial staff at the Catholic University of America,
William J. McDonald, ed. in chief.

CONTENTS: A compilation of authoritative articles dealing
with every aspect of the Catholic Church, its teachings, history,
organization, and activities throughout the world. The more
than 17,000 signed articles include selected bibliographies.
Many illustrations and maps are provided, and there is an
index volume.

The encyclopedia is not limited to ecclesiastical matters, but
includes general articles (e.g., on American literature) as well
as articles on "persons, institutions, religions, philosophies, scientific developments, and movements that have affected Catholicism." The treatment of all subjects "reflects a Catholic
sense of values."

METHOD OF ORGANIZATION: Alphabetical. Vol. 15 contains the
encyclopedia's detailed, analytical index.

USEFULNESS: The best place to check on questions of Catholic
doctrine and history. Because of its recent publication, the encyclopedia presents a modern view of Catholicism, reflecting
"the ecumenical spirit of the day."

EXAMPLES: Among the numerous subjects treated are the following: Catholic dogma, Church history of each country, history of missionary efforts, canon law, church-State relations,
Catholic social work, Catholic literature and press, Catholic education, art and music, philosophy, relation of physical sciences
to Christian life, biographies of deceased figures (works of living figures are discussed in pertinent articles—see index). The
individual articles vary in length, from a paragraph-length item
on Anchorites to a chapter-length article on St. Augustine.

RELATED REFERENCE WORKS: The work is a successor to the old
Catholic Encyclopedia (New York: Gilmary Society, 1907–
1914, 1922, 1950–1954).

Those wishing only quick and brief information can consult
the one-volume *A Catholic Dictionary,* ed. by Donald Attwater
(New York: Macmillan, 3rd. ed., 1958).

183] *Universal Jewish Encyclopedia*

New York: Universal Jewish Encyclopedia, Inc., 1939–1944.
11 vols. Ed. by Isaac Landman, *et al.*

CONTENTS: A multivolume "presentation of Jews and Judaism since the earliest times," containing more than 10,000 articles on Jewish history, religion, culture, and customs, as well as numerous biographical sketches. Articles are signed, and in many cases provide selected bibliographies for further study. Many illustrations.

METHOD OF ORGANIZATION: Alphabetical, from Aaron to Zweig, Stefan.

Vol. 11, *A Reading Guide and Index,* is more of a reading guide than an index, presenting the student with 100 outlines for reading. The major articles of the encyclopedia are classified and grouped under seven headings: History; Literature; Religion; Jewish Life; Jews and Non-Jews; General Subjects; Jewish Contributions to Civilization. A student looking for information about a particular subject (e.g., Jewish violinists, or Jewish history in New England) will be referred to the appropriate individual articles in the encyclopedia.

USEFULNESS: The most up-to-date multivolume reference work on Jewish history, religion, lore, and culture. Thorough, yet easy to read. Excellent coverage of American topics.

EXAMPLES: Here are a few article titles, chosen at random, found listed under the first letter of the alphabet: Ab, Fifteenth of; Abelard, Abinu Malkenu; Ablutions; Adler, Alfred; Adoption; Adultery; Africa; Afternoon Service; Aged, Care of; Aliyah; Alphabet; Amen; American Jewish Committee; American Literature on and by Jews; Anathema; Angels; Anger; Aqueducts in Palestine; Ark of Noah; Asch, Sholom; Assimilation; Athletics; Atonement. The individual articles vary in length from a paragraph-long article on Abraham's Bosom to a chapter-length article on Anti-Semitism.

RELATED REFERENCE WORKS: Another multivolume work, more scholarly in its treatment but somewhat dated, is the *Jewish Encyclopedia,* ed. by Isidore Singer, *et al.* (New York: Funk & Wagnalls, 1901–1906).

For quick reference, consult *The Standard Jewish Encyclopedia,* ed. by Cecil Roth (Garden City: Doubleday, 1959); this one-volume work treats the subject accurately and concisely. It is also useful as a supplement to the multi-volume works of earlier date.

184] *The Interpreter's Dictionary of the Bible*

New York: Abingdon Press, 1962. 4 vols.
Ed. by George A. Buttrick, *et al.*

CONTENTS: Identifications and explanations of "all proper names, significant terms, and subjects in Holy Scriptures, including the Apocrypha." Articles are written and signed by experts; brief biographies for further study are included. Many illustrations—pictures, maps, and charts.

METHOD OF ORGANIZATION: Alphabetical. Numerous cross references. No index.

USEFULNESS: A good place to check on Biblical references, to obtain interpretations, and to acquaint oneself with the latest findings in Bible studies.

EXAMPLES: For each name, term, or subject listed, the following information is given: pronunciation (when needed), the Hebrew or Aramaic or Greek original and its root meaning if known, followed by an identification and explanation. References, unless otherwise indicated, are to the Revised Standard Version of the Bible.

Most entries are short, from one paragraph to a page; but some articles run to essay length, e.g., 6 pages on Abraham, 13 pages on Acts of the Apostles, 12 pages on Government, 27 pages on Jesus Christ, 10 pages on Moses, 13 pages on Love, 6 pages on Song of Songs, 11 pages on Tribes, 34 pages on Versions of the Scriptures.

RELATED REFERENCE WORKS: Among other well-known Bible dictionaries are the *Catholic Biblical Encyclopedia,* ed. by John

E. Steinmueller and K. Sullivan (New York: Wagner, 1956), and a recently revised one-volume edition of James Hastings' *Dictionary of the Bible,* ed. by Frederick C. Grant and H. H. Rowley (New York: Scribner, 1963).

There are, of course, numerous Biblical commentaries, e.g., *Peake's Commentary on the Bible,* ed. by Matthew Black and H. H. Rowley (New York: Nelson, 1962); *A Catholic Commentary on Holy Scripture,* ed. by Bernard Orchard (New York: Nelson, 1953).

Also of interest are Burton Stevenson's *The Home Book of Bible Quotations* (New York: Harper, 1949), and the *Westminster Historical Atlas of the Bible,* ed. by George E. Wright and Floyd V. Filson (Phila.: Westminster Press, 1956).

185] *Butler's Lives of the Saints*

New York: Kenedy, 1956. 4 vols. Ed., rev., and
supplemented by Herbert Thurston and Donald Attwater.
(1st ed., 1756–1759.)

CONTENTS: Brief biographies of over 2,500 saints "who are either venerated liturgically in the Western church or whose names are generally familiar to Catholics of English speech."

Selected, annotated bibliographies are appended.

METHOD OF ORGANIZATION: Biographies appear under the days on which saints are commemorated, from January 1 to December 31; thus one either has to know the saint's feast day or consult the "General Index of Names" at the end of vol. IV before one can locate his biography.

USEFULNESS: Brief summaries of the lives of the major Christian saints.

Useful for checking literary or historical references.

EXAMPLES: The length of the average biography is one page, although some lives are given in one paragraph and others run to two pages or more—e.g., there are 8 pages on St. Augustine; 6 pages on St. Catherine of Siena; 6 pages on St. Ignatius of Loyola; 5 pages on St. Peter in the main entry (but note that the index lists more than one day associated with this saint, so there will be other entries).

RELATED REFERENCE WORKS: One-volume biographical dictionaries of saints, good for rapid consultation, are *A Biographical Dictionary of the Saints,* ed. by Frederick G. Holweck (St. Louis: Herder, 1924); and *The Book of Saints,* compiled by the Benedictine Monks of St. Augustine's Abbey, Ramsgate (New York: Crowell, 5th ed., 1966).

186] *Handbook of Denominations in the United States*

New York: Abingdon-Cokesbury, 4th ed., 1965.
Compiled by Frank S. Mead.

CONTENTS: Brief articles on over 250 religious denominations in the U.S.A., giving for each "a compact account of the history, doctrines, distinctive characteristics, organization and present status."

METHOD OF ORGANIZATION: Alphabetical, from "Adventists" to "Volunteers of America." But similar bodies are grouped together; e.g., the various Baptist denominations are listed under "Baptists." Consult the detailed table of contents, or the index, which lists religions, subjects, and names.

The book also has three appendixes: addresses of the headquarters of the various denominations; a table of church membership in the U.S.; a brief glossary of religious terms.

USEFULNESS: The handbook provides an up-to-date account of the numerous religious bodies; plans call for periodic revisions. The work attempts to be objective ("concerned only with factual truths"), comprehensive, and concise.

It is a good place to find a brief summary of the pertinent facts about a religious sect with which one is not too familiar.

EXAMPLES: Here are just a few of the denominations described: American Ethical Union; Black Muslims; Buddhist

Churches of America; Church of Christ, Scientist; Mormons; Russian Orthodox Church; Friends (Quakers); Jewish Congregations; Lutherans; Methodists; Salvation Army; Roman Catholic Church; Unitarians.

II. L.
SOCIOLOGY

187] *International Bibliography of Sociology*

London: Tavistock; and Chicago: Aldine (early volumes, Paris: UNESCO), 1952—. Annual; covers 1951—. Prepared by the International Sociological Association.

CONTENTS: A comprehensive annual bibliography of current publications—books, pamphlets, periodical articles—in sociology. The coverage is international. More than 5,000 items are listed in the latest volume.

No annotations. An index is provided.

METHOD OF ORGANIZATION: Since 1955, divided into six major sections: History & Organization of Social Studies; Theories & Methods of Sociology; Social Structure; Social Control & Communication; Social Change; and Social Problems & Social Policy. Then further divided by topics or geographic areas within each major section. In each subdivision, items are listed alphabetically by authors.

The index lists authors and subjects. References are to item numbers, not to pages.

USEFULNESS: The basic bibliographical tool in the field, listing all noteworthy publications of the year.

EXAMPLES: Here are two sample entries; the first a book, the second an article:

4640. **Dunne, G. H.** (ed.) *Poverty in plenty.* New York, P. J. Kenedy 64, 142 p.

2263. **Turner, R. H.** "Upward mobility and class values," *Soc. Probl.* 11(4), Spr. 64: 359–371.

Titles of works in languages other than English or French are cited in the original language, followed by an English translation. References to principal reviews of books are given, preceded by the symbol "CR:." For full titles of periodicals, see the "List of Periodicals Consulted" at the front of each volume.

RELATED REFERENCE WORKS: *Current Sociology*, a journal issued three times a year (London: Basil Blackwell, 1952—) is a companion work to the *Bibliography*. It should be consulted for its valuable *annotated* bibliographies.

Sociological Abstracts (our no. 188); *Public Affairs Information Service Bulletin* (our no. 89). Advanced students might want to consult the multivolume *London Bibliography of the Social Sciences* (London: School of Economics, 1931—).

188] *Sociological Abstracts*

New York: Sociological Abstracts, Inc., 1952—.
Published several times during the year (currently 8 issues annually). Ed. by Leo P. Chall.

CONTENTS: Abstracts—short summaries—of current books and periodical articles of interest to students of sociology. The coverage is international. Currently published eight times annually, approximately 5,000 items are now abstracted in a year.

METHOD OF ORGANIZATION: Summaries are grouped by 21 subject classifications (see the table of contents in each issue), from Methodology and Research Technology to Social Change and Economic Development to Urban Structures and Ecology to Social Problems and Social Welfare. These major subject areas are each divided into a number of subsections. The abstracts in each subsection are arranged alphabetically by authors.

The final issue of each volume contains a cumulative index for that year, listing subjects and authors. References are to item numbers, not to pages.

USEFULNESS: A quick way to check on whether or not it's worth one's time to read a particular book or article.

Also good for checking on what is currently being published in the field.

EXAMPLES: The following information is given for each work abstracted:

Abstract number; author's name and professional affiliation; title of book or article (in caps)—translated into English if in foreign language; for a book, the city, publisher's name, year, number of pages, and price—for an article, the name of journal (underlined), year, volume, number, month, and page numbers.

A brief, signed summary of the work's contents follows, usually between 100 and 200 words long.

RELATED REFERENCE WORKS: *International Bibliography of Sociology* (our no. 187).

189] A Guide to the Study of the United States of America

Washington, D.C.: Library of Congress, General
Reference & Bibliography Division, 1960.
Ed. by Donald H. Mugridge and Blanche P. McCrum.

CONTENTS: A fully annotated bibliography of books in English dealing with the United States, its people, society, history, government, customs, and culture. The work covers not only the social sciences, but also such topics as literature, music and art, sports, science, and technology. About 6,500 titles are described, and there is an index.

METHOD OF ORGANIZATION: Divided into 32 chapters according to general topics—e.g., Periodicals and Journalism; The American Indian; Diplomatic History & Foreign Relations; Intellectual History; Local History; Population, Immigration, & Minorities; Society; Communications; Medicine & Public Health; Education; Religion; Land & Agriculture; Economic Life; Constitution & Government; Law & Justice. Each chapter is headed by an introductory summary-essay on the field. The individual chapters are subdivided into sections according to subtopics or time periods; within each subdivision, items are listed alphabetically by authors.

Consult the index, which lists subjects, persons, and authors and titles of books described. References are to item numbers, not to pages.

The detailed table of contents could be used as a study guide for a researcher's particular field of interest.

USEFULNESS: A widely used reading and research guide for students of American sociology, history, and political science, noted for its full, descriptive annotations of the major books on the United States published up to about 1955–1958. The book descriptions are helpful in determining whether or not a particular work is relevant to the student's purposes.

EXAMPLES: The following information is given for each book listed: author; title; edition; city of publication, publisher, and date; number of pages; Library of Congress call number; pages of bibliography in book; followed by a relatively full description of the book's contents (often running to more than 200 words), and references to related books on the same topic.

RELATED REFERENCE WORKS: *Sources of Information in the Social Sciences: A Guide to the Literature*, ed. by Carl M. White, *et al.* (Totowa, N.J.: Bedminster Press, 1964); *International Bibliography of Sociology* (our no. 187).

190] *Handbook of Modern Sociology*

Chicago: Rand McNally, 1964. Ed. by Robert E. L. Faris.

CONTENTS: A collection of essays in which the theories and findings of recent research in the various areas of sociology are summarized. The aim of the work is to treat all major aspects of our culture and other cultures.

Many charts and tables are supplied. Extensive bibliographies of the works referred to or summarized are appended to each chapter, and there is an index.

METHOD OF ORGANIZATION: Divided into 27 chapters, according to the special areas of sociology—e.g., The Discipline of Sociology; Population & Society; Position & Behavior Patterns of Youth; Social Effects of Mass Communications; Industrial Relations; Race & Ethnic Relations; Sociology of Science; Mathematical Models & Computer Simulation, and others.

The index lists names and subjects.

USEFULNESS: These succinct summaries of current theories and research in the field enable the student to get an overall view. The bibliographical references, although they are not annotated, provide a good guide for further research.

RELATED REFERENCE WORKS: Those interested in a particular aspect of sociology may want to consult the specialized works in these areas, e.g., *The Negro Handbook,* compiled by the editors of *Ebony* (Chicago: Johnson Publishing Co., 1966); *Encyclopedia of Criminology,* ed. by Vernon C. Branham and Samuel B. Kutash (New York: Philosophical Library, 1949). The specialized works of interest can be located by using the *International Bibliography of Sociology* (our no. 187).

191] *A Dictionary of the Social Sciences*

New York: The Free Press of Glencoe, 1964.
Ed. by Julius Gould and W. L. Kolb.

CONTENTS: A volume of brief articles that "describe and define approximately one thousand basic concepts used in the social sciences." Compiled under the auspices of UNESCO.

The articles are signed, and they cover the fields of sociology, political science, economics, social anthropology, and social psychology.

There are cross references and bibliographies provided in the body of the work.

METHOD OF ORGANIZATION: Alphabetical, from Abnormal to Zonal Hypothesis.

Most articles (average length 1 page) are divided into two or more sections, labeled "A," "B," and so on. Section "A" gives the meaning(s) of the term. Sections "B," etc. give historical background and more detailed discussion on the subject.

USEFULNESS: Valuable both as a dictionary of terms for quick identifications, and as a handbook in which the history and theories associated with these terms are succinctly summarized and explained.
Useful for students of sociology and the related social sciences.

EXAMPLES: Here is a brief sample list of entries, chosen at random from the first letter of the alphabet:
Absentee Ownership; Absolutism; Acceleration Principle; Accommodation; Acculturation; Adjustment; Affinity; Age and Area Hypothesis; Aggregate; Agitation; Agnation; Alienation; Animism; Anomie; Apportionment; Aristocracy; Assimilation; Atomism; Authority; Autistic Thinking.

RELATED REFERENCE WORKS: *Dictionary of Sociology*, ed. by Henry P. Fairchild (New York: Philosophical Library, 1944), contains over 4,000 very brief definitions of sociological terms.

For a multivolume work, see the *International Encyclopedia of the Social Sciences* (our no. 7).

192] *Encyclopedia of Social Work*

New York: National Association of Social Workers, 1929—.

CONTENTS: A record of current social work that appears irregularly, at intervals of several years. Until 1965 it was published as *Social Work Year Book*. Each volume contains: encyclopedia-length articles on the history, organized activities, programs, and methods of social work in the U.S. and Canada, with a brief look at social problems and welfare in other parts of the world; and a directory of public and voluntary social work agencies.

Articles are signed, and contain selective up-to-date bibliographies.

METHOD OF ORGANIZATION: The format varies slightly in individual volumes. Vols. 1–12 (1929–1954) are each divided into two main parts; vols. 13–14 (1957–1960) into three main parts. Vol. 15 (1965) is divided into the following four main parts: (1) history (3 chapter-length articles); (2) around 100 medium-length topical articles with about 90 short biographical sketches of deceased leaders in the field—arranged alphabetically; (3) statistics; and (4) a directory of close to 500 agencies.

The index to the later volumes lists subjects, title articles, names, names of agencies, and cross references. There is no cumulative index.

USEFULNESS: An authoritative, one-stop source for students of social work. The latest volume is a combination history, encyclopedia, biographical dictionary, source-book for statistics, and directory of agencies.

EXAMPLES: Articles in the encyclopedic portion of the work deal with such topics as: Adoption; The Aging; Child Welfare; Community Organization; Day Care; Employment, Wages, and Standards of Living; The Law and Social Welfare; Medical Care; Migrants, Transients, and Nonresidents; Public Health; Unmarried Parents; Vocational Rehabilitation; Youth Services. Each article defines the term under examination and summarizes the historical background, contemporary developments, new knowledge and methods, research plans, and activities of social agencies in the area; a bibliography for further study follows.

Part III

SPECIALIZED REFERENCE WORKS for the PHYSICAL SCIENCES

III. A.

GENERAL REFERENCE WORKS

193] *Applied Science and Technology Index*

New York: H. W. Wilson, Co., 1958—.
Monthly, with quarterly and annual accumulations.

CONTENTS: Known from 1913 to 1957 as the *Industrial Arts Index*, this work lists about 70,000 articles yearly from 220 English-language periodicals, of which 20 are British, on almost every practical aspect of science—aeronautics, mining, automation, construction, metallurgy, industrial and mechanical arts, transportation, air pollution, noise control, nutrition, and electronics.

METHOD OF ORGANIZATION: Arranged alphabetically by subject only.

USEFULNESS: This is the work to consult for finding the newest and most up-to-date articles on applied science and technology.

EXAMPLES: Here is a sample entry:

Transfer Mechanisms
Increased integration of transfer saves floor space. L. W. Collins, Jr. il diag MACH 67:108–15 + Ja '61

Under the subject heading Transfer Mechanisms; the article is titled "Increased Integration of Transfer Saves Floor Space." The author is L. W. Collins, Jr. The article is illustrated, with a diagram, and is in the periodical *Machinery*, volume 67, pages 108 through 115 and other pages, in the January, 1961, issue.

194] *Nuclear Science Abstracts*

Washington: United States Atomic Energy Commission,
1948—. Semi-monthly.

CONTENTS: This work "covers technical reports of the U. S.
Atomic Energy Commission and its contractors, technical reports of U. S. Government agencies and other governments,
universities, industrial and research organizations, as well as
books and journals of literature on a world-wide basis."

During 1963, 42,427 "indicative and informative" abstracts
were included.

All titles are translated into English, and the abstracts are
always in English.

METHOD OF ORGANIZATION: Arranged in 14 alphabetical
classes, usually with subdivisions: Biology and Medicine;
Chemistry; Engineering; Geology and Mineralogy; Health and
Safety Instrumentation; Isotope Technology; Mathematics and
Computers; Metals, Ceramics, and Other Materials; Meterol-
ogy; Physics; Reactor Technology; Waste Disposal and Process-
ing; and General and Miscellaneous.

There is a detailed author and subject index.

USEFULNESS: This is an invaluable source for brief, objective
summaries of books, articles, and papers on every phase of nuclear science.

EXAMPLES: Here is a sample entry:

Radiation Detector. H. N. Wilson and F. M. Glass (to U. S.
Atomic Energy Commission). U. S. Patent 2,936,401. May
10, 1960.

A radiation detector of the type is described wherein a
condenser is directly connected to the electrodes for the purpose of performing the dual function of a guard ring and to
provide capacitance coupling for resetting the detector system.

RELATED REFERENCE WORKS: *A Guide to the World's Abstracting and Indexing Services in Science and Technology* (Washington: United States Library of Congress: Science and Technology Division, 1963). Covers about 2,000 titles published in
40 countries. Indexed by country and by subject. Extremely

valuable because it serves as a guide to the literature of science and technology and lists the major indexing and abstracting services published in the United States and abroad.

195] *Van Nostrand's Scientific Encyclopedia*

New York: Van Nostrand, 3rd ed., 1958.

CONTENTS: A basic reference work on science and engineering, on mathematics and medicine, this huge volume, written in clear and readable prose, defines about 15,000 terms in "aeronautics, astronomy, botany, chemistry, chemical engineering, civil engineering, computer technology, electrical engineering, electronics and radio, geology, guided missiles, mathematics, mechanical engineering, medicine, metallurgy, meteorology, mineralogy, navigation, nuclear science and engineering, photography, physics, statistics, zoology, and such related areas astrophysics, biochemistry, biophysics, nautical astonomy and others."

Entries range in length from a 20-word definition of Atmospheric Inversion to a 7,000-word entry on computers.

There are about 1,500 illustrations; no bibliographies and no biographies.

METHOD OF ORGANIZATION: Arranged alphabetically with an extensive system of cross references.

USEFULNESS: Probably the best one-volume reference work in the physical sciences. Has excellent definitions of terms. Both for the student and the layman.

EXAMPLES: Such sample entry titles as Aasvogel, Aciniform Glands, Air, Amines, Amplifier, Anthracene, Carbon, Cosmic Rays, Cucurbitaceae, Density, Differential Equation, Dye and Dyeing Textile Fibres, Electric Circuits, Embryo, Flower, Frequency Modulation (FM), Isotope, Magneto, Plastics, Spectrum, Stress, Television, and Vitamins, should give you an idea of the scope of this comprehensive volume.

RELATED REFERENCE WORKS: *Harper Encyclopedia of Science,* ed. by James R. Newman (New York: Harper and Row, 1963, 4 vols.). An excellent reference work, covering astronomy, biochemistry, biophysics, biology, chemistry, geology, history and philosophy of science, mathematics, and physics. Signed articles by about 450 specialists. Bibliography in volume 4; detailed index.

196] *McGraw-Hill Encyclopedia of Science and Technology*

New York: McGraw-Hill Co., 1960. 15 vols.

CONTENTS: Specifically designed for the college undergraduate in science and engineering, this comprehensive encyclopedia is written in clear and precise English by over 200 specialists, most of them American. There are well over 7,000 entries, of about 100 to 15,000 words each, on "the basic subject matter of all the natural sciences and all their major applications in engineering, agriculture, forestry, industrial biology, and food." Clinical medicine and psychiatry are excluded, but physiological and experimental psychology are represented.

Biographical and historical articles have been omitted, and "the philosophical basis of many subjects has been slighted."

Some of the longer articles are signed and have short bibliographies appended to them.

There are over 9,000 illustrations, some of them in color.

METHOD OF ORGANIZATION: Arranged alphabetically with cross references (there are about 50,000).

The index, volume 15, should be consulted to locate topics not given in separate entries.

USEFULNESS: The general articles, especially on botany and mathematics, provide a good survey of the various branches of science and technology. They are more detailed and specific than mere introductions; nevertheless, they should never take the place of books in the field.

EXAMPLES: There is great variety and scope in this encyclopedia. Some of the entries are on:

Acanthocephala; Acid and Base; Air Pressure; Analytic Geometry; Atomic Structure and Spectra; Fingerprint; Flower; Food; North America; Oxime; Parathyroid Gland; Uncertainty Principle; Vacuum Tube; Velocity Analysis; and X-Ray—to name just a few.

RELATED REFERENCE WORKS: *Van Nostrand's Scientific Encyclopedia* (our no. 195). Also see *Modern Men of Science* (our no. 198).

197] *Chambers's Technical Dictionary*

New York: The Macmillan Co., 3rd ed., 1958.

CONTENTS: This specialized dictionary defines over 16,000 important technical terms in pure and applied science and in all branches of engineering.

The definitions are very brief, clear, to the point, and usually no more than 30 words long.

No etymology is given, but each term is followed by the name of the field in which it is used.

METHOD OF ORGANIZATION: Arranged alphabetically.

USEFULNESS: Good source for very brief definitions of terms used in all the physical sciences.

EXAMPLES: Here is a typical entry:

Phloém (Bot.). The conducting tissue present in vascular plants, chiefly concerned with the transport of elaborated food materials about the plant. When fully developed, phloém consists of sieve tubes, companion cells, and Parenchyma, but companion cells may not be present.

RELATED REFERENCE WORKS: *A Dictionary of Science,* 3rd ed., revised by Alan Issacs (Harmondsworth, Middlesex: Penguin, 1964). A first-rate work, this consists of about 5,000 entries, primarily in pure science—Astronomy, Molecular Biology,

Chemistry, Mathematics, Physics, etc. Definitions range from 20 to some 2,000 words in length.

198] *Modern Men of Science*

New York: McGraw-Hill, 1966.

CONTENTS: Designed as a supplement to the 15-volume *Mc-Graw-Hill Encyclopedia of Science and Technology* (our no. 196), this one-volume biographical dictionary "seeks to provide both essential biographical data and extended descriptions of the most significant achievements of a substantial number of contemporary scientists." The coverage is international, but the majority are American.

Of the 426 articles in the volume, 300 were written by the scientists themselves and the others by qualified persons in the field (e.g., Professor L. Wilke of the Max-Planck Institut wrote the article on Karl Ziegler).

All the articles are short, ranging from about 200 to 750 words each, and are mostly on living men. Niels Bohr is one of the exceptions.

There are 426 illustrations.

METHOD OF ORGANIZATION: Arranged alphabetically by names. There are two alphabetical indexes at the back, an analytic and a classified.

The analytic index provides a guide to persons, subjects, books, and institutions mentioned in the text.

The classified index lists major scientific fields (e.g., Analytic Chemistry, Astronomy, Biology, Medicine, Microbiology, Nuclear Physics, etc.), followed by the names of the men closely associated with them.

USEFULNESS: A good source for brief biographical information on a modern scientist and a summary of his contribution to his particular field.

RELATED REFERENCE WORKS: *Asimov's Biographical Encyclopedia of Science and Technology,* by Isaac Asimov (New York: Doubleday, 1964). Contains biographies, often running to several columns, of scientists from ancient Greece to the space age. Indexed by name and subject.

American Men of Science, ed. by Jacques Cattell (Tempe, Arizona: Arizona State University, 1960–1962, 5 vols.). The tenth and latest edition gives the name, address, field of concentration, place and date of birth, degrees, and memberships of about 120,000 United States men of science.

BIOLOGY

199] *Biological and Agricultural Index*

New York: H. W. Wilson Co., 1964—. Monthly.

.CONTENTS: This monthly's contents are equally divided between the biological (Botany, Zoology, Genetics, Entomology, Microbiology, Physiology) and the agricultural sciences.

The *Biological and Agricultural Index* covers the literature in about 150 periodicals, all of them in English.

METHOD OF ORGANIZATION: Arranged alphabetically by subject only.

There are no cumulations; there is no author index.

USEFULNESS: This is a good work to consult to find some of the newest and most up-to-date articles in biology. It should be used in conjunction with *Biological Abstracts* (our no. 200).

EXAMPLES: Here is a sample entry:

Absorption (Physiology) Interrelation of amino acids and PH on intestinal iron absorption. D.J. Kroe and others, bibliog il Am J Physiol 211:414–18 Ag '66

The article, on the subject Absorption (Physiology), is titled "Interrelation of Amino Acids and PH on Intestinal Iron Absorption." The authors are D. J. Kroe and others. There are a bibliography and illustrations, and the article will be found in the *American Journal of Physiology*, volume 211, pages 414–18, issue dated August, 1966.

200] *Biological Abstracts*

Philadelphia: University of Pennsylvania Press, 1926—.
Semi-monthly, with annual cumulations.

CONTENTS: This is a comprehensive, semi-monthly guide to the literature of theoretical and applied biology, exclusive of clinical medicine. It summarizes the significant contents and conclusions of articles from about 5,000 journals, published in 90 countries, as well as annual institutional reports, review annuals, proceedings of conferences and symposiums, unclassified research reports from U. S. Government agencies. The abstracts themselves range from 25 to 300 words, are always in English, and are signed.

Titles are given in the original language (Oriental languages and Russian are transliterated) with English translations.

METHOD OF ORGANIZATION: The abstracts are arranged by topics; each topic is divided into subtopics. Within each subtopic, the abstracts are arranged alphabetically by authors. At the beginning of each issue is a Subject Classification Outline, which lists the subtopics included under each main topic, along with an alphabetical table of contents. There is an author index at the back of each issue.

USEFULNESS: This is one of the most valuable reference works in biology because it enables the student to keep up with periodical scholarship in this field throughout the world. Therefore indispensable (1) for summaries of important papers and articles, and (2) as a bibliographical guide to the field.

EXAMPLES:

64–6856. Anderson, Theodore G., Lowrain E. McCrea, and Anna T. Settembrino (Temple Univ. Sch. Med., Philadelphia, Pa., U.SA.) *Viruses as the etiologic agents of urinary tract infections.* Jour. Urol. 90 (1): 92–93. 1963.—Tissue culture studies of the urine of 24 patients with chronic urinary tract disease failed to reveal the presence of a recognized virus. Urine specimens from 13 patients caused a change in the cell pattern, but this change could not be reproduced beyond two passages in monkey kidney cells.—Erwin Neter.

RELATED REFERENCE WORKS: *International Abstracts of Biological Sciences* (London: Pergamon, 1956—). This important monthly gives signed informative abstracts covering such fields as anatomy, biochemistry, cytology, experimental botany, zoology, genetics, immunology, and experimental pathology, microbiology, and physiology. Quarterly subject and author indexes.

Abstracts of Human Development Biology (Amsterdam: Excerpta Medica Foundation, 1961—). Monthly with annual subject and author index. Covers "experimental and clinical aspects of normal and pathological human development."

201] *The Encyclopedia of the Biological Sciences*

New York: Reinhold, 1961. Ed. by Peter Gray.

CONTENTS: Succinct, accurate, and well-written, this 1,100-page encyclopedia describes and explains over 2,000 subjects in the biological sciences "as viewed by experts in their developmental, ecological, functional, genetic, structural and taxonomic aspects." Also included are short biographies of men who played an important part in the development of biology.

Most of the entries vary between 500 and 5,000 words in length; they are signed by their authors, biologists in the United States, Europe, and Asia.

Short bibliographies are appended to each article. Occasional pictures, diagrams, and tables appear next to appropriate article.

METHOD OF ORGANIZATION: Alphabetical. There is an index at the back.

USEFULNESS: This is a good general reference work for students majoring in biology.

It is especially valuable for those who may need information about biology even though this is not their field of specialization.

EXAMPLES: Here is a very brief sample list of entries to show the scope of this encyclopedia:

Actinopoda; Animal Kingdom; Bacterial Nucleus; Bone; Chordata; Egg; Fermentation; Krebs Cycle; Leaf; Migration; Nervous System; Oestrous Cycle; Primates; Social Insects; Space Biology; Toxins; Viruses.

202] A *Dictionary of Biological Terms*

Princeton: Van Nostrand. 1963. By I. F. Henderson and W. D. Henderson. 8th ed. by J. H. Kenneth.

CONTENTS: This dictionary gives the pronunciation, derivation, part of speech, and definition of about 18,000 terms in biology, botany, zoology, anatomy, physiology, cytology, genetics, and embryology, and some terms in other related subjects.

Definitions range in length from single-word synonyms to 60-word definitions.

Specific names of plants and animals are omitted (e.g., one will not find a definition of elephant here), as are references to the sources of terms.

METHOD OF ORGANIZATION: Alphabetical.

USEFULNESS: The *Dictionary of Biological Terms* is good for introductory, very brief, and concise definitions of biological terms.

Definitions in this work, however, should never be used as substitutes for those in an encyclopedia or a text.

EXAMPLES: Here is a sample of the information given in this work:

Concha (Kŏng′Kă) N. (GK. Kongché, shell.)

The cavity of the external ear, which opens into the external acoustic meatus; a superior, middle, and inferior projection from lateral wall of nasal cavity; turbinate body; one of two curved plates of Sphenoidal bone; a marine shell.

RELATED REFERENCE WORKS: A *Dictionary of Biology*, by Michael H. Abercrombie and M. L. Johnson (Chicago: Aldine,

1962). About 2,600 definitions of biological terms. Terms from palaeontology and anthropology included.

203] *Biology Data Book*

Washington, D.C.: Federation of American Societies for Experimental Biology, 1964. Compiled and ed. by Philip L. Altman and Dorothy S. Dittmer.

CONTENTS: Compiled by 470 biologists, zoologists, and basic medical scientists, this large and valuable reference work gives, in clear, easy-to-read charts, the important, established data in the biological and medical sciences.

Each chart is signed by the contributor.

Bibliographies, often very extensive, are appended to each chart.

METHOD OF ORGANIZATION: Arranged in 12 sections:

Genetics and Cytology; Reproduction; Development and Growth; Morphology; Nutrition and Digestion; Metabolism, Respiration, and Circulation; Blood; Biological Regulators and Toxins; Biophysical and Biochemical Characteristics; Environment and Survival; Parasitism; Materials and Methods.

There are 8 appendixes, and a detailed index.

USEFULNESS: This is a compact, easy-to-read, and easy-to-use compilation of the most important data in biology.

The index is especially useful for obtaining information on a particular animal order or plant family.

The appendixes provide information on Taxonomic Classification; Conversion Factors; and Sources of Supplies.

EXAMPLES: The following titles, chosen at random, should indicate the scope and depth of this work:

Body Weight and Height of Men of Different Nationalities at Different Years of Their Life; Respiration Rate of Bacteria; Classification of Acid-Base Disturbances in Man; Effect of Temperature on the Inactivation and Survival of Animal Viruses; Vascular and Capillary Pressures in Vertebrates; Blood Coagulation Theories; and Culture Media in Animal Tissues.

CHEMISTRY

204] *Chemical Abstracts*

Easton, Pa.: American Chemical Society, 1907—.
Bi-weekly, with annual volumes.

CONTENTS: Broad in scope and thoroughly indexed, this comprehensive reference work of pure and applied chemistry gives complete coverage of the world's chemical literature in papers, articles, and patents. It examines more than 7,000 scientific, technical, and trade periodicals from over 90 countries. Titles are given in the original language with English translations. The abstracts themselves range from 25 to 500 words, are always in English and signed.

METHOD OF ORGANIZATION: Each issue is divided in 33 sections, with a table of contents at the front. An author index is at the back of each annual volume; a separate subject index is issued twice annually; but there is no title index. The reader must, therefore, know the author or the subject to use this work.

The full titles of journals to which *Chemical Abstracts* refers in abbreviated form are found in the "List of Periodicals Abstracted by Chemical Abstracts," published at five-year intervals.

USEFULNESS: Indispensable (1) for summaries of important papers, articles, and patents published throughout the world, and (2) as a bibliographical guide to the field.

EXAMPLES: *Effect of irradiation on quality of ground pork and cooking conventionally and electronically.* Eulalia Lim,

Joan Yen, Faith Fenton (Cornell Univ., Ithaca, N.Y.). "Food Research" 24, 645–58 (1959).

Radiation resulted in significantly lower aroma, flavor, color, juiciness, moisture, and thiamine content. Radiation did not affect pH or a:b color ratio of the cut surface of either cooked or raw meat. Electronic cooking resulted in higher juiciness scores, evaporation loss, moisture, and thiamine content and lower aroma, flavor and color scores, cooking drip loss, peroxide, and fat content. In electronic cooking, % retention of thiamine was lowest in the control lot which required the longest cooking, and highest in the 6×10^6 r.e.p. added monosodium glutamate lot which required the shortest cooking.

C. R. Fellers

RELATED REFERENCE WORKS: *Index Chemicus* (Philadelphia: Institute for Scientific Information, 1960). Bi-weekly. Original articles (about 10,000 a year) are abstracted "graphically" (i.e., the structural and molecular formulae) as well as verbally. Quarterly and biennial index.

205] *International Encyclopedia of Chemical Science*

Princeton, N.J.: D. Van Nostrand, 1964.

CONTENTS: One of the newest and best encyclopedias of chemical terms, this 1,300-page volume has over 12,000 entries, most of them between 25 and 150 words long. It was designed specifically to meet the needs of "chemists and non-chemists, teachers and students, those who are interested in pure or applied chemistry, in chemical research, engineering or technology."

In keeping with trends in modern chemistry, "this book places equal emphasis upon the facts of chemistry and the principles which have been developed to explain and correlate them. The organic substances are discussed in comprehensive entries for each type of compound. In the entries for the individual elements, their inorganic and representative organo–metallic compounds have generally been discussed by periodical groups, and in accordance with present-day concepts of molecular structure and reaction mechanism."

METHOD OF ORGANIZATION: Alphabetical. The last section contains four multilingual indexes: French–English; German–English; Russian–English; and Spanish–English.

USEFULNESS: This is a good source for brief explanations of terms.

EXAMPLES:

Chromophoric Electrons
Electrons in the double bonds of the chromophoric groups. Such electrons are not bound as tightly as those of single bonds and can thus be transferred into higher energy levels with less expenditure of energy. Their electronic spectra appear at frequencies in the visible or near ultra violet region of the spectrum.

RELATED REFERENCE WORKS: *The Encyclopedia of Chemistry,* 2nd ed., ed. by George L. Clark and Gessner G. Hawley (New York: Reinhold, 1966).

206] *Condensed Chemical Dictionary*

New York: Reinhold, 6th ed., 1961.
Ed., compiled, rev., and enl. by Arthur and Elizabeth Rose.

CONTENTS: Designed specifically for working chemists as well as for teachers and students, the *Condensed Chemical Dictionary* defines chemical terms.

Each definition includes physical properties, shipping regulations, derivations, uses, sources, grades, methods of manufacture, and the trade name wherever possible.

METHOD OF ORGANIZATION: Alphabetical.

USEFULNESS: This dictionary is a valuable reference tool because it covers important practical uses of chemicals as well as definitions.

EXAMPLES: Here is a sample entry:

Magnesium Formate Mg (CHO2) 2 • 2H2 O.
   Properties: Colorless crystals; soluble in water; insoluble in alcohol and ether.
   Derivation: By the action of formic acid on magnesium oxide.
   Grades: Technical.
   Containers: Boxes; glass bottles.
   Uses: Analytical Chemistry; Medicine.
   Shipping Regulations: None.

RELATED REFERENCE WORKS: *The Dictionary of Chemical Names,* by Walter Edgar Flood (New York: Philosophical Library, 1963). This work gives the history and derivation of chemical names.
   Concise Chemical and Technical Dictionary, ed. by H. Bennett, 2nd ed. (New York: Chemical Publishing Co., 1962). About 59,000 definitions, including sections on nomenclature and pronunciation. "Appendices cover conversion tables, indicators and important organic ring systems."

207] *Handbook of Chemistry and Physics*

   Cleveland: The Chemical Rubber Co., 46th ed., 1966.
   Editor-in-Chief, Robert C. Weast.

CONTENTS: The aim of this ready-reference book of chemical and physical data, laid out in charts and tables, "has been to present in condensed form as large an amount of accurate, reliable, up-to-date information in the fields of chemistry and physics as was consistent" with a large one-volume work.
   An excellent section dealing with the history of the elements is included.

METHOD OF ORGANIZATION: In six sections:
   Mathematical Tables; Elements and Inorganic Compounds; Organic Compounds; General Chemical; General Physical Constants; Miscellaneous. There is no index.

USEFULNESS: A compact, easy-to-read, and comprehensive collection of reference data in chemistry and physics, selected especially for college students.

There is a good section on mathematical data.

EXAMPLES: The following titles, chosen at random, should give a good idea of the scope of this invaluable work:

Five-Place Logarithms; Haversines; Radians to Degrees and Decimals; Elliptic Integrals of the First Kind F (k,ø); Physical Constants of Minerals; Physical Constants of Organic Compounds Table; Steroid Hormones; Organic Analytic Reagents; Vapor Pressure of Inorganic Compounds; X-Ray Spectra; Diffraction Data for Curic Isomorphs; Density of Moist Air; and Surface Tension of Various Liquids.

RELATED REFERENCE WORKS: *Handbook of Chemistry*, ed. by Norbert A. Lange and Gordon M. Forker (New York: McGraw-Hill, 10th ed., 1961).

Handbook of Chemical Data, ed. by F. W. Atack (Altrincham, England: Sherratt, 1957).

MATHEMATICS

208] *Mathematical Reviews*

Lancaster, Pa.: The American Mathematical Society, 1940—.
Monthly with annual accumulations.

CONTENTS: This key reference work publishes signed abstracts
of articles on mathematics and allied fields—quantum mechanics, statistical physics, and relativity, for instance.
Over 600 magazines published in almost every country in the
world are examined for pertinent articles.
The abstract is usually in English. Sometimes, however, it is
in German or French.
Reviewers are from various countries.

METHOD OF ORGANIZATION: Divided into categories and fields:
e.g., General; History and Biography; Logic and Foundations;
Combinational Analysis; Theory of Numbers; Fields of Poly-
nomials; Linear Algebra; Homological Algebra; Topological
Groups and Lie Theory; Measure and Integration; Probability;
Differential Geometry; Astronomy; Geophysics, etc.
There is an author index at the back of each monthly issue.

USEFULNESS: This work is invaluable for brief objective summaries of articles on mathematics and allied fields published
throughout the world.

EXAMPLES: Here is a sample entry:

Barnes, D. W.
Lattice Isomorphisms of Associative Algebras.
J. Austral. Math. Soc. (1966), 106–121.
The author studies the following problem: If A and B are

associative algebras (over a field) having isomorphic lattices of subalgebras, how are A and B related? One of his results (among many others) is that if A is the ring of matrices of degree 3 over 9 finite-dimensional division algebra, then there is a one-to-one semi-linear map from A onto B which is either multiplicative or antimultiplicative.

J.E. McLaughlin (Ann Arbor, Mich.)

RELATED REFERENCE WORKS: *Statistical Theory and Method Abstracts* (our no. 209).

209] *Statistical Theory and Method Abstracts*

Edinburgh: Oliver & Boyd, 1959—. Annual.

CONTENTS: This annual publishes, in English, signed abstracts of the most important papers, including "special collections of papers as published in reports of conferences, symposia and seminars together with the published reports of experiment and other research stations" in 500 periodicals in the statistical and allied fields. The periodicals are from every country and in every language. The abstracts vary in length from 120 to 200 words each.

METHOD OF ORGANIZATION: Divided into 11 categories, with a different-color paper for each category: Mathematical Methods (white); Probability (pink); Frequency Distribution (green); Sampling Distribution (light blue); Estimation (yellow); Hypothesis Testing (purple); Relationships (grey); Variance Analysis (biscuit); Sampling Design (orange); Design of Experiments (blue); Stochastic Theory and Time Series Analysis (red); Miscellaneous (cream).

There is an author index.

USEFULNESS: An invaluable work for obtaining brief, objective summaries of papers in statistics and allied fields that are published throughout the world.

EXAMPLES: Here is a sample entry:

Shrikhande, S.S. (Bombay University) A note on mutually orthogonal Latin squares—In English Sankhyā (1961) 23, 115–116 (7 references)

It is proved that the existence of a set of (N–3) mutually orthogonal Latin squares of order N implies the existence of a complete set of (N–1) such squares and hence the existence of a finite projective plane PG (2,N).

(Author's Summary)

RELATED REFERENCE WORKS: *An Index of Mathematical Tables,* by Alan Fletcher (Reading, Massachusetts: Addison-Wesley, 1962). The second edition of this work, compiled in two volumes, gives an "important index to well-known tables of functions and to other less-known tables appearing in books and periodicals."

Guide to Tables in Mathematical Statistics, by Joseph Arthur Greenwood and H. O. Hartley (Princeton: Princeton University Press, 1962).

Mathematical Reviews. (See our no. 208)

210] *Universal Encyclopedia of Mathematics*

New York: Simon and Schuster, 1964.

CONTENTS: Clearly written, accurate, sensibly arranged and succinct, this encyclopedia was designed specifically for high school and college students.

It contains "a large collection of formulae (arithmetical, algebraic, geometric, trigonometric, special functions, series, differential and integral calculus). There are also tables of mathematical functions (powers, square and cube roots, logarithms, trigonometrical functions, exponential functions, length of arcs and angles in degrees and radians and tables of differences)."

Higher branches, such as group theory or algebraic topology, are not treated.

Biographies are not included, and history is not emphasized.

METHOD OF ORGANIZATION: Arranged alphabetically. There is no index.

USEFULNESS: Mainly, entries are intended to "explain the elements of a concept or method, indicate its connections and relations with other parts of mathematics, and give the reader the proper bearings and a good start in following up, if he is so inclined, by consulting appropriate texts and monographs."

EXAMPLES: A few among the concepts and methods covered in this book are:

Angles; the design and operation of calculating machines; conic sections; continued fractions; mathematical induction; regular polygons; the Pythagorean theorem; the real number system; infinite series; nomography; logarithms; linear transformations; the solution of equations; the binomial distribution; complex numbers; Archimedes' spiral; the computation of interest; the indefinite integral; Pascal's triangle; the Roman number system; rigid motions; Platonic solids.

211] *International Dictionary of Applied Mathematics*

Princeton, N.J.: D. Van Nostrand, 1960.
Ed. by W. F. Freiberger

CONTENTS: This dictionary "defines the terms and describes the methods in the applications of mathematics to thirty-one fields of physical science and engineering. These definitions and descriptions have been chosen to comprise those terms in general use and those methods which have proved most fruitful in practical calculations and analysis."

The well over 7,000 entries are between 10 and 500 words long; they are written in clear, precise, readable English.

METHOD OF ORGANIZATION: Arranged alphabetically.

USEFULNESS: A source for brief definitions of mathematical terms and concepts.

A useful feature of the dictionary is the group of four foreign language indexes, which list alphabetically the French, German, Russian, and Spanish equivalents of the terms defined in this book, with their English equivalents.

EXAMPLES: The following terms, selected at random, should give an idea of the range and scope of the *International Dictionary:*

Abel Identity; Adiabatic Process; Analysis of Variance; Beta Distribution; Boulvin Diagram; Chebyshev Polynomials; Curvilinear Orthogonal Coordinates; Diesel Engine; Dispersion Relations; Electromagnetic Units; Feynman Positron Theory; Huygens' Principle; Lagrangian Formalism for Field Systems; Raman Effect; Relativistic Quantum Field Theory; Shockwave; Valence Force in Polyatonic Molecules.

RELATED REFERENCE WORKS: *Mathematical Handbook for Scientists and Engineers,* by G. A. Korn and T. M. Korn (New York: McGraw-Hill, 1961). "A comprehensive reference collection of mathematical definitions, theorems, and formulas . . . concluding with numerical tables and a glossary of symbols and notations."

Mathematics Manual, by Frederick S. Merritt (New York: McGraw-Hill, 1962), gives important definitions, principles, theorems, corollaries, relationships, and methods "of the most commonly used branches of mathematics."

212] *Mathematics Dictionary*
(Multilingual Edition)

Princeton, N.J.: D. Van Nostrand, 1959.
Ed. by Glenn and Robert C. James.

CONTENTS: Accurate and well written, the definitions in this dictionary include explanations of basic terms in arithmetic, differential geometry, theory of functions of real and complex variables, advanced calculus, differential equations, theory of groups and matrices, theory of summability, point set topology, integral equations, calculus of variations, analytic mechanics, theory of potential as well as modern algebra, vector spaces, and numerical analysis.

METHOD OF ORGANIZATION: Arranged alphabetically. The appendix contains many useful tables, as well as an extensive list of mathematical symbols.

USEFULNESS: A source for brief definitions of mathematical terms and concepts.

A useful feature of this dictionary is the group of four foreign language indexes, which list alphabetically the French, German, Russian, and Spanish equivalents of the terms defined in this book, with their English equivalents.

EXAMPLES: Abel's Problem; Annuity; Coefficient; Density; Determinant; Ellipse; Factor; Green's Formulas; Integral; Line; Logarithm; Metric; Parabola; Pole; Radical; Root; Series; Symmetric; Trigonometric; and Velocity, are some of the terms defined.

RELATED REFERENCE WORKS: The *International Dictionary of Applied Mathematics* (our no. 211).

III. E.

PHYSICS

213] *Science Abstracts. Section A: Physics Abstracts*

London: Inst. of Electrical Engineers, 1898—. Monthly.

CONTENTS: This valuable monthly abstracts articles from about 800 journals published in almost every country and in every major language in the world. Yearly volumes contain about 60,000 entries.

The abstracts are generally between 10 and 300 words in length; they cover every aspect of physics, are often signed, and always appear in English. Titles never appear in the original language but are translated into English.

METHOD OF ORGANIZATION: Arranged by subjects, usually about twenty in number (e.g., General; Mathematical Physics; Vibrations; Waves, Acoustics; Heat; and often ending with Astrophysics and Biophysics).

A detailed author and subject index is published separately every year; a cumulative author and subject index is printed every fifth year; a detailed author index at the back of bound monthly volumes. Numbers next to the author's name make it possible for the user readily to locate the abstract of an author's work.

EXAMPLES:

67–12577 Surface-Wave Propagations on an Impedance Surface in a Medium with a Negative Permittivity.
N. S. Orlova
Izv. VUZ Radiofiz. (USSR), 1965, No. 5, 1047–9. In Russian.

English Translation In: Soviet Radiophys. (USA), 1965, No. 5, 757–9 (Sept.–Oct.).

Discusses aspects of the propagation of surface waves guided by an impedance surface in a medium with negative permittivity. Surface-wave propagation on a plane impedence surface lying in a semi-infinite plasma medium is considered. The plasma, assumed homogeneous and isotropic, is characterized by a relative permittivity Ep whose value can vary from unity to large negative values.

USEFULNESS: One of the most valuable reference works in physics, this work enables the student to keep up with periodical scholarship in his field throughout the world. Therefore, indispensable (1) for summaries of important papers and articles, and (2) as a bibliographical guide to the field.

214] *Encyclopaedic Dictionary of Physics*

New York: Pergamon Press, 1961.
8 vols. plus supplementary vol. Ed. by J. Thewlis.

CONTENTS: Detailed, scholarly, and well written, this 8-volume work covers not only physics proper but also such related subjects as mathematics, astronomy, aerodynamics, hydraulics, geophysics, metrology, physical metallurgy, radiation chemistry, physical chemistry, structural chemistry, crystallography, medical physics, biophysics, and photography.

The *Dictionary* contains over 20,000 signed articles by eminent physicists in the English-speaking world (including, for example, Glenn Seaborg, R. H. Dicke, U. Opik, and C. W. Moak), ranging from a 45-word entry on alkyl substitution to a 5,000-word entry on thermodynamics.

At the end of most of these articles will be found various cross references to other articles, where additional information can be obtained, together with a bibliography of useful sources for further reading. There are no biographies.

METHOD OF ORGANIZATION: Arranged alphabetically. Vol. 8 has a subject index and an author index. The supplementary volume, published in 1964, has a glossary in English, French, German, Spanish, Russian, and Japanese.

USEFULNESS: This *Dictionary* "should be useful not only to physicists (and would-be physicists) but to those who are concerned with any of the branches of science . . . which have a physical basis. The articles are, in general, of graduate or near-graduate standard."

EXAMPLES: The reader will find entries on such terms and concepts as:

Absorption of Radiation; Actinide Elements; Amplifier; Astronomical Instruments of Position; Betatron; Calculus of Residues; Exchange; Gaseous Equilibrium; Geomagnetic Field; Hydrogen Bombs and Diffraction Analysis; Legendre Functions; Mass; Motion Pictures; Paramagnetic Relaxation; Proton–Proton Scattering; Structure Types; Ultrasonics; X-Ray Absorption.

RELATED REFERENCE WORKS: *The Encyclopedia of Physics*, ed. by Robert M. Besancon (New York: Reinhold, 1966). This excellent one-volume encyclopedia has signed articles by 300 specialists, both in this country and abroad, ranging from one half a page to six pages. Subject index at the back.

215] *Dictionary of Physics*

London: Longmans, Green, 1958. Ed. by H. J. Gray.

CONTENTS: "Short and succinct articles on all the traditional and the newer sub-divisions of physics including quantum mechanics, atomic and nuclear physics."

The *Dictionary of Physics* also includes entries covering applied physics and touching on closely related subjects—e.g., astronomy and mathematics.

Key articles may run to several pages, with numbered subdivisions, e.g., Photometry, Diffraction of Light, Fluorine.

Very brief biographies and some literature references given.

METHOD OF ORGANIZATION: Arranged alphabetically.

USEFULNESS: This is a good source for brief articles defining the most important terms and concepts used in traditional and modern physics.

EXAMPLES:

Layer Structure. Crystalline arrangement in which the forces between atoms along one general direction are weaker than those at right angles or nearly at right angles to this direction, so that the atoms tend to form layers.

RELATED REFERENCE WORKS: *The International Dictionary of Physics and Electronics* (our no. 216).

Dictionary of Physics and Mathematics, ed. by David D. Polon (New York: The Odyssey Press, 1965). This is a dictionary of abbreviations, signs, and symbols and of nothing else. Valuable as an adjunct to handbooks and technical aids.

216] *International Dictionary of Physics and Electronics*

Princeton, N.J.: D. Van Nostrand, 2nd ed., 1961.
Ed. by W. C. Michels.

CONTENTS: This one-volume dictionary was primarily designed for students in physics and professional physicists, especially those who do not have an extensive background in mathematics.

The more than 12,000 terms defined, usually in about 75 words or less, include "laws, relationships, equations, basic principles and concepts, as well as the most widely used instruments and apparatus."

The fields covered include "mechanics, heat and thermodynamics; low temperature physics; the properties of gases, liquids, and solids; acoustics; optics; electricity; electronics; nuclear physics; mathematical physics; and representative topics in relativity and a few other of the more advanced and specified fields."

METHOD OF ORGANIZATION: Arranged alphabetically.

USEFULNESS: This *International Dictionary of Physics and Electronics* gives brief definitions of the most important terms in physics and related physical sciences.

An extremely useful feature is the group of multilingual indexes in French, German, Spanish, and Russian.

EXAMPLES: The following entry will show the kind of scope and depth one can expect from this dictionary:

Yield Point. The minimum unit *stress* at which a structural material will deform without an increase in the *load* is called the yield point. Some materials do not have a yield point and in others it is not a well-defined value. Consequently, in these cases it has become common practice to use a quantity called the *yield strength*. The yield strength is the unit stress corresponding to a specific amount of permanent unit *deformation*.

217] *Handbook of Physics*

New York: McGraw-Hill, 2nd ed., 1967.
Ed. by E. U. Condon and H. Odishaw.

CONTENTS: One of the important standard handbooks in physics, this work has "chapters by specialists, encyclopedic in nature."

METHOD OF ORGANIZATION: Arranged in nine sections: mathematics; mechanics of particles and rigid bodies; mechanics of deformable bodies; electricity and magnetism; heat and thermodynamics; optics; atomic physics; solid state; and nuclear physics.

Each section is divided into chapters; the chapters are arranged by categories. Chapter One of Section One, for example, is called "Fundamentals" and is divided into 2 parts: (1) Numbers and Arithmetic Operations, and (2) Logical Foundations of Arithmetic.

There is a detailed bibliography at the end of each chapter.

USEFULNESS: The *Handbook* contains good essays, many of them in depth, on the most important concepts in physics and related sciences.

EXAMPLES: The student will find entries here on such concepts as:

Ordinary Differential Equations; Kinematics; Orbital Motion; Quantum Dynamics; Gravitation; Rheology; Acoustics; Conduction of Electricity in Gases; Electromagnetic Waves; Molecular Optics; Thermionic Emission; and Neutron Physics —to name just a few.

RELATED REFERENCE WORKS: *American Institute of Physics Handbook,* ed. by Dwight E. Gray (New York: McGraw-Hill, 1963). Good treatment of "mathematical aids to computation, mechanics, acoustics, heat, electricity, magnetism, optics, atomic and molecular physics, nuclear physics, and solid-state physics." Selected bibliographies are included.

Part IV

AIDS FOR RESEARCH

HOW TO USE
THE LIBRARY

The library stores systematically, in books, magazines, pamphlets, and bulletins, "the best which has been thought and said in the world" from ancient times to the present. And the heart of any library is the card catalogue. Know how to use it and you know how to research any subject with confidence and efficiency.

The card catalogue consists of alphabetically filed cards that list every publication shelved in the library, either in the stacks, in the reference room, or in other parts of the building or the college. (In addition, your school may have departmental libraries, which you should get to know.)

These cards are filed alphabetically by author (called "author cards" or "main cards"), by title of the publication (called "title cards"), and by subject (called "subject cards"). Author cards are filed under the author's last name, title cards under the first word in the title (articles do not count), and subject cards under the subjects that the books in question treat. Any given publication then may be listed under three cards; thus you can find this publication if you know either the name of the author, its title, or the subject.

Here are six library cards, as they will most likely appear in your library card catalogue, and a key to the information they contain:

AUTHOR CARD OR MAIN ENTRY:

325.73   Kennedy, John Fitzgerald, *Pres. U. S.*, 1917–1963.
K35N2   A nation of immigrants ₍by₎ John F. Kennedy. Rev. and
         enl. ed. Introd. by Robert F. Kennedy. New York, Harper
         and Row ₍1964₎

            xi, 111 p.   illus., fold. map.   21 cm.

            Bibliography: p. 95–101.

            1. U. S.—Emig. & immig.   2. U. S.—Foreign population.
         I. Title.

         JV6453.K4   1964   325.73   64–7830

         Library of Congress   ₍4–1₎

1. "Kennedy, John Fitzgerald, *Pres. U. S.*, 1917–1963." gives the name of the author (last name first), his identity, and the date of his birth and death.

2. 325.73
   K35N2 is the call number (symbols used by the library to identify the book) according to the Dewey Decimal System, a numerical classification for all books.

3. "A nation . . . 1964" gives the title of the book; the author's name, this time written in standard order; information about this particular edition (it has been revised and enlarged); the name of the person who wrote the introduction; the place of publication; the name of the publisher; the date of publication.

4. "xi . . . pp. 95–101" tells that the book has eleven pages numbered in Roman numerals and 111 in Arabic numerals. It also has illustrations, a fold-out map, is 21 centimeters in height, and has a bibliography which can be found on pages 95–101.

5. "1. U. S. . . . Title" tells the subject categories under which you can find the book in your card catalogue. You will find President Kennedy's book listed under "United States— Emigration and Immigration," "United States—Foreign Population," and under its title.

6. "JV6453.K4 1964" is the Library of Congress call number and the date on which the book was catalogued.
7. "325.73" is the general classification number under the Dewey Decimal System.
8. "64–7830" tells the order number used by librarians.

TITLE CARD: Title cards are author cards with the title typed in above the author's name.

A nation of immigrants.

325.73
K35N2

Kennedy, John Fitzgerald, *Pres. U. S.*, 1917–1963.
A nation of immigrants ₍by₎ John F. Kennedy. Rev. and enl. ed. Introd. by Robert F. Kennedy. New York, Harper and Row ₍1964₎

xi, 111 p. illus., fold. map. 21 cm.

Bibliography: p. 95–101.

1. U. S.—Emig. & Immig. 2. U. S.—Foreign population. I. Title.

JV6453.K4 1964   325.73   64–7830

Library of Congress   ₍4–1₎

SUBJECT CARD: Subject cards are author cards with the subject typed in above the author's name.

U. S. – EMIGRATION AND IMMIGRATION

325.73
K35N2

Kennedy, John Fitzgerald, *Pres. U. S.*, 1917–1963.
A nation of immigrants ₍by₎ John F. Kennedy. Rev. and enl. ed. Introd. by Robert F. Kennedy. New York, Harper and Row ₍1964₎

xi, 111 p. illus., fold. map. 21 cm.

Bibliography: p. 95–101.

1. U. S.—Emig. & Immig. 2. U. S.—Foreign population. I. Title.

JV6453.K4 1964   325.73   64–7830

Library of Congress   ₍4–1₎

PERIODICAL ENTRIES: Books and monographs always have an author card unless, of course, the author is unknown. Periodicals, however, are not listed under author cards as such but under their title, their subject, and under the organizations that publish them. This last card functions as an author card.

TITLE CARD OR MAIN ENTRY:

```
Periodical
QH324
 .C9      Cryobiology.  v. 1-
            Sept./Oct. 1964-
            ₁Rockville, Md. ?₁
                 v.in      illus.

              Vol. 1, no. 1 preceded by a number dated July/Aug. 1964, called
              Supplement 1.
              Journal of the Society for Cryobiology.


              1. Cold—Physiological effect—Period.  2. Hypothermia—Period.
            3. Lyophilization—Period.    I. Society for Cryobiology.

            QH324.C9                                          65-9853

            Library of Congress              ₁1₁
```

SUBJECT CARD:

```
Periodical COLD - PHYSIOLOGICAL EFFECT - PERIODICALS
QH324
 .C9      Cryobiology.  v. 1-
            Sept./Oct. 1964-
            ₁Rockville, Md. ?₁
                 v.in      illus.

              Vol. 1, no. 1 preceded by a number dated July/Aug. 1964, called
              Supplement 1.
              Journal of the Society for Cryobiology.


              1. Cold—Physiological effect—Period.  2. Hypothermia—Period.
            3. Lyophilization—Period.    I. Society for Cryobiology.

            QH324.C9                                          65-9853

            Library of Congress              ₁1₁
```

NAME OF PUBLISHER
FUNCTIONING AS AUTHOR CARD:

DOCUMENTATION
OF THE RESEARCH PAPER:
FOOTNOTES AND BIBLIOGRAPHY

DOCUMENTATION

The two main purposes of "documenting" your research paper are: (1) to enable a reader to find easily the source you have quoted or paraphrased in your paper; (2) to acknowledge your debt to the people whose words or ideas you have used.

Note that such an acknowledgment is both necessary and advantageous: necessary because a reader may want to check the accuracy of your reference or read further in the book or journal quoted from; necessary because you have borrowed another author's property (unacknowledged borrowing is considered theft or "plagiarism"); advantageous because you are backing up your findings or opinions by naming authorities whose words usually carry more weight than yours.

The documentation of the research paper properly falls into two parts: (1) footnotes; (2) the bibliography.

Footnotes pinpoint the exact location of a quote or idea used; hence the specific pages referred to are cited (as well as the author's name, the title of the work, city and name of publisher or magazine title, and date of publication). The bibliography provides the reader with an alphabetical check list of the works you have consulted or quoted from in your paper (an extremely valuable service to the reader who may want to do further reading or research on the same subject himself).

Proper documentation—that is, documentation that is both clear and consistent—is relatively easy to achieve by following the rules spelled out in the style sheet or style book of your particular field of study.

For your convenience, we have summarized, below, the basic documentation rules that are currently in common usage. These rules or conventions are, with slight variations, acceptable in most fields of the humanities and social sciences.[1]

FOOTNOTES

(1) FORMAT Footnotes are numbered consecutively. Footnote numbers should be added at the end of the quotation or paraphrase in the text of the paper, typed slightly above the line. The footnotes themselves should be placed at the bottom of each page, separated from the text by a triple space (not by a line). The first line of each footnote is indented. The note begins with the appropriate "superior" number, and ends with a period. Single-space footnotes, but leave a double space between them.[2]

(2) FIRST REFERENCES
(a) *Books.* The information is given in the following order:
  —full name of author (in normal order, followed by a comma)
  —title of book (underlined), with no punctuation at end unless the title itself ends with a punctuation mark
  —city of publication (followed by a colon): name of publisher (followed by a comma), year of publication (all within parentheses)
  —exact page number or numbers (preceded by a comma and by "p." or "pp." and followed by a period)

---

[1] Before typing your research paper, ascertain whether or not your instructor or department or school has its own style sheet. If so, follow its rules. The most widely used style manual in the humanities is *The MLA Style Sheet* (New York: Modern Language Association of America, 1961). Rules for the documentation of papers for the physical sciences can be found by consulting a leading journal in the specific field. Or see such manuals as the *Style Manual for Biological Journals* (Washington, D.C.: American Institute of Biological Sciences, 1964) or the *Publication Manual of the American Psychological Association* (Washington, D.C.: American Psychological Association, 1957).

[2] This holds true for research papers written for school; but for articles written for publication in scholarly journals, type the footnotes on separate pages (headed "Footnotes"), double-space within the footnotes, and leave triple spaces between them.

EXAMPLE:

¹ Harold J. Laski, *The American Democracy* (New York: Viking Press, 1948), p. 125.

(b) *Articles in Periodicals.* The information is given in the following order:
   —full name of author (in normal order, followed by a comma)
   —title of article (in quotation marks, followed by a comma within the quotation marks)
   —name of periodical (underlined, followed by a comma)
   —volume number (in capital Roman numerals)
   —month or season of issue, and year (separated by a comma; all within parentheses; followed by a comma)
   —exact page number or numbers (without "p." or "pp."; followed by a period)

EXAMPLE:

² Thomas E. Connolly, "Joyce's 'The Sisters,'" *College English,* XXIV (December, 1965), 192–93.

(c) *Articles in Newspapers and Weekly Magazines.* The information is given in the following order:
   —full name of author if article is signed (in normal order, followed by a comma)
   —title of article (in quotation marks, followed by a comma within the quotation marks) *or* title of article (in quotation marks) followed by an identifying label, e.g. editorial or anon. rev. (in parentheses, followed by a comma)
   —name of newspaper (underlined, followed by a comma)
   —full date of newspaper (month, day, year, followed by a comma)
   —exact page number or numbers (preceded by "p." or "pp." and followed by a period)

EXAMPLES:

³ Ronald Maiorana, "Birth Rate Decline Attributed to Contraceptives," *New York Times,* Nov. 13, 1967, p. 16.

[4] "Strategy for Vietnam Peace" (editorial), *New York Times,* Nov. 12, 1967, sec. 4, p. 10.

(d) *Essays in a Collection.* The information is given in the following order:

—full name of author of essay (in normal order, followed by a comma)

—title of essay (in quotation marks, followed by a comma within the quotation marks)

—title of the collection (underlined, followed by a comma)

—name of editor of collection (preceded by "ed.")

—city of publication (followed by a colon), name of publisher (followed by a comma), year of publication (all within parentheses)

—exact page number or numbers (preceded by a comma and by "p." or "pp." and followed by a period)

EXAMPLE:

[5] Sigmund Freud, "The Theme of the Three Caskets," *The King Lear Perplex,* ed. Helmut Bonheim (San Francisco: Wadsworth, 1960), p. 60.

(e) *Articles in Encyclopedias.* In general, such references can be treated as though they were essays in a collection (see "d" above); but note the following differences:

—city of publication, name of publisher and editors need not be given if the encyclopedia is a standard work

—edition number and/or year of publication should be cited

—if the work consists of more than one volume, the volume number should be given (in Roman numerals), followed by the exact page number or numbers (without "p." or "pp." if the volume number is given)

—for unsigned articles in encyclopedias and other books of information, follow the same procedure, but begin footnote with title of article

EXAMPLES:

[6] Kathleen Schlesinger, "Horns," *Encyclopaedia Britannica,* 11th ed. (1911), XIII, 698–99.

[7] "Woman's Suffrage," *Columbia Encyclopedia,* 3rd ed. (1963), p. 2112.

(f) *Other Complications.*

—*more than one author:* list full names of all authors, up to three names; if book has more than three authors, give the first author listed only, followed by "*et al.*" (and others)

EXAMPLE:

[8] Albert C. Baugh, *et al., A Literary History of England* (New York: Appleton-Century-Crofts, 1948), p. 1372.

—*translation:* cite the translator's name after the title of the book, preceded by "trans."

EXAMPLE:

[9] Giovanni Boccaccio, *The Decameron,* trans. Frances Winwar (New York: Modern Library, 1955), pp. 213–14.

—*introductions:* treat references to introductions as if they were essays in collections (see "d" above)

EXAMPLE:

[10] Robert Penn Warren, "Introduction," *An American Tragedy,* by Theodore Dreiser (Cleveland: World Publishing Co., 1962), p.9.

(3) SUBSEQUENT REFERENCES

(a) *General Rules.* Full bibliographical descriptions are given for first references only. Second and later references to the same work need not (and, indeed, should not) repeat the information contained in the first footnote. Hence, such subsequent footnotes need to give only the following information: the author's last name and the page number(s).

EXAMPLES:

[first reference]
[1] Harold J. Laski, *The American Democracy* (New York: Viking Press, 1948), p. 125.

[subsequent reference]
[11] *Laski,* pp. 275–76.

[first reference]
[2] Thomas E. Connolly, "Joyce's 'The Sisters,' " *College English,* XXIV (December, 1965), 192–93.

[subsequent reference]

¹² Connolly, p. 191.

(b) *Variations and Complications.* When two or more *consecutive* references are made to the same work, the abbreviation *"Ibid."* (for *ibidem;* meaning "in the same place," i.e., in the work cited immediately preceding) may be used instead of the author's name.

EXAMPLE:

¹³ Erika Ostrovsky, *Céline and his Vision* (New York: New York Univ. Press, 1967), p. 188.

¹⁴ *Ibid.,* p. 194.

However, the use of *"Ibid."* and other Latin abbreviations, such as *"op. cit.,"* is on its way out. Therefore, you would be within your rights (and within the modern tradition) if you were to forget about *"Ibid."* and instead were to treat consecutive references in the same way you treat other subsequent references; i.e., give the author's last name and the page number(s). Thus, footnote no. 14 would read:

¹⁴ Ostrovsky, p. 194.

And footnote no. 15 would read:

¹⁵ Ostrovsky, pp. 199–200.

But whichever method you choose, remember that you must be consistent! (Either use *"Ibid."* throughout your paper, or don't use it at all.)

—When your paper contains references to two or more works by the same author, you must clearly distinguish between those works in subsequent footnotes. Hence, in those cases, you will have to add the title of the work (or a shortened form of the title).

EXAMPLES:

[first references]

⁵ Sigmund Freud, "The Theme of the Three Caskets," *The King Lear Perplex,* ed. Helmut Bonheim (San Francisco: Wadsworth, 1960), p. 60.

¹⁶ Sigmund Freud, *The Basic Writings of Sigmund Freud,* trans. A. A. Brill (New York: Modern Library, 1938), p. 602.

[subsequent references]

¹⁷ Freud, "The Theme of the Three Caskets," p. 6o.
¹⁸ Freud, *Basic Writings,* p. 6o6.

The same holds true when your paper contains references to two authors with identical last names; here, again, you will have to add the title of the work to avoid confusion.

BIBLIOGRAPHY

A bibliography—a full list of the works cited or used in the preparation of the paper—must be appended to every research paper.

The following general rules should be observed:

(1) NAMES
—works are listed alphabetically according to the author's last name
—the author's last name is given first (followed by a comma and his first and middle names)
—second (and other) works by the same author are listed alphabetically under his name according to titles (dashes take the place of the author's name in second and later entries)
—works of more than one author are listed under the name of the first author; the second and third authors' names are given in normal order (first name, middle name, last name); for works of more than three authors, the name of the first author only is given, followed by *"et al."* (and others)
—anonymous works are listed in the same alphabetical list according to the first important word in the title

(2) PAGES
—page numbers for books are not given
—for periodical articles, the page numbers of the complete article are given
—for essays in collections, encyclopedia articles, and newspaper articles, the page numbers of the complete item are given

(3) PUNCTUATION
—the main parts of bibliographical entries are separated by periods (not by commas as in footnotes)

—each entry begins with a capital letter and ends with a period (as is true of each footnote)

(4) FORMAT

—the bibliography should begin on a new page
—items are *not* numbered
—the first line of each entry is flush with the left margin; second lines are indented
—entries are single-spaced, with double spaces between items

EXAMPLE:

Baugh, Albert C., et al. *A Literary History of England.* New York: Appleton-Century-Crofts, 1948.

Boccaccio, Giovanni. *The Decameron.* Trans. Frances Winwar. New York: Modern Library, 1955.

Connolly, Thomas E. "Joyce's 'The Sisters,'" *College English,* XXIV (December, 1965), 189–95.

Freud, Sigmund. *The Basic Writings of Sigmund Freud.* Trans. A. A. Brill. New York: Modern Library, 1938.

————. "The Theme of the Three Caskets," *The King Lear Perplex.* Ed. Helmut Bonheim. San Francisco: Wadsworth, 1960, pp. 62–64.

Galin, Saul, and Peter Spielberg, *Reference Books: A Practical Guide for College Students.* New York: Random House, 1969.

Graves, Robert. *The Greek Myths.* 2 vols. Baltimore: Penguin Books, 1955.

Laski, Harold J. *The American Democracy.* New York: Viking Press, 1948.

Maiorana, Ronald. "Birth Rate Decline Attributed to Contraceptives," *New York Times,* Nov. 13, 1967, p. 16.

Ostrovsky, Erika. *Céline and his Vision.* New York: New York University Press, 1967.

Random House Dictionary of the English Language (Unabridged Edition). New York: Random House, 1966.

Schlesinger, Kathleen. "Horns," *Encyclopaedia Britannica,* 11th ed. (1911), XIII, 697–706.

"Strategy for Vietnam Peace" (editorial), *New York Times,* Nov. 12, 1967, sec. 4, p. 10.

United States. *Congressional Record.* 80th Cong., 2nd Sess., 1948, XCIV, Part 8, 9650.

Warren, Robert Penn. "Introduction," *An American Tragedy* by Theodore Dreiser. Cleveland: World Publishing Co., 1962.

"Woman's Suffrage," *Columbia Encyclopedia,* 3rd ed. (1963), pp. 2111–2114.

INDEX

Mythology of All Races, 103, 181,
  221
  described, 179–80

Names, 134, 156, 253
  pronunciation of, 50–52
  See also Nicknames
Napoleonic Wars, 85
Narcotics, 213, 217
*National Cyclopaedia of American
  Biography,* 38
  "Current Series" of, 40, 43–44
National income, 118, 121
Nautical astronomy, 241
Navigation, 241
Near East, *see* Middle East
Negro Handbook, The, 234
Negroes, 144, 228, 234; *see also*
  Slavery
Netherlands, *see* Holland
Neurology, 215, 218, 249
New American Nation Series, The,
  142
New Cambridge Modern History,
  150
New Catholic Encyclopedia, 224
New Century Classical Handbook,
  148, 178–79
*New Century Cyclopedia of
  Names,* 50–51, 176
  described, 12–13
*New Century Handbook of English
  Literature,* 171, 175–76
*New College Encyclopedia of
  Music, The,* 193–94
*New Dictionary of British History,
  A,* 145–46
New Dictionary of Quotations, 35
*New English Dictionary (New
  English Dictionary on
  Historical Principles, NED),*
  see Oxford English
  Dictionary
New Golden Bough, The, 104
New Oxford History of Music,
  198–99
*New Schaff-Herzog Encyclopedia
  of Religious Knowledge,*
  222–23
New Serials Titles 1950–1960, 61
New Serials Titles 1961–1964, 61
New York Times, The, 278–79,
  283
New York Times Index, The, 55,
  62–63
New Yorker, The (magazine), 56
Newnes Dictionary of Dates, 152
Newspapers (press, journalism),
  177, 208, 232

biographical material in, 39,
  45–46, 62
documentation on, 278–79, 282–
  283
fact-book information on, 74
historical American, 170
indexes to, 54–55
  descriptions of, 62–65
  suitable to individual needs,
    55
Nicknames, 49, 211
*Nineteenth Century Readers' Guide
  to Periodical Literature,* 54,
  59
North America, 180, 243
  fact-book information on, 73, 76
  history of, 139
  Indians of, 100–101
  See also Canada; United States
Norway, 190, 199
Norwegian language, 158, 166, 214
Novels, 171, 176, 187–88, 190
  criticism of, 164, 185
Nuclear physics, *see* Atomic
  physics
Nuclear Science Abstracts, 240–41
Numerical tables, 260
Nursing, psychiatric, 218
Nutrition (food), 122–23, 239,
  241–43, 250
  cooking and, 251–52
  encyclopedia entries on, 8, 14
  See also Eggs; Feeding
    problems; Restaurants

Oats, 123
Obituaries, 53
  in fact books, 73, 79
  newspaper, 39, 62
Occupation, *see* Employment
Occupational therapy, 218, 236
Oceania, 111, 134, 180–81
Oceans, 83–84
*OED, see Oxford English
  Dictionary*
Official Congressional Directory,
  207–8
Official Index, The (London
  Times), 63
Old English language, 159, 164,
  174
Opera, 12, 187, 190
  music reference works on, 191,
    195–98
  opera characters, 186
Opera houses, 198
Optics, 265–67
Oratorios, 197
Orchestral music, 193, 196

About the Authors

SAUL GALIN is Assistant Professor
of English at Brooklyn College.
He received his A.B. from New York University
and a master's degree and doctorate from
Columbia University. His colleague,
PETER SPIELBERG, is also an Assistant
Professor of English at Brooklyn College.
Dr. Spielberg received his A.B. from City
College of New York, took an M.A. at New York
University, and a Ph.D. at the University
of Buffalo.